WRONGFUL ENRICHMENT

This book analyses enrichment law and its development and under-pinning in social culture within three geographical regions: the United States, western members of the European Union and the late Ottoman Empire. The regions correspond, though imperfectly, with three different legal traditions: the American, continental and Islamic traditions.

The book argues that we should understand law as a mimetic artefact. In so doing, it explains how typical patterns and exemplary articulations of wrongful enrichment law capture and reiterate vocal cultural themes found in the respective regions. The book identifies remarkable affinities between poetic tendencies, structures and default dispositions of wrongful enrichment law and cultural world views. It offers bold accounts of each region's law and culture providing fertile grounds for external and comparative elucidations of the legal doctrine.

International Studies in the Theory of Private Law: Volume 13

International Studies in the Theory of Private Law

This series of books edited by a distinguished international team of legal scholars aims to investigate the normative and theoretical foundations of the law governing relations between citizens. The context for such investigations of private law systems is set by important modern tendencies in systems of governance. The advent of the regulatory state marks the withdrawal of the state from direct control and management of social and economic activity, and the adoption instead of procedural regulation and co-regulatory strategies that promote the use of private law techniques of ordering and self-regulation in social and economic interactions between citizens. The tendency known as globalisation and the corresponding increases in cross-border trade produce the responses of transnational regulation of commerce and private governance regimes, and these new systems of governance challenge the hegemony of traditional national private law systems. Furthermore, these tendencies towards transnational governance regimes compel an interaction between different national legal traditions, with their differences in culture and philosophy as well as their differences based upon variations in market systems, which provokes questions not only about competing policy frameworks but also about the nature and adequacy of different kinds of legal reasoning.

The series encompasses a diverse range of theoretical approaches in the examination of these issues including approaches using socio-legal methods, economics, critical theory, systems theory, regulation theory, and moral and political theory. With the aim of stimulating an international discussion of these issues, volumes will be published in Germany, France, and the United Kingdom in one of the three languages.

Current Editors

Hugh Collins, *All Souls College, University of Oxford*
Christian Joerges, *University of Bremen*
Gunther Teubner, *Frankfurt University*

Former Editors

Antoine Lyon-Caen
Horatia Muir Watt
James Q Whitman

Volumes published with Hart Publishing, Oxford

1. David Campbell, Hugh Collins und John Wightman (eds), *Implicit Dimensions of Contract: Discrete, Relational and Network Contracts* (2003).
2. Christian Joerges, Inger-Johanne Sand and Gunther Teubner (eds), *Transnational Governance and Constitutionalism* (2004).
3. Oren Perez, *Ecological Sensitivity and Global Legal Pluralism: Rethinking the Trade and Environment Debate* (2004).
4. Harm Schepel, *The Constitution of Private Governance* (2004).
5. Nili Cohen and Ewan McKendrick, *Comparative Remedies for Breach of Contract* (2005).
6. Marc Amstutz and Gunther Teubner (eds), *Networks: Legal Issues of Multilateral Co-operation* (2010).

7. Gunther Teubner (edited and with an Introduction by Hugh Collins), *Networks as Connected Contracts* (2010).
8. Christian Joerges and Josef Falke (eds), *Karl Polanyi, Globalisation and the Potential of Law in Transnational Markets* (2011).
9. Poul F Kjaer, Gunther Teubner and Alberto Febbrajo (eds), *The Financial Crisis in Constitutional Perspective: The Dark Side of Functional Differentiation* (2011).
10. Jean Braucher, John Kidwell and William C Whitford (eds), *Revisiting the Contracts Scholarship of Stewart Macaulay: On the Empirical and the Lyrical* (2013).
11. Thomas Dietz, *Global Order Beyond Law: How Information and Communication Technologies Facilitate Relational Contracting in International Trade* (2014).
12. Anna Beckers, *Enforcing Corporate Social Responsibility Codes: On Global Self-Regulation and National Private Law* (2015).

Volumes published in German by Nomos Verlagsgesellschaft, Baden-Baden

1. Peer Zumbansen, *Ordnungsmuster im modern Wohlfahrtsstaat: Lernerfahrungen zwischen Staat, Geseelschaft und Vertrag* (2000).
2. Dan Wielsch, *Freiheit und Funktion: Zur Struktur- und Theoriegeschichte des Rechts der Wirtschaftsgesellschaft* (2001).
3. Marc Amstutz, *Evolutorisches Wirtschaftsrecht: Vorstudien zum Recht und seiner Methode in den Diskurskollisionen der Marktgesellschaft* (2001).
4. Christian Joerges and Gunther Teubner, Gunther (eds), *Rechtsverfassungsrecht: Recht-Fertigungen zwischen Sozialtheorie und Privatrechtsdogmatik* (2003).
5. Gunther Teubner, *Netzwerk als Vertragsverbund: Virtuelle Unternehmen, Franchising, Just in Time in sozialwissenschaftlicher und juristischer Sicht* (2004).
6. Daniel Dédeyan, *Macht durch Zeichen: Rechtsprobleme der Kennzeichnung und Zertifikation* (2004).
7. Dietrich Claus Becker, *Von Namen und Nummern: Kollisionen unverträglicher Rechtsmassen im Interent* (2005).
8. Vagias Karavas, *Digitale Grundrechte: Elemente einer Verfassung des Informationsflusses im Intenet* (2007).
9. Peter Korth, *Dritthaftung von Ratingagenturen* (2009).
10. Cordula Heldt, *Baukooperation und Franchising als multilaterale Sonderverbindung. Vertragsnetzwerke—Parallelschuldverhältnisse—Personengesellschaften* (2010).
11. Jan Lüsing, *Die Pflichten aus culpa in contrahendo und positiver Vertragsverletzung* (§ 241 II BGB): *Über den hybriden Charakter der Schutzpflichten und zur Selbstbindung ohne Vertrag* (2010).
12. Moritz Renner, *Zwingendes transnationales Recht: Elemente einer Wirtschaftsverfassung jenseits des Staates* (2011).
13. Christoph Lüscher, *Zur Konzeptualisierung von Verbrauchervertragsrecht unter besonderer Berücksichtigung des schweizerischen und europäischen Verbrauchervertragsrechts. Eine Untersuchung im Schnittfeld von Vertragsrecht, Systemtheorie und Ökonomie* (2011).
14. Daniel Klösel, *Compliance-Richtlinien. Zum Funktionswandel des Zivilrechts im Gewährleistungsstaat* (2012).
15. Chunyi Qi, *Rechtstransfer in Chinas Produktionsregime? Zur Kontrolle der Allgemeinen Geschäftsbedingungen im deutschen und chinesischen Recht* (2013).

Wrongful Enrichment

A Study in Comparative Law
and Culture

Nahel Asfour

·H A R T·
PUBLISHING
OXFORD AND PORTLAND, OREGON
2017

Hart Publishing
An imprint of Bloomsbury Publishing Plc

Hart Publishing Ltd
Kemp House
Chawley Park
Cumnor Hill
Oxford OX2 9PH
UK

Bloomsbury Publishing Plc
50 Bedford Square
London
WC1B 3DP
UK

www.hartpub.co.uk
www.bloomsbury.com

Published in North America (US and Canada) by
Hart Publishing
c/o International Specialized Book Services
920 NE 58th Avenue, Suite 300
Portland, OR 97213-3786
USA

www.isbs.com

HART PUBLISHING, the Hart/Stag logo, BLOOMSBURY and the
Diana logo are trademarks of Bloomsbury Publishing Plc

First published 2017

© Nahel Asfour 2017

British Library Cataloguing-in-Publication Data
A catalogue record for this book is available from the British Library.

ISBN: HB: 978-1-78225-705-9
ePDF: 978-1-78225-707-3
ePub: 978-1-78225-706-6

Library of Congress Cataloging-in-Publication Data
Names: Asfour, Nahel, author.

Title: Wrongful enrichment : a study in comparative law and culture / Nahel Asfour.

Description: Oxford ; Portland, Oregon : Hart Publishing, an imprint of Bloomsbury
Publishing Plc, 2017. | Series: International studies in the theory of private law ;
volume 13 | Based on author's thesis (doctoral—University of Vienna.
Rechtswissenschaftliche Fakultèat, 2013) issued under title: The cultural perspective
of wrongful enrichment law. | Includes bibliographical references and index.

Identifiers: LCCN 2017023831 (print) | LCCN 2017024029 (ebook) |
ISBN 9781782257066 (Epub) | ISBN 9781782257059 (hardback : alk. paper)

Subjects: LCSH: Unjust enrichment—European Union countries. | Unjust enrichment—
United States. | Unjust enrichment—Turkey—History. | Law—Social aspects—European
Union countries. | Law—Social aspects—United States. | Law—Social aspects—Turkey—History.

Classification: LCC K920 (ebook) | LCC K920 .A824 2017 (print) | DDC 346.02/9—dc23
LC record available at https://lccn.loc.gov/2017023831

Typeset by Compuscript Ltd, Shannon
Printed and bound in Great Britain by TJ International Ltd, Padstow, Cornwall

To find out more about our authors and books visit www.hartpublishing.co.uk. Here you will find
extracts, author information, details of forthcoming events and the option to sign up for our newsletters.

To Sally Awad Asfour and my Three N(s)

Preface

There was an aura of mystery emanating from the decorated walls. I was with some colleagues who fled the raucousness of their cities that Saturday afternoon. They travelled long distances seeking some quiet time. It was not spiritual devotion they were after. None of them was religious. It was my slow-paced home town which captured their imagination. Lacking a more zestful plan for the day, we ended up gazing at the walls of the Annunciation Basilica. The mosaics on the wall were indeed astonishing in detail, but were equally perplexing. For a long time, local mosaics of 'Mary and the Child' had a cliched effect, or no effect at all, on sightseers. We were no exception. It was the Asian lady with her child which caught our attention. This mosaic was hanging on the wall of the upper church. Mary and Jesus had almond-shaped eyes with epicanthic folds. Their black hair was smooth, dark and thick. The child had a square jaw and a wide flat nose. The two figures were dressed in traditional kimonos. They were clearly not of Mediterranean origin, or at least, they did not reflect portrays of the Virgin and Child I used to recognise.

It was a mosaic piece sent by a Japanese Christian community to the Basilica sometime after the erection of the church. But it was only one mosaic out of more than 40 mosaics, all depicting the same biblical figures but in different national variations. There were, for example, the African, Indonesian, German, Egyptian, Bolivian, Ukrainian, and Irish Mary and Jesus. Each mosaic portrayed the figures in local eyes. Their reproduction of the biblical theme seemed bound by materials locally available to each community. By that I refer to the distinguishing physical traits of the people, their costumes, their tools and belongings, their residence, greenery and firmament. It was the distinctive mixture of colours, shapes and materials making up each community's world or how each community came to see, feel and experience its own reality. A community's local materials shaped its produced artefacts, I was sure. And if facts are artefacts, it was a vocal triumph for a claim I used to make every now and then, that culture was so powerful it could rewrite facts. At least I had the temporary support of the Basilica's mosaics for that.

My company was not persuaded. Indeed, the claim was a bit odd. It had the rhetorical force of an argument that the distinctive shape of a nationally manufactured vehicle's headlamp could be an imitation of the ethnic eye shape of that nation. It seemed a refutable argument. Function and aesthetics were leading elements of any artefact, far more than a unique world perception. At any rate, a degree of cultural imitation in any product seemed inescapable. This is how forgeries could be scientifically detected. Forgery is a novel composition which uses the patterns, techniques, colours and methods of the authentic work to falsely lead consumers to think they hold an original. Any artefact is necessarily immersed in the composer's spatiotemporal dimensions. An artefact inevitably imitates 'the culture, style, and features of its era and place of creation'. Thus, forgers are never able to conceal their cultural identity. They are never capable of committing the 'perfect crime'.[1] At any rate, it was not the themes of the individual mosaics which interested me. It was why these themes were there and how the mosiaics came to convey different variants of the same figures which intrigued me.

We had to turn to a local tourist guide for some revelation. Our lengthy conversation disclosed two provocative insights. The first is that the mosaics were not spontaneously drawn, but were invited contributions. Christian communities around the world were invited to visualise the biblical figures in their own eyes and to expressly include distinguishing traits of their local communities. It was a devastating earthquake to the artefact-as-culture argument. The second insight was no less dramatic. The guide hinted that not all pieces were actual mosaics. Some were merely paintings imitating the pattern of mosaic art. Later, we were challenged to detect those 'imitations' and it was no easy task. We were never fully confident that we had traced an imitation. The claims of artefact-as-culture or artefact-because-of-culture in a straightforward sense seemed far-fetched that day. But it was not an all-or-nothing case. Indeed, processing cultural materials into cultural products is not an exact formula but a complex phenomenon not fully comprehensible to the keenest of observers. Still, it seemed plain that imitation was part of that process. Whether consciously practised or inadvertently present, imitation had metamorphosing powers. It was a connecting force of human artefacts and culture needing some attention.

Nahel Asfour
Nazareth

---

[1] N Asfour, 'Art and Antiquities: Fraud' in *The Encyclopedia of Transnational Crime and Justice* (2012) 20–21.

Acknowledgements

This book culminates seven years of research commencing as a doctoral project in the Department of Civil Law at the Faculty of Law, University of Vienna. I was fortunate to have the warm support of many people, programmes, grants and institutions along the road. Without their endorsement, this book would not have been written. I owe a great debt of gratitude to Christiane Wendehorst my outstanding mentor for offering indispensable advice and leading with great wisdom and shrewdness, to Ken Oliphant and Judith Schacherreiter who also read, challenged and advised, and to my colleagues at the University of Vienna, Barbara Lyszczarz and Vanessa Wilcox with whom I had many eye-opening discussions. I also want to thank the organisers and professors at the International Osnabrück Summer Institute for the Cultural Study of Law who imbued me with endless passion to the interdisciplinary study of law, notably Director Peter Schneck, Sabine Meyer, Rosemary Coombe, Brook Thomas, Martin Zeilinger and my colleagues Francesca Vitali, Serena Bravi, Adil Khan, Mai-Linh Hong and Katja Kurz. I am also indebted to Randy Gordon and Maksymilian Del Mar, organisers of the 'Exemplary Narratives: Interdisciplinary Perspectives' workshop at the IVR Congress, Goethe University, Frankfurt where I staged and debated an early concept of this research. Deep gratitude is also owed to the directors of the Max Planck Institute for Comparative and International Private Law, Reinhard Zimmermann, Jürgen Basedow and Holger Fleischer who offered me an exceptional opportunity to pursue my research at the Institute, to Claudia Holland the Institute's Library Director, and to my colleagues at the Institute, Ivan Romashchenko, Donike Qerimi, Hao Jiang, Bernhard Burtscher, Katharina Au, Marella Stanzione, Renato Neto, Endri Barmbek, Bevan Marten, Natia Chitashvili, Perry Spolaore, Rodrigo Vaz Sampaio, Akawat Laowonsiri and Béatrice Jaluzot, each adding his or her own insight and voice to this book. I am also grateful to former Dean of the Faculty of Law at Tel-Aviv University, Ron Harris and Vice Dean Roy Kreitner for supporting my first steps in Israeli academia, and to Raef Zreik with whom I discussed the whole thesis of this book. Thanks are also owed to my students at the University of Vienna and the University of Tel Aviv, who provoked many bright ideas over the years, to my friends Amin Asfour and Nizar Farraj who patiently listened and offered me thoughtful feedback, and to Khaled Hamdan and Rawa Zoabi for making many valuable Sharia and Ottoman sources available. I also wish to thank the series editors at Hart Publishing, Hugh Collins, Christian Joerges and

Gunther Teubner who perceptively commented with enriching suggestions, and to Bill Asquith, Francesca Sancarlo, Anne Flegel, Anne Bevan and the rest of the team at Hart Publishing who made this book possible. I owe this book to my parents Nabeel and Omaima, sisters Gida and Shahd, and my wife and children, Sally, Nour, Nabil and Neil Samuel for their patience, support and encouragement. Many grants aided me at different stages of this research, notably from the University of Vienna, Max Planck Institute for Comparative and International Private Law in Hamburg, and the International Osnabrück Summer Institute for the Cultural Study of Law to whom I am deeply indebted. All errors and inaccuracies found in this book remain mine.

Contents

Transliteration and Translation Notes

Romanised script of Ottoman Turkish words is as found in sources or as commonly used in English (eg, *Tanzimat*). Otherwise, transliteration is produced according to Birnblaum 1967 standards: E Birnbaum, 'The Transliteration of Ottoman Turkish for Library and General Purposes' (1967) 87(2) *Journal of the American Oriental Society* 122.

Transliteration of Arabic is produced according to ALA-LC Arabic (2012) Romanizing Table, available at: www.loc.gov/catdir/cpso/romanization/arabic.pdf.

Transliteration of Hebrew is produced according to ALA-LC Hebrew and Yiddish (2011) Romanizing Table, available at: www.loc.gov/catdir/cpso/romanization/hebrew.pdf.

Translations into English are as in cited sources. Otherwise, translations are produced by the author. English translation of titles is added immediately following transliterated ones.

Table of Cases

Table of Legislation

Table of DCFR and EU Projects

Table of EU

Table of Restatements

Introduction

IN SPITE OF a 'long and immensely successful career', to borrow John Dawson's words,[1] Pomponius's famous maxim that 'nobody should be made richer through loss and wrong to another'[2] continues to articulate one of the most elusive ideas in the history of obligation law. Perhaps this is the way with ethical prescriptions in general. When we attempt to carve them out as detailed legal doctrines, we confront their amorphous nature. The more we seek, the less we find. This condition is typical of ideals like justice, fairness, equity and good faith but it is also evident in maxims of obligation law such as 'one should keep his promise' or 'one should not harm another'. Regardless of their ostensible degree of graspability, these maxims are equally meagre in instructive content. Their teleological allure suspends our critical senses and conceals their wily nature. Though ethical prescriptions enjoy strong moral appeal, their high versatility renders them short of coping thoroughly and comprehensibly with the intricacies of human conduct.

On a historical level, however, the elusive content of Pomponius's maxim did not erode the dictum's continuing presence in the legal arena. As early as Roman law, the maxim presented a 'common denominator' for all Roman *condictions*, such as *Condictio indebiti, Condictio causa data causa non secuta* and *Condictio ex causa furtiva* and a general principle on which remedies could be drawn in aberrant cases.[3] Today, Pomponius's dictum marks the intellectual keystone of well-developed corpuses of restitution, unjust and unjustified enrichment law around the world.[4] Probing the conversion of this fundamental dictum into detailed norms of gain-based laws, dominant accounts often highlight the role of doctrinal development and jurists, notably legal scientists and Reporters of early Restatement of Restitution, as major forces behind the construction of current laws.[5] These accounts rest chiefly on an internal approach to law. According to

---

[1] J Dawson, *Unjust Enrichment: A Comparative Analysis* (New York, William S Hein & Co, 1999) 3.

[2] P Birks, *An Introduction to the Law of Restitution* (Oxford, Oxford University Press, 1985) 23.

[3] R Zimmermann, *The Law of Obligations: Roman Foundations of the Civilian Tradition* (Cape Town, Juta, 1992) 852.

[4] M Gergen, 'What Renders Enrichment Unjust?' (2000–01) 79 *Texas Law Review* 1927, 1927.

[5] *cf* H Dagan, *The Law and Ethics of Restitution* (Cambridge, Cambridge University Press, 2004) 13.

Christiane Wendehorst, an internal approach, also known as 'working *in* the law', addresses law as a normative framework with bending norms. Doctrinal development is, hence, a quest for the 'perfect' law which perpetually sorts and endorses the supposedly 'right' legal answer.[6]

These accounts are often trapped in dry disciplinary elucidations and are incapable of providing any contextual illumination. A comprehensive approach does not ignore external perspectives. An external approach addresses law as a factual framework and 'works *on* the law', notes Wendehorst. It takes a descriptive standpoint and sorts statements into 'true' and 'false'.[7] External approaches could be historical, social, economic, cultural, philosophical and more. An economic approach, for example, accentuates the dictum as a matter of promoting the autonomy of agents and the element of efficiency. According to some studies, wealth mobility should manifest the exercise of one's free and unerring will. This is why consent, absent, vitiated or qualified, is often the crux of enrichment law. Respecting consent promotes the autonomy of social agents and is deemed cost-efficient. Restitution works to overturn wealth shifts which disregard consent. By quashing the misplaced value, it creates a strong economic incentive for agents to reach an agreement where possible, or at least be careful when relocating portions of their wealth.[8] Niva Elkin-Koren and Eli Salzberger suggest a distinction between enrichment law as allocator of 'entitlements' and as a 'remedy' to protect such 'allocation'. Economic analysis of the doctrine as allocator in wrongful enrichment proves it an inefficient device, they assert, since it does not maximise wealth or decrease costs. As a legal redress, however, they add that the doctrine quashes illicit profit, enriches a court's toolbox for protecting entitlements and makes a useful addition to Calabresi–Melamed property, liability and inalienability rules.[9]

In his monograph *Bereicherungsrecht als Wirtschaftsrecht* (*Enrichment Law as Economic Law*), Christian Joerges urges the use of enrichment law as an instrument to achieve economic goals. Structural changes in the market and economic system justify, he asserts, a more programmed scheme of incentives and restrictions based on this law. Joerges skilfully reorients the legal functions of performance action (*Leistungskondiktion*) and intervention action (*Eingriffskondiktion*), prominent in German law, to implement desired policies, notably with regard to contractual services and

---

[6] C Wendehorst, 'The State as a Foundation of Private Law Reasoning' (2008) 56 *American Journal of Comparative Law* 567, 569–70.

[7] ibid.

[8] W Farnsworth, *Restitution: Civil Liability for Unjust Enrichment* (Chicago, IL, University of Chicago Press, 2014) 9–11.

[9] N Elkin-Koren and E Salzberger, 'Towards an Economic Theory of Unjust Enrichment Law' (2000) 20 *International Review of Law and Economics* 551, 555–570.

protection of goods. He exemplifies how these norms can be used to monitor and control competitive and anti-competitive practices in the market. He discusses the need for a 'paradigm shift' in enrichment law which would utilise the elastic and expansive functionality of this law to serve as an economic regulative tool when needed.[10] Joerges' thesis is another eloquent example of economic elucidations of enrichment law.

A different path was taken by Charlie Webb in his recently published research *Reason and Restitution*. In his research, Webb explores enrichment law with a philosophic orientation and utilises practical logic for that purpose. Webb's account perceives enrichment cases principally as a breach of the 'condition' of consent since each person has a legally protected entitlement to decide what is done with his wealth. The doctrine provides a qualified protection to that person's proprietary interest therewith.[11] Though unlike former accounts, Webb's thesis does not rest on resource management and decision-making analysis, it still sets the doctrine on a rational axis. Human conduct, however, is not necessarily rational. It is often not driven by informed and logical choices. Life, in general, is more ambivalent and unpremeditated. And it cannot be summed up as the aggregate of human rational activities in which each person pursues his best interests. Law is a cultural artefact. And as Marshal Sahlin puts it, 'no cultural form can ever be read from a set of "material forces", as if the cultural were the dependent variable of an inescapable practical logic'. Logic itself is integrated with a 'cultural system' and is a 'lifeless' drive if detached from the cultural properties that give it force and meaning.[12]

Resting on the former critique, one rewarding approach is the study of enrichment law with culture in mind. The current book embraces such an approach. It abandons the positivistic assumption that law is a product of rational design or a failed form of the ideal law,[13] and seeks instead a *verstehen* approach, namely meaning-driven elucidations. To that end, the book treats enrichment law as a cultural artefact. Doctrinal accounts have expectedly not done so, and interdisciplinary ones have forsaken the cultural mission. Restrained to a literal comprehension of law-as-culture, a barren method approaches enrichment law via content-detectors, seeking to trace direct shifts of substance between law and culture. Ultimately, it ends up assigning only a minor and marginal role for culture in the shaping of this law, thus the absence of culture in such accounts.

---

[10] C Joerges, *Bereicherungsrecht als Wirtschaftsrecht: Eine Untersuchung zur Entwicklung von Leistungs- und Eingriffskondiktion* (Köln, Otto Schmidt, 1977).

[11] C Webb, *Reason and Restitution: A Theory of Unjust Enrichment* (Oxford, Oxford University Press, 2016) 75–76.

[12] M Sahlins, *Culture and Practical Reason* (Chicago, IL, University of Chicago Press, 1978) vii–x, 206–08.

[13] P Kahn, *The Cultural Study of Law* (Chicago, IL, University of Chicago Press, 1999) 92, 97.

An example of this method may be found in a central work generated by European legal scholarship, namely, the *Principles, Definitions and Model Rules of European Private Law: Draft Common Frame of Reference (DCFR)*. The DCFR authors understand law-and-culture as an issue of content absorption. In their endeavour to take account of 'cultural diversity', they assure that certain DCFR Articles allow for local commercial practices and native language uses.[14] Nevertheless, they argue that 'where a certain aspect of life has not only cultural content but also a strong functional content' the need to preserve the cultural content relinquishes in favour of higher goals, such as solidarity, promotion of welfare and the internal market, goals that are profoundly enhanced by the European Union polity and institutions.[15]

The object of enquiry in such a method is those gateways to culture which explicitly allow cultural content into the domain of law. In contract law, for example, these gateways are found in norms that bend contract parties to local practices[16] or impose the use of comprehensible language—as a cultural medium—in different contractual instances.[17] They are also traceable in tort law norms which define scopes of liability or standards of conduct by reference to the so-called 'reasonable person',[18] the 'avatar' who supposedly embodies 'typical cultural and social practices found in the community'.[19] Similar gateways are also detected in family law norms which endorse cultural practices in marital contracts, and in criminal law norms which consider cultural motives in questions of guilt or allow cultural evidence in courtrooms.

Approaching many countries' enrichment laws with these examples in mind, one can hardly locate comparable gateways. A permissive approach could mark, for instance, certain standards of 'reasonableness',[20] 'moral duties',[21] 'prevailing practices'[22] or 'public policy'[23] as prospective

---

[14] C von Bar, E Clive and H Schulte-Nölke et al (eds), *Principles, Definitions and Model Rules of European Private Law: Draft Common Frame of Reference (DCFR)*, Outline Edition (Munich, Sellier, 2009) 15–16.

[15] ibid.

[16] eg ibid 178 [Art II.-1:104(2)].

[17] eg ibid 188, 222, 290, 468, 471, 494 [Arts II.-3:102(2)(c) and (3); II-9:109; IV.A. 6:103(1)(e); IX.-3:310(1)(d); IX.-3:319(2); IX-7:210(3)].

[18] F Busnelli, G Camandé and H Cousy et al (eds), *Principles of European Tort Law: Text and Commentary* (Vienna, Springer, 2005) 1–10 [Arts 3:201(a); 4:102(1)].

[19] D Engel and M McCann, 'Introduction: Tort Law as Cultural Practice' in D Engel and M McCann (eds), *Fault Lines: Tort Law as Cultural Practice* (Stanford, CA, Stanford University Press, 2009) 2.

[20] eg von Bar, Clive and Schulte-Nölke et al (eds) (n 14) 413, 417 [Arts VII.-2:101(4)(b) and (c); VII.-5:101(2) and (5)]; A Burrows, *A Restatement of the English Law of Unjust Enrichment* (Oxford, Oxford University Press, 2012) 7, 42–43 [Art 7(3)(a)].

[21] See, eg, *Larner v London County Council* [1949] 2 KB 683; G Virgo, *The Principles of the Law of Restitution* (Oxford, Oxford University Press, 2006) 150, 726.

[22] See, eg, Burrows, *A Restatement of the English Law of Unjust Enrichment* (n 20) 19, 150 [Art 31(2)].

[23] Virgo (n 21) 44–45.

pathways to cultural content. Dominant accounts, however, are reluctant to do so. Wittingly or not, they usually choose to emulate judiciary decisions and legal commentaries in their meagre production of cultural elucidations of enrichment law. Though in general cultural elucidations of law have set firm footing in legal scholarship, it is not infrequently charged as pseudo-science. This *acultural* stand could be explained by the general tendency, inspired by analytic, formalistic and positivistic tropes, to split scientific explanations into justification-based and causation-based explanations, favouring the former in legal scholarship and dismissing causation-based explanations as irrelevant. Cultural approaches to law have been categorised with the second type of explanations and, thus, were always held suspicious.

According to Alon Harel and Yair Lorberbaum, the imprudent transition of law-and-culture scholarship from the 'trivial' claim that culture affects law, namely that culture is a 'cause' of law, to the 'erroneous' one that law is culture or culture 'justifies' law, is extremely flawed. Law, they argue, exercises legitimate 'normative-control' over its sources and content. This control preserves the legal system and its most precious resource: the 'legal ethos' of 'objectivity and neutrality'. The 'leakage' of culture into the legal domain, a matter generated by the captivating and 'imperialistic' appeal of law-and-culture scholarship, they assert, puts this resource along with the whole legal project at serious risk of legitimacy crisis, and thus needs to be inhibited.[24]

This call to restrain cultural enquiries of law, I think, is problematic, if not perilous. It undermines the contingency of its own terminology as well as the prospective fruits of law-and-culture scholarship. Law constitutes and is constituted by social realities. It engages in reciprocal and indivisible ties with culture. At one time, law imitates culture, at another, it is the other way around. The latter manifests the perpetual social discourse of 'domination and resistance'.[25] It is important to note that the ostensible dichotomy between law and culture, on which the 'cause' versus 'justification' thesis stands, is not static but dynamic. It dwells alongside ongoing 'struggles for identity, recognition, and legitimacy' to use Rosemary Coombe's words.[26] A common example of this reciprocity condition may be the legal recognition of indigenous peoples' rights to their traditional knowledge and folklore as intellectual property rights.

---

[24] A Harel and Y Lorberbaum, 'Hirhurim 'l Sakanot Mishpat yi Tarbut' ('Reflecting on Dangers of Law and Culture') (2011) 40 *Mishpatim* 939, 941–43, 950, 968, 971–73.
[25] S Hirsch and M Lazarus-Black, 'Introduction—Performance and Paradox: Exploring Law's Role in Hegemony and Resistance' in S Hirsch and M Lazarus-Black (eds), *Contested States: Law, Hegemony and Resistance* (New York, Routledge, 1994) 4.
[26] R Coombe, 'Contingent Articulations: A Critical Cultural Studies of Law' in A Sarat and T Kearn (eds), *Law in the Domains of Culture* (Ann Arbor, MI, University of Michigan Press, 2003) 21–23.

According to Coombe, 'law provides means and fora both for legitimating and contesting dominant meanings and the social hierarchies they support'.[27] Turning a blind eye to this aspect of law and the regenerative role of culture in this process could prove detrimental to the very ethos Harel and Lorberbaum are eager to protect. A legal craft which relentlessly refrains from internalising social and cultural vicissitudes, which ignores changes in social powers, and which abstains from justifying its choices forthrightly, is a maladaptive and underdeveloped craft. It generates resentments and lacks the equilibrating means necessary for its endurance. A craft of this sort would rapidly suffer serious allegations of *instrumentalisation* and politicisation prompting a major crisis of 'legitimacy' and loss of 'public trust'.[28]

Though law is necessarily fashioned by culture, in this research I wish to abandon the justification-causation dichotomy as a presumable indicator of legitimacy and public trust, and suggest that these issues are, in fact, very dependent on culture. To be more accurate, they are very dependent on the mimetic faculty of legal crafting with regard to culture. And by no means do I refer to a direct 'content absorption' process or law's classic gateways to cultural substance. Culture is only infrequently a direct and unmediated 'cause' of law. More so, it can be described as a distal cause which leaves a discernible watermark or fingerprint on the artefact of law. Thus, instead of a necessarily logical, or even historical, cause–effect relationship, the book seeks and exhibits significant 'congruence', meaningful 'adequacy' and 'elective affinity' between law and culture, to use but some of Max Weber's thought-provoking terms in his monograph on *The Protestant Ethic and the Spirit of Capitalism*.[29] It is vital to point out, however, that traced affinities between legal patterns and cultural perceptions do not seek to obliterate other grounds for such affinity notably doctrinal, theoretical, historical or policy-related. I also do not set the task of identifying all cultural elements having such affinities with traced legal patterns.

This approach, I believe, is one possible way to avoid analytical fantasies and dead-end enquiries. While it should not be undermined that culture provides the fora, discourses and themes in which the law develops, treating affinities in terms of 'scientific' evidence can, in fact, be frustrating and at times even misleading. The task this book sets to accomplish is a cultural elucidation. Admittedly, enrichment law has earned a reputation for being extremely technical and dry. Many perceive it as exemplary

---

[27] R Coombe, 'Critical Cultural Study of Law' (1998) 10(2) *Yale Journal of Law & the Humanities* 463, 479.

[28] *cf* M Mautner, *Law and the Culture of Israel* (New York, Oxford University Press, 2011) 162–63.

[29] M Weber, *The Protestant Ethic and the Spirit of Capitalism: And Other Writings* (New York, Penguin, 2002) xxiv.

of rational thinking and pure logic, a product made by professionals for professionals. This condition has convinced that enrichment law cannot foster any cultural insight. But this conclusion is fallacious and does not stand the tests of law-and-culture scholarship. Due to the cultural nature of meaning, no matter how dry the law seems, culture as a pool of meanings, values, attitudes and discourses cannot be filtered out. Enrichment law, like any other law, necessarily embodies and fleshes out the values, themes and cultural perceptions of the era in which it is produced. This data is worthy of scholarly attention, and this is the working assumption of the current research.

A notable study which went along this road is Hanoch Dagan's groundbreaking research entitled *Unjust Enrichment: A Study of Private Law and Public Values*. In his book, Dagan proposes an eloquent theory which purports to explain the different 'dynamics' of wrongful enrichment law across three different legal systems: American, Jewish and international law, with reference to each one's 'socio-economic ethos'. His thesis produces a 'translating scheme' which identifies the rationales underlying the monetary measures available, notably compensation, restitution and disgorgement. He argues that such measures correspond with 'public values', ranging from the 'communitarian value of sharing', the 'utilitarian value of well-being', and to the 'libertarian value of control'. Furthermore, he argues that the normative selections between the different measures accentuate those values and the 'socio-economic ethos' of each culture. Dagan readjusts his thesis noting that the societal meaning of the invaded property and the degree with which it is perceived as extension of the 'Self' affect the level of legal redress provided.[30]

Dagan refines some of his arguments in later works, notably his book *The Law and Ethics of Restitution*.[31] In this book, Dagan abandons the cultural approach to restitution law in favour of 'legal realism'. In Wrongful Enrichments chapter, he does not provide cultural explications of the law or any study of cultures. He notably endorses, instead, a theoretical tool proposed by Ernest Weinrib's theory of corrective justice entitled 'Correlativity'.[32] Correlativity accentuates the need to justify any legal redress on the merits of equivalency between the disadvantaged person and the enriched person. Any choice of remedy should be explainable by reference to both parties—the plaintiff and the defendant.[33] Thus, for example, disgorgement of profits while explainable in terms of the

---

[30] H Dagan, *Unjust Enrichment: A Study of Private Law and Public Values* (Cambridge, Cambridge University Press, 1997) 12–49, 214.

[31] Dagan, *The Law and Ethics of Restitution* (n 5).

[32] ibid 224–28.

[33] E Weinrib, 'Restitutionary Damages as Corrective Justice' (1999) 1 *Theoretical Inquiries in Law* 1, 3–4.

enriched person's ill-behaviour, fails the correlativity test since it cannot justify the disadvantaged's right to those profits. The adoption of this remedy, therefore, should be questionable, argues Dagan.[34]

I think Dagan's law-as-public values thesis is remarkably insightful but like any theoretical work it has a few downsides. The work does not engage in a traditional cultural study of enrichment law. Dagan's aim to provide an 'analytic tool' with which it is possible to evaluate existing rules as well as inform or prescribe future legal outcomes, comes at the expense of a classic cultural analysis of law. The outcome is a fully rational thesis offering mathematical accuracy. This trait makes Dagan's thesis too perfect in a slightly drawback sense. Culture, in general, is not a web of neatly defined themes with a tidy order. It is not necessarily systematic, logical or predictable. Dagan's decision to embrace correlativity enhances this positivistic hyper-rational part of Dagan's thesis, for better and worse.

As some critics of Dagan's work point out, the legal dynamics of wrongful enrichment are not necessarily dictated by public values and social ethos.[35] Good testimonies for this critique are found in the statutes and cases which do not comply with Dagan's thesis.[36] One critic explicates this point noting that 'in his attempt to elucidate a causal relationship true of all cultures', Dagan 'tends to assume a direct link between legal doctrine and the values of the broader community', thus ignoring the role of 'the legal community' in forming these dynamics.[37] Dagan's aim to provide a useful tool entailed abstractions, inductions, reductions and sorting materials into 'one-fits-all' scales. The fabric of cultures tolerates these analytical processes but it tends to end up a bit worn, losing parts of its unique, rich and colourful texture.

These comments aim neither to dismiss Dagan's thesis which remains a useful analytical tool nor to downplay culture's impact on this field of law. Culture's unique traits should be brought into further consideration avoiding as much as possible all mechanic-like phraseologies. Regrettably, Dagan's pioneer work has not persuaded others to address the cultural question of enrichment law, and to date the field remains largely silent with only sporadic, and mostly unverified, comments on the important role of the cultural factors in the shaping of unjust(ified) enrichment and restitution law around the world.[38] Perhaps, it remains the case, as one

---

[34] Dagan, *The Law and Ethics of Restitution* (n 5) 225–26.

[35] C Rotherham, 'Unjust Enrichment and the Autonomy of Law: Private Law as Public Morality' (1998) 61 *Modern Law Review* 580, 580, 588; H MacQueen, 'Book Review: Unjust Enrichment: A Study of Private Law and Public Values' (1998) 47 *International & Comparative Law Quarterly* 740, 741.

[36] ibid (Rotherham); cp *Olwell v Nye & Nissen* [1946] 173 P 2d 652 as discussed in Dagan, *The Law and Ethics of Restitution* (n 5) 210–30.

[37] ibid 580, 588 (Rotherham).

[38] M McInnes, 'The Canadian Principle of Unjust Enrichment: Comparative Insights into the Law of Restitution' (1999) 37 *Alberta Law Review* 1; K Barker 'Understanding the Unjust

critic puts it, that though the field 'will inevitably be affected by societal mores, this correlation is liable to be' and stay—I will add—'indirect and obscure'.[39]

In this book, I embark on a new voyage to study this territory. But in this exploration, I embrace different angles and postulates. I dismiss the presumption of strictly causal effect between law and culture, favouring instead a more holistic and meaning-oriented explication of this reciprocity. I settle for culture's watermark in the law seeking conspicuous correspondence between cultural perceptions and various law dispositions. I also acknowledge the important role of jurists and the professional community in legal craftsmanship. Furthermore, I do not aim to explicate the dynamics of enrichment law but the poetics of its static construction and default choices. Bearing in mind the endless ways in which any legal norm can be structured, the book does not target the question of 'what' the legal content is, but 'how' that content is structured and delivered.

In the following chapters I elucidate typical—and by typical, I mean representative, exemplary, archetypal or modular—patterns of legal crafting and the telling congruence of these patterns with culture. I target those exemplars, orientations or dispositions of wrongful enrichment law which emulate cultural perceptions of wealth and wealth acquisition. It is important to note that 'culture' has been defined in various ways.[40] In this book, I embrace an expansive definition of the term. By 'culture' I mean the pool of shared meanings, values, attitudes, perceptions, patterns, ideas and symbols with which humans understand their reality, interpret their life experience and shape their actions. Culture concerns both clear and implied 'patterns of thought and perception' which at times 'act below conscious levels'.[41] It is manifested and discernible in a variety of cultural mediums such as language, myths, art, literature, architecture, politics, media, law and more.[42]

In a later chapter I expound on certain processes that have been invoked by the late Ottoman Empire with the intention to 'Ottomanise' culture. The said processes revitalised Islamic themes, icons and motifs, aiming to assert the Empire's unity with Islamic tradition. The discussion of these processes may be described as a study of political ideology rather than one of culture. This ostensible inconsistency begs an explanation.

Enrichment Principle in Private Law: A Study of the Concept and its Reasons' in J Neyers, M McInnes and S Pitel (eds), *Understanding Unjust Enrichment* (Oxford, Hart Publishing, 2004) 81–83.

[39] Rotherham (n 35) 580, 588.

[40] M Minkov, *Cross-Cultural Analysis: The Science and Art of Comparing the World's Modern Societies and Their Cultures* (Thousand Oaks, CA, Sage, 2013) 10–11.

[41] 'Culture', *Oxford Dictionary of Sociology* (3rd edn, 2009) 153.

[42] A Amsterdam and J Bruner, *Minding the Law* (Cambridge, MA, Harvard University Press, 2002) 40, 263, 282–83.

Ideology, notes Michael Minkov, refers to the 'desirable' meanings, merits, attitudes and perceptions that a person wishes 'to see' in other people, 'which may or may not overlap with' his own. For example, a high official may loathe corruption in the corridors of power, but may himself accept bribes to ease certain financial difficulties.[43] Minkov's definition is a general version of the more common term of political ideology which denotes proposals, proclamations and ideas of a cohesive and idealised socio-political programme manifested in systematic processes of propagandising.

At first sight, ideology seems unrelated to culture. Such observation, however, is inaccurate. In his 'Ideology as a Cultural System', Clifford Geertz reminds us that culture is an indispensable ground of ideology. The latter, he argues, 'does not grow out of disembodied reflection' but 'is always bound up with the existing life situation of the thinker'. Resting on people's cultural context, ideology utilises contradictions, problematises themes and 'interworks' meanings embedded in a given culture to evoke emotional attitudes and responses.[44] For our purpose, discussing *Ottomanising* as processes of political ideology does not forsake cultural explications. On the contrary, it provides a deeper understanding of sensible cultural postulates which nurtured and facilitated those political processes. In fact, I use the Ottoman Empire's example to illustrate an exceptional case where legal crafting does not only imitate culture, but is more so designed to provoke cultural imitation of law.

It is perhaps here that I need to stress the 'integrative' trait of culture. Culture is formed as a web of 'interrelated' themes. Discussion of any theme often leads to a discussion of another. It is up to the researcher to discern those interwoven themes that seem most revealing on the subject at hand. Furthermore, 'culture' is a 'complex' phenomenon. Any 'unit of analysis' is both overgeneralised and reductive. Any culture necessarily contains many 'subcultures' while is itself only a portion of a bigger containing culture. No 'unit of analysis' is ever comprehensive or critic proof. Like culture, cultural themes are often 'diffused' terms which resist rigid taxonomies. A diffused concept, explains Minkov, is one 'whose boundaries cannot be determined in a way that will result in universal consensus'. Themes are not legal terms and are not prone to bear single titles and definitions. Many intra-related terms such as 'profit', 'gain' and 'money' can be interchangeable in describing and elucidating one theme.[45]

As noted earlier, culture is neither the output of reason nor a planned scheme of rational decisions. It is the output of the 'cumulative and balanced resultant of many selections of many individuals' notes

---

[43] Minkov (n 40) 42–43.

[44] C Geertz, 'Ideology as a Cultural System' in C Geertz (ed), *The Interpretation of Cultures* (New York, Basic Books, 1973) 193–94, 197, 207.

[45] Minkov (n 40) 22, 24–25, 29.

Talcott Parsons and his colleagues, or as Minkov puts it, 'even when people think that they have made a deliberate collective choice', their decision is eventually embedded, fashioned and 'imposed on them by economic, political, and historical factors'.[46] Hence, a useful method of discerning collective significances of a culture is invoking an eagle-eyed perspective and tracing general patterns. Cultural themes, patterns and perceptions resist intellectual depth. The deeper one seeks for rationalised details, the fewer answers one finds. It is a state of 'intrinsic incompleteness' to use Geertz terms. The latter described this condition picturesquely with a folklore anecdote. It tells of an Englishman who enquired into indigenous belief about the Earth's pillars. The reply he got was that the world 'rested on the back of an elephant which rested in turn on the back of a turtle', and afterwards it was 'turtles all the way down'.[47]

In his book on the 'enrichment' component of enrichment law, Andrew Lodder identifies three 'competing' concepts of enrichment. The first is 'value'-based. This concept focuses on the shift of monetary quantifiable values. The second is 'right'-based. This one perceives the case as a transfer of rights and a release of obligations. The third concept is 'wealth'-based. This concept accentuates the enrichment as a 'net accumulation of things having a value, whether through exchange', 'income' earning 'or otherwise'. The latter perception, stresses Lodder, 'elides the concepts of value and rights in the umbrella concept of "wealth"'.[48] Expectedly, dominant accounts of enrichment law conceive enrichment as 'wealth', wrongfulness as a matter of wealth 'misplacement',[49] a 'disapproved' acquisition of wealth or simply a 'reversible' wealth,[50] and restitution as a 'decision to undo nonconsensual shifts of wealth'.[51]

It is with this understanding of enrichment law doctrine that I intend to explore cultural themes. Two further enhancements are made to this study aiming to seek 'core' cultural attitudes about wealth acquisition. One is confining the study to intentional wrongs. The second is confining it to tangible property. These choices place the research, satisfactorily, in the overlapping area of the three supra-systems I intend to study. They are the European, the American and the late Ottoman. In legal terms, the case would largely be part of unjustified enrichment law for the former,

---

[46] ibid 32.

[47] C Geertz, 'Thick Description: Toward an Interpretive Theory of Culture' in C Geertz (ed), *The Interpretation of Cultures* (New York, Basic Books, 1973) 3, 29.

[48] A Lodder, *Enrichment in the Law of Unjust Enrichment and Restitution* (Oxford, Hart Publishing, 2012) 13, 30.

[49] F Giglio, 'A Systematic Approach to "Unjust" and "Unjustified' Enrichment"' (2003) 23(3) *Oxford Journal of Legal Studies* 455, 455.

[50] Birks (n 2) 19.

[51] Gergen (n 4) 1930.

of restitution for wrongs for the intermediate, and of *gasb* (usurpation) for the latter. Reaping an economic value through the appropriation or exploitation of another person's tangible property is a classic case. It mirrors the three 'fundamental principles' of restitution law as described by Graham Virgo. It is a case of unjust enrichment, a case of wrongful profit and a case of interfering with a proprietary entitlement.[52] The interplay of these principles generated much taxonomical debate among restitution law scholars;[53] nevertheless they provide an indispensable condition for a cross-cultural study of the law. Rich in meanings and perceptions, the case is well fit for a comparative study as it provides various legal and cultural ways of perceiving the event, each asserting a different angle.

Furthermore, intentional wrongs provoke core cultural attitudes. Deliberate wrongdoing promptly defies our sense of 'fairness' and 'equity'.[54] They challenge our very 'basic instincts and values', uncompromisingly.[55] Ernest Weinrib describes deliberate misplacements of wealth as 'intuitively offensive to our moral sensibilities'.[56] These human intuitions, though universal in nature, seed our cultural perceptions of the event and how we grasp proper and improper wealth acquisitions. Thus, intentional wrongs are best suited to investigate core cultural perceptions. In a same realm, the book does not deal with intangible and intellectual property cases as it would be too much ground to cover. Though these cases share different elements with tangible property cases, they consist of a separate class of cases with distinctive values, beliefs, themes and attitudes.[57]

The book studies three supra-nations or supra-states. Though the 'nation state' has been a classic unit for cultural enquiries, the supra-state offers a new and auspicious unit with which it is possible to comprehend 'cross-national realities' like cultural reality. Culture often stops at no political border. It is often carried by many historical, economic, political and regional significances which bypass the single state.[58] The 'supra-state paradigm', however, does not aim at downplaying or marginalising state or national specificities. It only highlights additional inclusive dimensions

---

[52] Virgo (n 21) 7–8.

[53] See, eg, A Burrows, *The Law of Restitution* (Oxford, Oxford University Press, 2011) 5, 9; A Burrows, 'Quadrating Restitution and Unjust Enrichment: A Matter of Principle' (2000) 8 *Restitution Law Review* 257, 269; Birks (n 2) 1.

[54] Zimmermann (n 3) 853; Gergen (n 4) 1927, 1929.

[55] ibid 1929 (Zimmermann).

[56] Weinrib (n 33) 24–25.

[57] See, eg, R Coombe, *The Cultural Life of Intellectual Properties: Authorship, Appropriation, and the Law* (Durham, NC, Duke University Press, 1998).

[58] For an explanation of the term 'region', see R Ostergren and M Bossé. *The Europeans: A Geography of People, Culture, and Environment* (New York, Guilford, 2011) 3–5.

in which important cultural perceptions lie.[59] Furthermore, the spatial, temporal and geographical 'remoteness' of each supra-state from other supra-states serves two purposes. It crystallises the impact each culture had on its respective law while minimising possible reciprocities between the different supra-nations. It also underplays the possible differences traceable at national, state- and other micro-levels providing, instead, broad and overarching lines of delineation. Perhaps not accidentally, these lines correspond, though imperfectly, with rooted divisions of legal families, namely continental law, common law and Islamic law traditions.

The book is produced in eight chapters. The first elucidates my theoretical framework concerning the law-as-culture paradigm and mimesis in legal crafting. The next six chapters are thematically divided in pairs. Each two handle, respectively, the law and culture of a single supra-state. Hence, the second and third chapters are dedicated to the European context. The fourth and fifth chapters examine the American context. And the sixth and seventh chapters discuss the late Ottoman context. The division of law and culture chapters in each pair aims at sustaining separate frameworks and hindering the impression of causality while explaining the elective affinity between the two at the end of each cultural chapter. Furthermore, I decided to avoid division according to doctrinal elements of wrongful enrichment as such division does not necessarily correlate with cultural thematic divisions. I dedicate the final chapter to conclusions and reflection on the comparative and collective levels. For convenience purposes, I use the DCFR terms of 'enriched' and 'disadvantaged' to denote the two parties of a wrongful enrichment case. To avoid gender-biased writing, I alternate between genders in each chapter.

---

[59] See, eg, G Joffé, 'Regionalism—A New Paradigm?' in M Telò (ed), *European Union and New Regionalism* (Hampshire, Ashgate, 2007) xiii, xiii–xiv; U Hedetoft and M Hjort, 'Introduction' in U Hedetoft and M Hjort (eds), *The Post-national Self* (Minneapolis, MN, University of Minnesota Press, 2002) vii, vii–xxxi.

1

Law as a Mimetic *Craft*

IN HIS EXPLICATION of the term 'tradition', H Patrick Glenn points at 'forms of capture'. These are objects of physical or visual traits, like art and archeological objects, which readily capture the past and communicate it to the present observer.[1] They contain knowledge, not only as to *what* they mean, but also as to *how* they mean. An ancient pot records data on historical and social practices primarily linked with its functional and aesthetic qualities. Yet it also exhibits the know-how on materials and crafting processes necessary to make the pot. This knowledge consists of rules formerly made as to how a pot is produced. These rules vary and are bound by place and time. They are mostly implicit in the work and rest on postulates valued by the community of craftspersons and often transmitted from one generation to another. These postulates communicate significant data for archeologists.

Like physical and visual objects, law is a 'form of capture'.[2] It communicates meanings on the levels of content and form. Ernest Weinrib defines content as the 'what-ness' of the matter. It sets what the matter is while differentiating it from what it is not. Content makes the matter 'determinate'. Form, however, is the qualities that 'renders content determinate'. Form, argues Weinrib, 'is not separate of content but is the ensemble of characteristics that marks the content as determinate'.[3] It is 'how' the matter is set and made. A legal craft records human thoughts and fleshes out their content. Law imposes form on cognitive substance using textuality as a chief instrument.[4]

Textuality is an important medium used in legal crafting. It captures meaning in two levels: form and content. Hermeneutics examines content and poetics targets form. Hermeneutics seeks to 'discover new and better interpretations' of the text and takes meanings as its pursued end. Poetics,

---

[1] H Glenn, *Legal Traditions of the World* (New York, Oxford University Press, 2007) 11.

[2] cp H Dagan, *Reconstructing American Legal Realism and Rethinking Private Law Theory* (Oxford, Oxford University Press, 2013) 51–52.

[3] E Weinrib, 'Legal Formalism: On the Immanent Rationality of Law' (1987–88) 97 *Yale Law Journal* 949, 958.

[4] See generally C Boeckx, *Language in Cognition: Uncovering Mental Structures and the Rules Behind Them* (West Sussex, Wiley-Blackwell, 2010). Against: J Hill and B Mannheim, 'Language and Worldview' (1992) 21 *Annual Review of Anthropology* 381, 382.

on the other hand, searches for those postulates that determine how meaning is constructed and delivered. It focuses on those 'conventions' or 'codes' that structure meaning and how one makes sense of content.[5] It exposes the postulates of meaning articulation.[6] One vital aspect of poetics is, what Tzvetan Todorov called, the 'verbal' aspect. It is the fictional image produced by the 'exposition', *descriptivity* and narrativity of the textual medium.[7] To communicate its message, law necessarily describes objects, persons, actions, occurrences, and settings. It engages in a 'labor of construction' which transforms 'a series of sentences' into 'an imaginary universe'. Through representative and performative acts the law constructs mental images; these are 'verbal representations of the fictional system' which help us make sense of what the law is.[8]

In this sense, legal crafting is like 'word painting', to use Rebecca McClanahan's term.[9] Law communicates meaning through verbal representation of reality and constructed images of life. Fragmented, shoddy and thin as they may be, these crafted images necessarily stand in some relation to the actual or imagined world. The capacity of simulacra to stand in juxtaposition with reality can be effectively examined in terms of mimesis.[10] Mimesis is a term originally used in art and literature theory, and later on employed in various fields of study, notably philosophy, history, psychology, sociology, anthropology and drama. Mimesis describes the relationship between a crafted image and reality in two senses: one is the 'reflective' sense, the other is the 'compositional' sense; both senses are inherent traits of mimesis.[11]

The 'reflective' sense, explains Matthew Potolsky, is the image's capacity to imitate reality or the external world. This mimetic trait is typically called the 'Platonic' trait. The other sense is the 'compositional' one. This sense perceives the image as 'a craft with its own internal laws and aims' working to reveal certain 'norms of human thought' rather than reflect the world. It is also referred to as the 'Aristotelian' trait. A simulacrum of any object does not reflect the object itself but our perception of that object. Reflective mimesis, thus, does not describe a relational tie to the ontological world but to the epistemological one. It concerns the distinctive way in

---

[5] J Culler, *Literary Theory: A Very Short Introduction* (Oxford, Oxford University Press, 2000) 60, 61, 62, 69; S Almog, *Mishpat yi Sifrut bi'idan Digitali* (*Law and Literature in the Digital Age*) (Shrigim-Leon, Nevo, 2007) 33–34.

[6] P Brooks, 'Introduction' in T Todorov, *Introduction to Poetics*, trans R Howard (Minneapolis, MN, University of Minnesota Press, 1984) vii, ix.

[7] K Polking, *Writing A to Z* (Cincinnati, OH, Writer's Digest Books, 1990) 106; R McClanahan, *Word Painting: A Guide to Writing More Descriptively* (Cincinnati, OH, Writer's Digest Books, 2000) 7.

[8] Todorov (n 6) 14–16, 27.

[9] McClanahan (n 7) 7.

[10] Todorov (n 6) 28.

[11] M Potolsky, *Mimesis* (New York, Routledge, 2006) 1–4, 6–7, 15, 19, 23, 33, 41, 42.

which we sort and organise the world around us, the postulates, meanings and concerns with which we assess and interpret reality, or in a simple word: culture. Reflective mimesis is tied to the 'social and historical context' of the product. 'Different cultures' notes Potolsky, have distinctive ways of perceiving the world. One culture's convention may seem odd to another culture.[12] Mimesis, hence, exhibits a crafted image in two senses: the image as a product of internal rules and the image as reflection of a unique cultural perception.

Utilising processes of mimesis, law produces an image which informs our understanding of legal norms. Anthony G Amsterdam and Jerome Bruner analogise law with literature. Like a work of literature, they assert, law 'imitates' life.[13] Law's mimetic traits facilitate a dialect between two shaping forces: one is law as a professional craft produced by jurists and adhering to certain postulates of legal knowledge; the other is law as manifestation of culture and the distinctive way in which we perceive and cluster the world around us. Clifford Geertz affirms this thesis. He argues that law is a 'craft of place'. Law works 'by the light of local knowledge', he says, and is 'part of a distinctive manner of imagining the real'. Law, he explains, is not occupied with events but with the 'representation' of those events.[14] Two views of law inform his argument. One is the 'functional' view which proceeds along consensual and established postulates, rules and protocols which inform us how to resolve conflicts.[15] This is law-as-knowledge.[16] The other is the 'construing' view. This view emphasises the visionary, generative and expounding 'powers' of law which not only shape human conduct but also interpret it. Those 'powers', Geertz notes, are 'rooted in the collective resources of culture rather than in the separate capacities of individuals'. This is law-as-culture.[17]

Like a work of art, a legal artefact is not only an interpretable product but is itself an interpretation of cultural materials. This understanding is borrowed from Ruth Lorand's aesthetic evaluation approach. Lorand explains her approach as one which lies on the axis of 'raw material' and 'final product'. According to this approach 'the product interprets the materials by demonstrating what can be done with them'. Thus, she proceeds, 'the product is not only an end but also a means for a new and

---

[12] ibid; Plato, *Republic*, trans A Bloom (New York, Basic Books, 1991) 279; Aristotle, *Aristotle's Theory of Poetry and Fine Art*, trans S Butcher (New York, Dover, 1951) 7.

[13] A Amsterdam and J Bruner, *Minding the Law* (Cambridge, MA, Harvard University Press, 2002) 3.

[14] C Geertz, 'Local Knowledge: Fact and Law in Comparative Perspective' in C Geertz (ed), *Local Knowledge—Further Essays in Interpretive Anthropology* (New York, Basic Books, 2000) 173.

[15] R Rorty, *Philosophy and the Mirror of Nature* (Princeton, NJ, Princeton University Press, 1981) 320–22; ibid 222–23 (Geertz).

[16] cp Geertz, 'Local Knowledge' (n 14) 215.

[17] ibid 167, 173, 184, 215.

better understanding of the materials'.[18] To discern the law-as-culture sense of a constructed image, we ought to know how law is a work of the legal profession, and what the postulates of law-as-knowledge are. These postulates are often traced in the different textual levels and the doctrinal dynamics, notably technicalities, style, mechanisms and functionality. They often leave their obvious mark on the cognitive image constructed by the law as well.

Take, for example, Articles 96 and 97 of the *Mecelle* (Ottoman Civil Code). The first titled 'disposal of another's property without permission' provides that 'it is impermissible for anyone to dispose of another's property without her permission'. The second is entitled 'laying hands on another's wealth' and states that 'it is impermissible for anyone to lay hands on another's wealth without a legal ground'. These Articles provide general and typical traits of law-as-profession. They are instructive, pithy and organised in their descriptions. Language is serious and even a bit dull. Persons are anonymous. Occurrences are specific but unhistoric.[19] Functionality is provided by rules, exceptions, contrasts and equilibrations. Mechanisms rest on categorisation and order. These traits affect the imaginary image which law produces in people's cognition. This image is mostly formal in content, pictorial in description, also magisterial but flat in tone. It depicts a two-dimensional world which lacks any significant depth. It is hardly artistic in composition and poorly aesthetic. The image, however, is evidently representational yearning to be naturalistic and lifelike. Contained figures can, to a great extent, be described as archetypal, simplified, thin and even pale. Objects seem typified and flat. And the whole occurrences contained are undramatically narrated.

Of course, these observations are not necessarily true for all forms of law. They may be apparent in a legislative act more than in a judicial decision. Judicial decisions usually evoke more vibrant and colourful images of life. Nevertheless, they are confined to the same variants of legislative artistry but differ in degree and intensity. Law-as-culture is prominent in other parts of the image. It is present in the semantic moulds and signification processes which construct the image and tell us what it depicts. It is not the theme of the image itself but how it is presented. And it is not what the crafted image means in doctrinal terms. It is rather how the image communicates its content to law's consumers. In our case, it is not about restitution or unjustified enrichment, but about how an archetypal

---

[18] R Lorand, *Aesthetic Order: A Philosophy of Order, Beauty and Art* (London, Routledge, 2000) 162–68; F Cucker, *Manifold Mirrors: The Crossing Paths of the Arts and Mathematics* (Cambridge, Cambridge University Press, 2013) 114.

[19] A Byyūmī, *Lughat al-Qānūn fī Daw' Lughat al-Naṣ: Dirāsa fī a-Ttamāsuk al-Khaṭṭī* (*The Language of Law in Light of Text Language: A Study in Textual Cohesion*) (al-Maḥ alla al-Kubra, Dar al-Kutub al-Qānūnyyah, 2010) 41–42, 51–59.

incident of wrongful gaining is drawn and conceived, which patterns and exemplars appear in the picture, and how the incident is narrated by the crafted image. In general, the more the observer zooms out and evades traits of functionality, the more she is revealed to the cultural dimension of the picture.

Remarkably no matter how much legal professionalism is invoked, law would continue to bear cultural baggage needing to be unpacked. Professionalism cannot inhibit cultural mimesis or filter out culture. One extreme example of legal professionalism is Legal Science. This was a powerful school of thought established by German scholars following heated debates on the proper way to codify German law in the mid- to late-nineteenth century. These scholars called for the application of 'formal logic' to produce systematic rules and principles. They collected 'raw' legal materials and then engaged in an 'inductive process' which synthesised concrete cases into different levels of abstraction, producing rules and principles of broad applicability, a process also known as 'logical expansion'. The process aimed at excluding 'intuition and subconscious' assumptions. It elevated pure rationalism, and sought analytic clarity rejecting all 'non-legal' data, be it cultural or historical.[20]

Oddly enough, the main idea behind the rise of German Legal Science was the rejection of revolution-based codification exemplified in the French civil code. Proponents of this school of thought persuasively argued that law is an 'organic product' peculiar to the people and their history. It accentuates their distinct '*Volksgeist*' (people's collective spirit). Any codification, they asserted, ought to rest on an extensive study of the law, its Roman law roots as adopted in Germany, and the 'historical context' of the law.[21] Their argument that cultural and historical data can be filtered out by professional work seems odd and inconsistent with their initial presumption that law is *necessarily* a product of specific time and place. In fact, this inconsistency was one of the primarily pitfalls of German Legal Science. Professional products are inherently locked in their social, cultural and historic backgrounds. The work of nineteenth-century jurists took place in an 'intellectual climate' which embraced liberal values such as 'individualism' and 'autonomy'. Their work eventually expressed those ideals and fleshed out many of their hidden beliefs.[22] A claim that professional legal work is capable of circumventing cultural data is, at best, fictitious ideality.

Hans-Georg Gadamer explains the indispensability of the spatiotemporal context in terms of 'historicity of consciousness' (*Wirkungsgeschichtliches*

[20] J Merryman, *The Civil Law Tradition: An Introduction to the Legal Systems of Europe and Latin America* (Stanford, CA, Stanford University Press, 2007) 61, 63–65; M Glendon, P Carozza and C Picker, *Comparative Legal Traditions in a Nutshell* (St Paul, MN, West, 2008) 33–43.

[21] Mautner (n 30) 42–44.

[22] Merryman (n 20) 3–32, 64–65; Glendon, Carozza and Picker (n 20).

Bewußtsein). According to Gadamer, understanding always occurs against the background of the agent's historical context and is considered an 'effect' of it. In phenomenological terms, jurists are situated within a particular horizon (*Horizont*) that is determined by the historical place in which they are situated. Their cognitive process belongs to a certain time. 'Belonging' is an inseparable condition of these processes.[23] It informs the meaning of the law and sets the path for its interpretations. Like literal textuality, law's textuality is inherently cultural. In his *Poetics of Culture*, Stephen Greenblatt criticises a number of literary theories like Formalism and New Criticism which consider textual products as autonomous entities. He fiercely rejects their claim that the residing links between the text and its historical-cultural context could be evaded. Greenblatt argues that the text is innately integrated with the total sum of social thought and practices of its time. Textuality is significantly informed by all cultural forces which shape the societal and historical conditions of the author. A text cannot be but part of the episteme informing society at a given time and place.[24] An attempt to tear law off its cultural context or culture off law is doomed to failure. Legal expertise does not oust cultural substance. It merely decides not to pursue cultural observations.

The law as a mimetic craft model rests on rooted theories of language and cognition. In his *Essay Concerning Human Understanding*, John Locke argues that mental concepts, namely the sorting, naming and expressing of things and ideas are 'as men, and not as Nature, makes them'.[25] They do not reflect an intrinsic essence. Rather, they exhibit the identity of their utiliser and the way she classifies and organises things in the world. An enquiry into these concepts discloses the cognitive perception of reality that is shared and communicated by the group. Though made centuries ago, Locke's argument persists in being accurate and is still supported by contemporary studies in cognition and psychology. According to these studies, our mental perception is processed through cognitive categorisation and application of previous knowledge to the produced categories. With these processes, we are able to make sense of reality and claim we understand it.[26]

Concepts are cognitive categories which sort things in the world as part of a functional service provided by the mind. Instead of mentally

---

[23] H Gadamer, *Method and Truth* (London, Continuum International, 2004) 252, 298, 335; Mautner (n 30) 86–100.

[24] J Veenstra, 'The New Historicism of Stephen Greenblatt: On Poetics of Culture and the Interpretation of Shakespeare' (1995) 34(3) *History and Theory* 174, 176, 177–78.

[25] J Locke, *An Essay Concerning Human Understanding* (London, Willian Tegg, 1849) 299, 333–34.

[26] See, eg, G Murphy, *The Big Book of Concepts* (Cambridge, MA, Massachusetts Institute of Technology, 2004); Z Salzmann, J Stanlaw and N Adachi, *Language, Culture and Society: An Introduction to Linguistic Anthropology* (Boulder, CO, Westview, 2011) 265–67.

processing a newly perceived item from scratch, concepts spare time and effort by offering a readily available category with which that item can be sorted and understood.[27] Using established categories, we know that the flying object is a 'bird' and the standing thing is a 'tree' even if we have not seen those specific objects before. By sorting them with an exemplar or a typified category we already have we can mentally grasp the item. In a similar manner, we understand abstract notions such as maturity, marriage or family by cognitive categories formerly constructed in line with the way we sort and arrange these issues in life. These cognitive entities organise our mental perception of the world, but more so, they 'tie our past experiences to our present interactions with the world'. Hence, define who we are and with whom we belong.[28]

Cognitive categories reflect the scheme of selections and assessments we made of reality. These choices are 'grounded in conceptions of *what matters* to ourselves and those on whom we depend'; they are an integral part of our perception. They create and sustain our collective identity by promoting 'the continuing adherence to a particular understanding of human affairs and the values by which they should be measured'.[29] Culture is, thus, defined as the pool of categories which we 'internalised' throughout our lives enabling us 'to grasp the world' in a certain way and limit our 'capacity' to do that in 'ways that digress the structure and content of these categories'.[30] These categories are not confined to cognition but also extend to language. Categories are communicated through language and reflected by it. According to Wilhelm von Humbold, language provides men with 'prior linguistic comprehension of the world' enabling them to create and sketch their conception of that world.[31] Humbold defines this phenomenon as *Weltansicht*, the way language conceives reality in preset moulds, templates and patterns. With *Weltansicht*, culture furnishes people with certain preset processes to communicate their needs, interpretations and ideas.[32]

The modern cogitators of the language-as-culture theory are Edward Sapir and his student Benjamin Lee Whorf. Both scholars argue that language is encoded with conceptions of culture, and thus, reflect and reproduce 'cultural patterns' of thoughts and ideas.[33] They assert that language

---

[27] Amsterdam and Bruner (n 13) 19–26.

[28] Murphy (n 26) 1, 385.

[29] Amsterdam and Bruner (n 13) 23, 24.

[30] M Mautner, *Mishpat yi Tarbut* (*Law and Culture*) (Ramat-Gan, Bar-Ilan University Press, 2008) 28.

[31] J Underhill, *Humboldt, Worldview and Language* (Edinburgh, Edinburgh University Press, 2009) 18.

[32] ibid 17; Salzmann, Stanlaw and Adachi (n 26) 309. cp O Jespersen, *Growth and Structure of the English Language* (Leipzig, BG Teubner, 1912) 17.

[33] E Sapir, *Selected Writings in Language, Culture and Personality*, (ed) D Mandelbaum (Berkeley, CA, University of California Press, 1985) 161–63.

fashions people's communication by fixating a 'grammar' of talk which sorts and organises perception in a certain way. They also add that rules of linguistic conception differ from one culture to another. Thus, how an idea is expressed in one language would be different from the way it is communicated in another.[34] In spite of its allure, the Sapir–Whorf hypothesis has been strongly contested, especially with regard to its deterministic claim. Empirical evidence shows that language as moulds which restrain people's thought and reason is an exaggerated claim.[35] Language, in fact, has an orienting impact. It tends to shape the way people think or as Claire Kramsch puts it 'the way a given language encodes experience semantically makes aspects of that experience not exclusively accessible, but just more salient for the users of that language'.[36]

According to Lev Vygotsky and Alexander Luria, language is itself a cultural artefact which develops alongside cultural progress. Like any tool made by humans, language is built to accommodate practices, serve needs and achieve goals important to that culture.[37] It reflects the knowledge, history, culture, world-view and experience of many generations.[38] In textuality, we find the 'social patrimony', 'symbolic capital' and 'know-how' of culture.[39] Textuality emulates the accumulated knowledge developed by a certain culture.[40] Joel Sherzer describes this phenomenon in terms of 'textual patterning' which both society and language produce and apply through the nexus of 'discourse'. The latter is manifested in 'the myths, legends, stories, verbal duels, and conversations that constitute a society's verbal life'.[41] Stuart Hall explains the condition referring to a 'conceptual map' which members of a culture construct as a shared way of interpreting signs and producing meanings. To share a culture, thus, is to 'see the world from within the same conceptual map and to make sense of it through the same language systems'.[42]

Culture informs the basic cognitive concepts with which the linguistic and textual dimensions are produced and interpreted in legal crafting.

---

[34] B Whorf, *Language, Thought and Reality: Selected Writings of Benjamin Lee Whorf* (New York, Technology, 1956) 212–15.

[35] See, eg, S Pinker, *The Language Instinct: How the Mind Creates Language* (New York, Harper Perennial Modern Classics, 2007) 60–61.

[36] C Kramsch, *Language and Culture* (Oxford, Oxford University Press, 2001) 13, 14.

[37] R Nisbett and A Norenzayan, 'Culture and Cognition' in D Medin and H Pashler (eds), *Stevens' Handbook of Experimental Psychology: Cognition*, vol 2 (New York, Wiley, 2001) 569–71; M Cole, *Cultural Psychology: A Once and Future Discipline* (Cambridge, MA, Harvard University Press, 2003) xiv.

[38] ibid xiv (Cole).

[39] Kramsch (n 36) 10, 14.

[40] Murphy (n 26) 432–33.

[41] J Sherzer, 'A Discourse-Centered Approach to Language and Culture' (1987) 89(2) *American Anthropologist* 295, 295–96, 305–06.

[42] S Hall, 'The Work of Representation' in S Hall (ed), *Representation: Cultural Representations and Signifying Practices* (London, Sage, 1997) 13, 19, 22, 24, 25.

No matter how much legal terminology deviates from the ordinary usage of language,[43] a legal artefact is inevitably situated in culture's unique concepts. It is unavoidably nurtured by the discourses and moulding themes of culture. Ruth Benedict defines themes as the 'patterns' according to which a certain society makes its choices out of the 'arc' of possible human and social concerns. Each culture, she argues, capitalises certain 'segments' of the full spectrum of these concerns, constructing its unique identity by way of defining what is relevant and vital and what is not. These are shared 'patterns', which pervade and integrate culture, imposing 'conformity' and 'uniformity' and affecting people's selections.[44] Clyde Kluckhohn perceives patterning themes as 'cultural configurations'. Filmer Northrop stresses their key role as defining people's notions, values and conceptions of reality. Morris Opler describes them as 'dynamic affirmations', conscious and unconscious, tacit and stated, which design people's actions and thoughts.[45]

Cultural themes have been under attack for their assertion of predictive, integrative and foundational powers. Themes cannot necessarily predict cultural developments. They are inaccurate in presuming full consistencies and they definitely do not mould cultures in a coercive and deterministic pattern.[46] Nevertheless, cultural themes are still valid for their descriptive and orienting traits. According to Geertz, the presence of incidental 'inconsistencies', be they 'illogical', 'historical' or 'accidental residues' of culture, does not invalidate the 'orienting' force of cultural themes. In fact, the actuality and utility of themes continue to be widely acknowledged across anthropology and social sciences.[47] Identification and explication of themes are a significant part of ethnography[48] and cultural studies.

---

[43] H Mattila, 'Legal Vocabulary' in P Tiersma and L Solan (eds), *The Oxford Handbook of Language and Law* (Oxford, Oxford University Press, 2012) 27, 28.

[44] R Benedict, *Patterns of Culture* (Boston, MA, Houghton Mifflin, 1934) 24, 48–49; H Sidky, *Perspectives on Culture: A Critical Introduction to Theory in Cultural Anthropology* (New Jersey, NJ, Pearson, 2004) 150–53. R Benedict and M Mead, *An Anthropologist at Work* (New Jersey, NJ, Rutgers-State University of New Jersey Press, 2011) 204.

[45] C Kluckhohn and E Hoebel, 'Covert Culture and Administrative Problems' (1943) 45(2) *American Anthropologist* 213, 218; F Northrop, 'Jurisprudence in the Law School Curriculum' (1948–49) 1 *Journal of Legal Education* 482, 489; M Opler, 'Themes as Dynamic Forces in Culture' (1945) 51(3) *American Journal of Sociology* 198, 198–99.

[46] See, eg, A Cohen, 'An Evaluation of "Themes" and Kindred Concepts' (1946) 52(1) *American Journal of Sociology* 41; A Cohen, 'On the Place of "Themes" and Kindred Concepts in Social Theory' (1948) 50(3) *New Anthropologist: New Series* 436, 437; S Moore, 'Law and Anthropology' (1969) 6 *Biennial Review of Anthropology* 252, 263, 276. For a reply, see M Opler, 'The Context of Themes' (1949) 51(2) *American Anthropologist* 323.

[47] Geertz, 'Local Knowledge' (n 14) 187.

[48] C Geertz, 'The Way We Think Now: Ethnography of Modern Thought' in C Geertz (ed), *Local Knowledge—Further Essays in Interpretive Anthropology* (New York, Basic Books, 2000) 157.

They also inspired the 'thematic approach' to data used in advanced qualitative analysis.[49]

These elucidations throw some light on the paradigm of law-as-culture, but they do not fully explain how and why a legal artefact imitates segments of culture. In this chapter, I will suggest preliminary answers to these questions based on the mimetic trait of artefacts in a general context. I will leave it to the rest of the book to look into these answers in concrete cases of wrongful enrichment. For now, let us examine some widely common artefacts in their cultural settings. Take, for example, the pink onesie, the pink cot bedding and the pink nursery walls. Pink is not innately girlish. In some cultures, however, it is a gender signifier and carries baby girl connotations. In fact, many artefacts are mimetically produced pink and expectedly replicate these meanings. A wedding ring is another example. It signals a married status. The mimetic artistry of wedding rings reproduces this preset meaning. Producing triangular bands or funny shoes, instead, would usually signal other meanings and jam the original one. Banners, billboards and signs are also mimetically reproduced in certain shapes as information carriers. We read them for data, announcements or advertisements. If the signage industry decided to use plants and trees as information carriers instead, it would seem odd and troublesome for consumers looking for this information.

An artefact usually possesses functional and aesthetic traits. But it often has a mimetic trait as well. The mimetic trait works to enhance meaning and naturalise it in a given cultural setting. It merges meaning with its complementing background. Mimesis, however, is not confined to physical objects but extends to verbal artefacts as well. Metaphors are a good example. Metaphors are verbal expressions, like words or phrases, which we apply to an object or action in spite of literal inapplicability. We do that to suggest resemblance or equivalency of some sort between the compared items. The use of metaphors is a work of mimesis. One can, for example, treat ideas as material things in metaphors like 'I have an idea', 'I gave you that idea' or 'put your idea on paper'.[50] A metaphor enhances meaning and makes the user's intention more intelligible to the listener. On a rhetorical level, a metaphors naturalises the comparison and legitimises derivative conclusions. Hence, for example, it would be more acceptable to advance proprietary solutions to inventive ideas in a society which uses such a metaphor, than in one which does not objectify ideas as is the case with many indigenous cultures.

---

[49] See, eg, J Underhill, *Ethnolinguistics and Cultural Concepts: Truth, Love, Hate and War* (Cambridge, Cambridge University Press, 2012); G Ryan and H Bernard, 'Techniques to Identify Themes' (2003) 15(1) *Field Methods* 85; M Miles and M Huberman, *Qualitative Data Analysis: An Expanded Sourcebook* (Thousand Oaks, CA, Sage, 1994) 56.

[50] G Lakoff and M Johnson, *Metaphors We Live By* (Chicago, IL, University of Chicago Press, 2003) 10.

Human action can also be treated as a cultural artefact with clear mimetic capacity. An academic who desires to look and sound like a senior professor, may wish to dress, act and speak like one. Imitative behaviour can naturalise the action and produce preliminary acceptance and legitimacy for the imitator. If I and some friends plan to open a restaurant, it would be welcoming to a greater number of clients if we just imitate the conventions of a food serving place instead of inventing such from scratch. In similar vein, a newly established radio station would find it very 'natural' to open news updates with conventional attention grabbing soundtracks and not a 'Looney Tunes' one. Listeners would perceive the former more recognisable and more acceptable. In similar manner, a startup company will often imitate conventions practised by other similar companies to run its business and workforce. This is a claim to greater productivity as accepted in that business sector. Mimesis transforms meaning and thus is a chief device of poetics. To put a wooden cross behind a podium would transform a regular hall into a chapel by imitative actions. If we allow in people with court dresses and wigs instead, that hall can turn into a courtroom or perhaps a performing theatre.

The mimetic trait of any human artefact utilises relevant themes and practices to optimise understanding, clear up intentions and increase effectiveness. It facilitates efficiency by sparing the time and effort necessary to construct meaning. It also legitimises the artefact, naturalises it and makes it more acceptable to social agents. A legal artefact is no exception. Along with functional and aesthetic traits, a legal artefact possesses a powerful mimetic capacity which utilises professional as well as social and cultural postulates. To be recognisable and acceptable, law needs to imitate the image of life as we recognise it. A law that reads like an essay in astrophysics would most likely be rejected. The work of mimesis communicates legal meaning and content in an identifiable and naturalised way. Through mimesis law maximises its meaning to the local ear and empowers normative justification. Like an indispensable language, law uses mimesis to convey meaning, authority and legitimacy.

In fact, the mimetic trait can be deliberately and purposefully utilised to decrease plausible refutations and anaesthetise potential objections. Life examples are abundant. Morally contested actions like prostitution can be sold to the doubtful by imitating postulates of casual service provision. Trade of illegal drugs to minors can regrettably be enhanced by deliberate imitation of candy shapes and colours. Fraudulent business practices can be concealed and naturalised by imitating certain business conventions. The aim of intentional mimesis of accepted postulates, which I refer to as *imitatio*, is to distort, mutate, conceal, euphemise or beautify original meaning by resting on familiar and acceptable postulates of the imitated action or object. With *imitatio*, the utiliser can achieve greater legitimacy in consumers' eyes, as well as greater degrees of social and cultural acceptance. Remarkably the terms 'legitimacy' and 'to legitimate' are themselves defined in terms of *imitatio* and its reaped benefits. The former is 'conforming to recognised principles or accepted rules and standards'. The latter is described in terms of lending 'authority or respectability' or showing and affirming 'to be justified'.[51]

In a similar vein, law can also involve a work of *imitatio*. Legalising or passing laws on debatable issues have the power to erode criticism to various degrees and normalise the balances offered by the law. For example, in many countries around the world, smoking bans in public areas were not the norm. In fact, many years ago they were very controversial. Using *imitatio* legislators overcame resistant public voices. Normalising these bans was not only the consequence of legal enforcement, but more so the result of these laws' capacity to introduce pervading powerful images of life in which healthy people are not smoking in public areas. These simulacrum images infiltrated people's life conceptions and increasingly became part of their *normal* social attitudes. Through legislation these images are infused in people's mind and culture. *Imitatio* demonstrates a complementing reciprocity with regard to the law-as-culture paradigm. It elucidates cases of counter-mimesis, where law does not imitate culture, but culture imitates law. In the following chapters I will examine the law of wrongful enrichment as a mimetic artefact and focus on the law-as-culture paradigm. In the seventh chapter, I will present and discuss the interesting case of legal *imitatio* as practised in the late Ottoman Empire.

---

[51] 'Legitimacy' and 'to Legitimate', *Merriam-Webster's Collegiate Dictionary*, 11th edn, Kindle edn (2006) locations 666245, 666260.

2

European Law

THE ROUTE TO EXEMPLARS

IN HIS CONTRIBUTION to the *International Encyclopedia of Comparative Law*, Peter Schlechtriem attempts to round up the many paths different legal systems around the world have taken to deal with property-related unjust enrichments. Perhaps it is this far-stretched aim which begot the need to commence his chapter with a warning to the readers. No 'fruitful results' would be yielded in a comparative legal analysis which assumes 'the existence of particular dogmatic categories' or seeks 'correlations among foreign legal systems', he asserts.[1] This may hold true for a global oriented study. One expects a more compromising view when confining the study to the laws of Europe. But this seems not to be the case. For example, the architects of the European codified model rules on unjustified enrichment, part of the so-called Draft Common Frame of Reference, have disclosed comparable doubts as to whether 'some minimum core' of any 'unjustified enrichment' rules could be forthrightly traced in all European Union (EU) Member States.[2]

Narrowing pan-European comparisons down to limited parts of Europe would not necessarily change these assertions. European laws are often too diverse to overlap, so the argument goes. But the complexity and dissimilarity of these legal rules should not lead to dereliction of, what I deem are, discernible exemplars in European law, unexclusive as they may be. Examining the law of Western continental members of the EU yields several undeniable consistencies and default patterns which ought to be highlighted and discussed. These perceptible voices of legal patterns found in the Romano-Germanic law of Western Europe should not be silenced even if additional patterns could be discerned. In many of these jurisdictions they are important moulds in which the case under study tends to be grasped.

---

[1] P Schlechtriem, 'Unjust Enrichment by Interference with Property Rights' in *International Encyclopedia of Comparative Law*, vol X (2007) 3.

[2] C von Bar and S Swann, *Principles of European Law: Unjustified Enrichment* (Munich, Sellier, 2010) 93.

WESTERN CONTINENTAL LAW

This section will provide a brief historical chronology of wrongful enrichment law. The aim is to offer a very broad sketch of the doctrinal development of European law since Roman law. For obvious reasons only highlights and major changes of the case's legal treatment will be covered. Subsequently, the current law of several Western European countries, confining examples to Germany, Austria, Italy and Spain will be reported. France, as a debatable case, will be discussed in a later section. To complement examination, the section will also discuss the Draft Common Frame of Reference. In these examinations, I neither aim at detailed accounts of law nor do I see a need to do so, especially when I risk pointless over-complications. Each account is instead offered in a manner which facilitates better discernment of the legal poetics I wish to discuss in the following sections.

Historical Overview

Roman law originally conceived a case of property appropriation or exploitation as a wrong of *furtum* or *furtum usus* (theft broadly defined).[3] Such cases often required bad faith and intention on the part of the enriched person to gain from his wrongful action. Roman law provided the disadvantaged person with different courses of action to seek remedy. Each course of action highlighted different perspectives of the case. One such course of action is the penal *actio furti*. This action stressed the bad behaviour of the enriched person. If the person was found guilty, he would pay back double (or more) the value appropriated. This action usually encompassed serious diminishing (and even abolition) of that person's reputation and social standing. The aim of the procedure was mainly to punish for dishonesty and condemn the enriched person's bad behaviour.[4] The main protagonist of this course of action was the enriched person whose misconduct was the gist of the adjudication process.

Another course of action which emphasised the enriched person and his wrongful behaviour was the *condictio ex causa furtiva*. This was a special case of the *condictio* (condition) actions addressing *furtum*. The action was subject to proof of wrongful conduct and pursued recovery of the disputed object rather than compensation or penalty. It obliged the enriched

---

[3] W Buckland and A McNair, *Roman Law and Common Law: A Comparison in Outline* (Cambridge, Cambridge University Press, 1965) 102–03, 353–54, 379; R Zimmermann, *The Law of Obligations: Roman Foundations of the Civilian Tradition* (Cape Town, Juta, 1992) 981–83.

[4] ibid 923, 932–33 (Zimmermann).

person to return the object or pay for it, if it had perished.[5] A more general and 'residual' claim was the *condictio sine causa* (condiction for lack of ground). In general terms, this condiction was used when no other specific condiction could be invoked. It addressed all wealth transfer cases which lacked legal basis (*causa*) and called for reversion. This condiction hinged on a proof of the object shifting hands rather than on wrongful conduct on the part of the enriched.[6]

Another redress which, like the *condictio sine causa*, shifted the weight to the disadvantaged and his proprietary autonomy was the *rei vindicatio* (vindication of the thing). This redress was available mostly for property owners on grounds of unapproved dispossession. Unlike the condictions which were *in personam* actions, this course of action was *in rem* in scope. The disadvantaged person could claim back his object against any holder with a *rei vindicatio*. The wrongful conduct of the enriched was alien to this procedure. A mere dispossession of the object was enough to satisfy the claim. That is unless the defendant had a valid defence. A successful action would eventually instruct the latter to return the object aiming at restoration and restitution.[7] Another course of action which did not directly address the case at hand, yet contributed to the formation of liabilities in unjustified enrichment later on was the *actio de in rem verso*. This claim originally addressed special cases which lacked express agency. The claim was often invoked by third parties against *paterfamilias* (head of family) or slave-owners to recover benefits conferred under transactions with children or slaves. These normally lacked legal capacity to contract or be sued and could not bind the head of the household.

As time passed, courses of action which highlighted the enriched person and his wrongful conduct increasingly lost status paving the way for redresses which turned attention to the disadvantaged person and his challenged domain. Although *furtum* and the penal *actio furti* were received in the *ius commune*, by the late Middle Ages/Early Renaissance they were steadily fading away in civil litigation and were instituted instead in the criminal arena as criminal act and prosecution process. Likewise, the *condictio ex causa furtiva* was losing its 'practical significance', and eventually was obliterated, by the modern law of delict and the *condictio sine causa*. At a later stage, it was mostly excluded from modern codes like the Napoleonic Civil Code (*Code Napoléon*) and the German Civil Code (*Bürgerliches Gesetzbuch* (BGB)). Adversely, the *rei vendicatio* and the *condictio sine causa* were gradually embraced as dominant redresses for the case being considered. The latter course of action increasingly gained

---

[5] ibid 941–942; J Dawson, *Unjust Enrichment: A Comparative Analysis* (New York, William S Hein & Co, 1999) 42–43.
[6] ibid 857 (Zimmermann).
[7] ibid 940–42, 947–48.

power as a general model which fostered a natural human tendency for fair treatment in cases of groundless enrichments.[8] These shifts eventually led to the elevation of *causa* as one key element in most legal enquiries of the case.[9]

By the early seventeenth century, it was arguably Hugo Grotius (1583–1645) who made the additional conceptual shift from the residual *condictio sine causa* to the general rule of 'enrichment without cause' as an independent source of obligation.[10] In his *De iure belli ac pacis* (*On the Law of War and Peace*) (1625), *Inleidinge tot de Hollandsche rechtsgeleerdheid* (*Introduction to the Jurisprudence of Holland*) (1631) and a letter to his brother Willem (1616), he expanded Aquinas's and Scholastic's ideas of *restitutio* (restitution) in cases of *inaequalittas* (inequalities) arguing that 'Obligation from deriving profit arises when someone without legal title derives or would derive profit from another person's property',[11] and more generally that 'inequality' which enriches a person at the expense of another demands restitution 'without regard to the way in which he came to acquire it'.[12]

These developments were utilised later by many scholars, notably Friedrich Carl von Savigny (1779–1861) and the historical school who called for a scientific study of the conditions. One of their important contributions was marking the changes in the patrimonial status of the parties as an important supplement to the question of *causa*. These ideas eventually generated modern models of unjustified enrichment liabilities like the German BGB which offered general provision for unjustified enrichment. The *actio de in rem verso* went into similar historical changes. The contractual basis between the disadvantaged and the intermediary (ie, slave or child) was increasingly left out and the emphasis was gradually put on the gain shifting hands. The three-party base of the action was broadened to include two-party cases, and the redress was generalised to include more and more cases of enrichment regardless of the mode of acquisition.[13]

The *actio de in rem verso* was eventually utilised by the late eighteenth/ early nineteenth centuries to shape different provisions of restitution especially in the Prussian *Allgemeines Landrecht* (General Land Law) 1794 [Article 262 (Part 1, Title 13) provides 'Derjenige, aus dessen Vermögen etwas in den Nutzen eines Andern verwendet worden, ist dasselbe entweder in Natur zurück, oder für den Werth Vergütung zu fordern

---

[8] ibid 853, 856, 878, 943–44, 948, 957, 961–62.
[9] Dawson (n 5) 46–47.
[10] R Feenstra, 'Grotius' Doctrine of Unjust Enrichment as a Source of Obligation: Its Origins and its Influence in Roman–Dutch Law' in E Schrage (ed), *Unjust Enrichment: The Comparative Legal History of the Law of Restitution* (Berlin, Duncker & Humblot, 1995) 197, 198–99.
[11] ibid 205.
[12] Zimmermann (n 3) 886.
[13] ibid 872–73, 881–84.

berechtigt' ('One, from whose assets a thing has been converted to the benefit of another, is entitled to have it back in nature, or to demand compensation for the value of it'] and the Austrian *ABGB* 1811 [Article 1041 provides 'Wenn ohne Geschäftsführung eine Sache zum Nutzen eines Anderen verwendet worden ist; kann der Eigenthümer sie in Natur, oder, wenn dieß nicht mehr geschehen kann, den Werth verlangen, den sie zur Zeit der Verwendung gehabt hat, obgleich der Nutzen in der Folge vereitelt worden ist' ('When without management of affairs, a thing has been used for the benefit of another, the owner can claim it in nature, or, if this is not possible, to require the value it had at the time of use, even if the benefits were not reaped')]. Like the *condictio sine causa* these provisions were mostly asset-oriented and less wrong-focused. In France too, the Cour de cassation (Court of Cassation) acknowledged in the famous *Boudier* case (1892)[14] the *actio de in rem verso* as a general enrichment action, thus adding to the provisions of the Civil Code regulating *condictio indebiti* (Articles 1376–81) and *negotiorum gestio* (Articles 1372–75).[15]

Current Law of Germany

Although cases of tangible property wrongs are usually handled by the German law of delict, a *restitutionary* response is mainly provoked by two models outside that law: (1) the property law model; (2) the unjustified enrichment law. The property law model offers proprietary claims for recovery of tangible objects (eg, chattel or land).[16] This model has its origins in the Roman action for protecting ownership, the *rei vindicatio* which was laid down as a special provision in Article 985 of the BGB.[17] This Article provides the basic vindication claim which states: 'Der Eigentümer kann von dem Besitzer die Herausgabe der Sache verlangen' ('The owner can require the possessor to surrender the thing'). The owner can also claim recovery of the *Nutzungen* (loosely translated as emoluments or utilisations). Article 100 (BGB) defines *Nutzungen* as 'the fruits of a thing or a right, and the benefits provided by the use of the thing or the right'. *Nutzungen* are extensions of the notion *Sache* (thing), either as *Früchte* (fruits) or *Vorteil* (benefit) from use.[18]

---

[14] Cass req 15 June 1892, DP 1892.1.596; S 1893.1.281 cited in J Cartwright and M Hesselink, 'Case 9' in J Cartwright and M Hesselink (eds), *Precontractual Liability in European Private Law* (Cambridge, Cambridge University Press, 2008) 258.

[15] Zimmermann (n 3) 881–84.

[16] G Dannemann, *The German Law of Unjustified Enrichment and Restitution: A Comparative Introduction* (Oxford, Oxford University Press, 2009) 88–89.

[17] Schlechtriem (n 1) 16.

[18] Dannemann (n 16) 311; J Beatson and E Schrage (eds), *Cases, Materials and Texts on Unjustified Enrichment* (Oxford, Hart Publishing, 2003) 43–45, 123–27.

The Code provides an elaborated scale of culpability, for example, Articles 987, 988, 990 (BGB) affecting the extent to which recovery is allowed.[19] The behaviour element of the wrongdoer, however, is minimally described and is mostly ethically neutral. For example, the basic vindication claim provided in Article 985 lacks any description of wrongful behaviour or any behaviour at all. Instead, the focus is on the asset component to be returned and its extensions. Similar drafting is noticeable in other Articles as well. For example, Article 987(1) states that 'Der Besitzer hat dem Eigentümer die Nutzungen herauszugeben, die er nach dem Eintritt der Rechtshängigkeit zieht' ('The possessor must return to the owner the emoluments he receives after litigation is pending'). Article 989 regulates a thing that is said to deteriorate or perish. An example of ethically neutral language is Article 988. The Article describes a property that is *erlangt* (acquired) rather than 'exploited' for example. In the same manner, Article 990 uses the word *Erwerb* (acquisition).

This property law model stands vis-a-vis an unjustified enrichment one. Wrongful enrichments are covered mostly by the so-called *Eingriffskondiktion* (Action for intervention) to the extent they are not covered by the property law model. The main rule is provided for in Article 812(1) alt 2 (BGB). It is classified within the category of non-performance-based enrichments (*Nichtleistungskondiktion*). Here too, enrichments are described in terms of an *etwas* (something) that is *erlangt* (acquired) by the enriched. The ethical aspect of the action is again absent. And the asset-focused orientation is predominant. The *Eingriff* (intervention) aspect mainly concerns absolute rights, for example, tangible/intangible property and personality rights, which are enjoyed against anyone (rather than against a particular person), and also legal prohibitions.[20] Following Walter Wilburg's and Ernst von Caemmerer's theory of attribution (*Zuweisungstheorie*), it is widely accepted that the *Eingriff* which gives rise to restitution is not tied to the 'unlawfulness' of the interference, but rather to an asset-oriented question. The enrichment is subject to restitution if it is attributable to the owner's right, namely, if the right to reap this particular enrichment is originally bestowed on the owner.[21]

---

[19] ibid 90 (Dannemann); N Foster and S Sule, *German Legal System and Laws* (Oxford, Oxford University Press, 2010) 507–10.

[20] ibid 91–92 (Dannemann); ibid 481–85 (Foster and Sule); Beatson and Schrage (n 18) 43–48; T Krebs, 'Unrequested Benefits in German Law' in J Neyers, M McInnes and S Pitel (eds), *Understanding Unjust Enrichment* (Oxford, Hart Publishing, 2004) 249–53; J Gordley and A von Mehren, *An Introduction to the Comparative Study of Private Law: Readings, Cases, Materials* (Cambridge, Cambridge University Press, 2006) 559.

[21] W Wilburg, *Die Lehre von der ungerechtfertigten Bereicherung nach österreichischem und deutschem Recht* (Graz, Leuschner & Lubensky, 1934) 27; E von Caemmerer 'Bereicherung und unerlaubte Handlung' in H Dölle, M Rheinstein and K Zweigert (eds), *Festschrift für Ernst Rabel*, vol 1 (Tübingen, Mohr, 1954) 333, 353; ibid 94 (Dannemann); ibid 54–55, 129 (Beatson and Schrage).

This model is in fact part of the so-called *Bereicherungsrecht* (enrichment law). As a non-performance-based claim, it suffices to show that the shift of wealth from one party to another had no legal or consensual basis, and was at the latter's expense. There is no need to prove that the appropriation or exploitation of the property was tortuous or wrongful as in common law trespass or conversion for example. As Schlechtriem explains, the gist of the matter here is neither sanctioning the faulty behaviour of the enriched person nor working to deter such conduct. It is rather the property interest which provides the owner with exclusive powers to enjoy his asset and make any such handling or use by another person without permission an unjustified enrichment.[22]

Current Law of Austria

Although the Austrian Civil Code (*Allgemeines Bürgerliches Gesetzbuch* (ABGB)), does not acknowledge a concept of 'unjustified enrichment' as such, the existence of a law of unjustified enrichment is widely accepted by courts and legal scholarship. Based on Roman law as received and modified, a number of condictions were enacted in legislation.[23] Scholars often distinguish between the condiction of performance (*Leistungskondiktion*) and that of interference with another's asset (*Verwendungsanspruch*). The latter (and under different conditions also delict law) handles, inter alia, cases of tangible property appropriation and exploitation. Section 1041 alt 1 of the AGBG provides: 'Wenn ohne Geschäftsführung eine Sache zum Nutzen eines andern verwendet worden ist; kann der Eigentümer sie in Natur ... verlangen,...' (...'If an asset has been used for the benefit of someone else without agency, the owner can demand the asset in kind'...). Here too the Code provides a scale of culpability which does not affect the right of the disadvantaged for restitution but mainly affects the extent of the restitutionary measure provided.[24]

As with German law, the *Verwendungsanspruch* projects a strong asset orientation. It opts for an ethically neutral description of the conduct involved. Furthermore, it neither stresses fault (eg, intention, negligence) on the part of the enriched party, nor damage to the disadvantaged one. The centre of the rule is the asset (*eine Sache*). The Austrian law scholar, Walter Wilburg, refers in his explanation to the power of property and

---

[22] Schlechtriem (n 1) 9.
[23] von Bar and Swann (n 2) 97–98.
[24] M Lehmert and M Rainer, 'Austrian Law of Unjust Enrichment' in E Schrage (ed), *Unjust Enrichment and the Law of Contract* (Hague, Kluwer Law International, 2001) 53, 54, 72; *Das Österreichische ABGB—The Austrian Civil Code*, trans P Eschig and E Pircher-Eschig (Vienna, LexisNexis, 2013) 254.

the need to protect the autonomy of the person. Monika Lehmert and Michael Rainer explicate this point adding that it is 'something belonging to a certain person' which is used by another 'to whose benefit the good is not dedicated' thus enjoying 'a benefit that the owner is entitled to'.[25] The Austrian Supreme Court (*Oberster Gerichtshof*) has stressed in numerous cases that it is sufficient for the proprietary sphere of the disadvantaged person to be violated, regardless of fault, to trigger a claim in unjustified enrichment against the enriched person.[26]

Austrian law provides tangible property owners with a concurrent right to vindicate and claim back appropriated property. This arrangement is mainly dealt with by section 366 of the ABGB. The section provides: 'Mit dem Rechte des Eigentümers jeden andern von dem Besitze seiner Sache auszuschließen, ist auch das Recht verbunden, seine ihm vorenthaltene Sache von jedem Inhaber durch die Eigentumsklage gerichtlich zu fordern' ('The right of the owner to exclude everyone else from possession of his asset includes also the right to claim the asset withheld from each holder by a claim of ownership at court').[27] As with a *rei vidicatio* claim, the property vindication claim rests on the owner's right to exclusive control over his asset and does not need to prove faulty conduct by the enriched person, or damage to prevail in his action. The term 'a thing' (*eine Sache*) stands out as one of the key concepts with which the law grasps these cases. *Sache* is defined in the widest manner possible. Section 285 (ABGB) provides that it includes *anything* other than humans which can be used by them.

Current Law of Italy

In Italy, proprietary wrongful enrichments are governed, inter alia, by the general action for unjustified enrichment as provided for in Article 2041 of the Italian Civil Code (*Codice Civile Italiano*).[28] The Article states that: 'Chi, senza una giusta causa, si è arricchito a danno di un'altra persona

---

[25] W Wilburg, 'Zusammenspiel der Kräfte im Aufbau des Schuldrechts' (1964) 163(4) *Archiv für die civilistische Praxis* 346, 347; ibid 53, 70–72 (Lehmert and Rainer).

[26] OGH 9.3.1960, 6 Ob 8/60, 'Rechtsprechung' Juristische Blätter, 82 Jahrganges 1960, Heft 22/23 (26 November 1960) 607; OGH 17.6.1993, 8 Ob 610/92, 'Rechtsprechung' Juristische Blätter, 116 Jahrganges 1994, Heft 8 (August 1994) 538; cf C Wendehorst 'No Headaches over Unjust Enrichment: Response to Daniel Friedman' in K Siehr and R Zimmermann (eds), *The Draft Civil Code for Israel in Comparative Perspective* (Tübingen, Mohr Siebeck GmbH & Co., 2008) 128.

[27] von Bar and Swann (n 2) 534; *Das Österreichische ABGB—The Austrian Civil Code* (n 24) 96.

[28] F Giglio, *The Foundations of Restitution for Wrongs* (Oxford, Hart Publishing, 2007) 68; G Alpa and V Zeno-Zencovich, *Italian Private Law* (Oxon, Routledge-Cavendish, 2007) 236.

è tenuto, nei limiti dell'arricchimento a indennizzare quest'ultima della correlativa diminuzione patrimoniale' ('A person who has enriched himself without cause at the expense of another shall, to the extent of the enrichment, indemnify the other for his correlative financial loss').[29] This general obligation dismisses the wrongful behaviour or faulty conduct of the enriched as a prerequisite to restitution.[30] Instead, it erects the claim on the typical civilian approach of enrichment without a ground (*arrichimento senza causa*). This legislation reinstates early decisions of Italian Courts of Cassation which recognised a general rule of patrimonial unjust enrichment (*ingiusta locupletazione*) on several occasions at the end of the nineteenth century.[31]

The codified rule asserts the need for a patrimonial reduction (*diminuzione patrimoniale*) on the part of the disadvantaged person. This widely defined prerequisite of economic loss along with its correlative enrichment is concretised in cases of property appropriation. The latter is covered under the second part of the Article. It provides that 'Qualora l'arricchimento abbia per oggetto una cosa determinata, colui che l'ha ricevuta è tenuto a restituirla in natura, se sussiste al tempo della domanda' ('If the enrichment consists of a specified thing, the person who received it is bound to return it in kind if it is still in existence at the time of the demand').[32] This obligation to return in kind the thing (*una cosa*) taken materialises the asset orientation. It reinforces the protected sphere which a property interest can bestow on its holder.

Commentaries often stress the rarity of invoking Article 2041 in practice. This could be explained by the ancillary character of the unjustified enrichment claim in Italian law. According to Article 2042, an enrichment claim cannot be raised if other actions are available. This rule works to prioritise the delict model of the code (eg, Article 2043) which offers claimants a compensatory response correlative to their damages and lost profits (eg, Article 1223). In addition, the Italian Supreme Court has interpreted Article 2042 to mean that concurrent claims, even if unavailable de facto (due to prescription for example) would still hinder a claim under Article 2041.[33] Another possible explanation for the infrequent use of unjustified enrichment in Italian legal practice is the need to prove loss.

---

[29] *The Italian Civil Code and Complementary Legislation*, trans Susanna Beltramo (New York, West, 2012) 431.

[30] Giglio (n 28).

[31] eg Corte Di Cassazione di Firenze, 24 febbraio 1898, *Il Foro Italiano* vol 23, Parte Prima: Giurisprudenza Civile e Commerciale (1898) (321–26) 321, 326; Corte di Cassazione di Torino, 18 marzo 1892, *Il Foro Italiano* vol 17, Parte Prima: Giurisprudenza Civile e Commerciale (1892), (433–51) 442.

[32] *The Italian Civil Code and Complementary Legislation* (n 29) 431.

[33] Corte di Cassazione; Sezione III civile, 4 maggio 1978, no 2078; *Il Foro Italiano*, vol 102, Parte Prima: Giurisprudenza Constituzionale e Civile (1979) (180–86).

An enrichment which is not joined by impoverishment falls outside the scope of the said Article.[34]

Francesco Giglio notes that unlike German law, the general clause of restitution in Italian law does not follow from the absence of a ground element but from an 'equitable' equilibrium which courts seek to establish in cases of unaddressed proprietary wrongs.[35] Indeed the subsidiary nature of Article 2041 makes it a gap-filler and a handy instrument for the judiciary to reach fairer results. This, however, neither relegates the fact that no faulty conduct or wrongful behaviour is necessary to trigger restitution nor do these legal thresholds distort the asset-oriented norm structuring of the case at hand in Italian law.

Current Law of Spain

Similar traits can be traced in Spanish law. Cases of wrongful proprietary enrichments are governed, inter alia, by proprietary and unjustified enrichment models. The Spanish Civil Code (*Código Civil*) provides concrete rules of possession which articulate the possessor's entitlement to be respected in his private sphere and regulates the need to restore him to his original position if his interest has been challenged. Article 446 of the *Código Civil* states: 'Todo poseedor tiene derecho a ser respetado en su posesión; y, si fuere inquietado en ella, deberá ser amparado o restituido en dicha posesión por los medios que las leyes de procedimiento establecen' ('Every possessor has a right in his possession; and if he is disturbed therein, he must be protected or possession must be restored to him by the means established in procedural laws').[36]

Article 348 of the Code provides for the owner's vindication right against holders. The Article defines ownership as the right to enjoy and dispose of a thing (*una cosa*). It reiterates the basic idea of the Roman *rei vidicatio* providing that 'El propietario tiene acción contra el tenedor y el poseedor de la cosa para reivindicarla' ('The owner has a right of action against the holder and the possessor of a thing to recover it').[37] Both Article 446 and Article 348 perceive the case in question neither in terms of faulty conduct nor in terms of damage. Although these two characters are arguably typical to property rules of many jurisdictions, they are highlighted since they can be discerned to a great extent also in the

---

[34] Corte di Cassazione; Sezione I civile, 21 ottobre 1988, no 5716; *Il Foro Italiano*, vol 112, Parte Prima: Giurisprudenza Costituzionale e Civile (1989) (764–80).

[35] Giglio (n 28) 70–71.

[36] *Civil Code of Spain*, trans J de San Pio (Bilingual edn, Madrid, International Legal Publications, 2009) 271.

[37] ibid 244.

applicable Spanish law of unjustified enriched (*Enriquecimiento sin causa*, enrichment without ground). Unlike the German BGB, the *Código Civil* does not provide a general clause for unjustified enrichment. Following the French Civil Code, it mainly regulates cases of managing another's affairs (*negotiorum gestio*) (Articles 1888–94) and undue debt collection (*indebiti solutio*) (Articles 1895–1901).[38] The case under consideration is, however, covered by the judicially consolidated *condictio sine causa generalis* (general lack of ground condiction), although some scholars prefer to discuss the more specific *condictio por intromisión* (condiction for interference).[39]

The judicial *condictio sine causa generalis* was based, inter alia, on an expanded interpretation of Article 1901. The latter allows retention of the benefit only if a valid legal, judicial or consensual basis (*a causa justa*) can be traced. Like the property law model, the misconduct, fault and mental state of the enriched person are mostly irrelevant for a right to restitution. They may, however, affect the measure and extent of recovery allowed. In the case at hand, the impoverishment element of the *condictio* could be satisfied when a proprietary interest belonging to the disadvantaged person has been invaded, encroached on or exploited by another. If damage occurs, the plaintiff usually has a concurrent claim in delict and in unjustified enrichment.[40] It is important to note that the subsidiary character of the *condictio* has been debated by scholars for some time. Different opinions were also expressed in case law and the decisions of the Supreme Court (Tribunal Supremo).[41] While in general terms the *condictio* is held ancillary to other claims based on specific laws, it appears that Spanish law retains a concurrent position for the *condicto* in delict cases and does not relegate it to an ancillary one.[42]

The Draft Common Frame of Reference

The economic, institutional and political alliances fostered by EU Member States introduced numerous challenges to the pan-European project.

---

[38] C Ligüerre, 'Disgorgement of Profits Under Spanish Law: Gain Based Remedies throughout the World' in E Hondius and A Janssen (eds), *Disgorgement of Profits* (Cham, Springer, 2015) 200; S Lapuente, 'Undue Payment' in S van Erp and A Vaquer (eds), *Introduction to Spanish Patrimonial Law* (Granada, Comares, 2006) 209; S Lapuente, 'Negotoirum Gestio' in S van Erp and A Vaquer (eds), *Introduction to Spanish Patrimonial Law* (Granada, Comares, 2006) 211.

[39] C Alvarez and D Picazo, *Manuel de la Cámara Alvarez and Díez-Picazo, Dos estudios sobre el enriquecimiento sin causa* (Madrid, Civitas Ediciones, 1991) 116.

[40] A Vaquer 'Unjustified Enrichment' in S van Erp and A Vaquer (eds), *Introduction to Spanish Patrimonial Law* (Granada, Comares, 2006) 198.

[41] eg España Tribunal Supremo (Sala de lo Civil, Sección 1) Sentencia núm. 1434/2003 de 3 de Marzo de 2003.

[42] von Bar and Swann (n 2) 101.

The need for law harmonisation in a climate of the highly diversified legal systems of the Member States has quickly materialised amid a growing integration of markets and the free movement of people, goods and services. To that end, an extensive work was done by scholars to find common principles and frames of reference for Member States to follow in their respective jurisdictions. European Union Private Law (EUPL) was one area of scholarship which gained much from these collaborations notably in contract, property and family law.[43] Although these efforts have not culminated in official EU legislation as such, it seems highly plausible that they would soon constitute a critical mass upon which future enactments could be made. Though the EU does not have broad competence to legislate in the field of private law, fragments of EUPL can be traced in areas like consumer law, free movement of goods, persons and services, and competition law.

In the area of unjustified enrichment, extensive work was done by scholars aided by law practitioners to produce coherent model rules. The project was undertaken by the Study Group on a European Civil Code and the Research Group on Existing EC Private Law (Acquis Group). The two groups embraced a revised version of earlier model rules of contract law, the Principles of European Contract Law (PECL),[44] originally produced in tripartite by a former group of scholars known as the Commission on European Contract Law. The new groups worked to extend the revised PECL in different directions, notably in specific contracts, unjustified enrichment, *negotiorum gestio*, non-contractual liabilities, and portions of movable property law (eg, acquisition, security for credit). Their goal was to promote the harmonisation of Member States' law and to draw nearer to a unified European private law.[45]

This work eventually culminated in the Principles, Definitions and Model Rules of European Private Law: Draft Common Frame of Reference (DCFR). The DCFR initial goal was to provide a draft upon which a later 'political' Common Frame of Reference (CFR) could be based. The CFR was in fact a project primarily induced by the European Commission's Action Plan on a More Coherent European Contract Law of 2003. The DCFR, however, continued to stress its scholarly independence and its potential to serve as academic and practical reference regardless of the

---

[43] eg H Schulte-Nölke, M Ebers and S Leible et al, *Principles of the Existing EC Contract Law (Acquis Principles)—Contract I: Pre-contractual Obligations, Conclusion of Contract, Unfair Terms* (Munich, Sellier, 2007); K Boele-Woelki, F Ferrand and C Beilfuss et al, *Principles of European Family Law Regarding Divorce and Maintenance Between Former Spouses* (Anwerp, Intersentia, 2004).

[44] O Lando and H Beale (eds), *Principles of European Contract Law: Parts I and II* (The Hague, Kluwer, 2000); O Lando, E Clive A Prüm et al (eds), *Principles of European Contract Law: Part III* (The Hague, Kluwer, 2003).

[45] von Bar and Swann (n 2) vii.

CFR initiative. Another notable aim identified by the DCFR is its capacity to exhibit similarities between Members' laws and the extent to which they 'may be regarded as regional manifestations of an overall common European legacy'.[46]

An advanced tentative edition of the DCFR was published in 2008 as an interim outline. A modified and revised edition was published year later in 2009 as a final outline edition. Later that year, a final edition came out.[47] The DCFR is elegantly organised into ten books. Each book covers a different substantive area, for example, non-contractual liability arising out of damage caused to another, benevolent intervention in another's affairs, acquisition and loss of ownership of goods and more. The law of unjustified enrichment is covered in book VII. The book is divided into seven chapters and 23 articles. Chapter 1 provides general basic rules. Chapter 2 defines when enrichment is deemed unjustified. Chapter 3 elaborates cases of enrichment and disadvantage. Chapter 4 explains the rules of attribution. Chapter 5 regulates the measures of reversals. Chapter 6 provides rules of defence. And chapter 7 provides miscellaneous rules pertaining mostly to relating book VII to other areas of law.

Book VII is intended to cover a wide range of cases often deemed part of unjustified enrichment, notably: (i) cases of mistaken confers; (ii) renders under fraud, threats and duress; (iii) rescission of contracts considered void *ab initio*; (iv) voluntary enhancement of another's property without obligation; (v) wrongful interference with another's property and rights; and (vi) paying off another person's debt. Some areas of unjustified enrichment are explicitly not covered, notably instances of reversals governed by contract law (eg, reversals following termination of a valid contract or governed by express contract rules) (Article 7:101(3)) and cases involving public bodies or governed by public law (Article 7:103).[48]

The major rules dealing with cases of intentional appropriation or exploitation of another person's tangible property are regulated in different Articles across book VII. They could be summed up as follows: a general rule stating that 'a person who obtains an unjustified enrichment which is attributable to another's disadvantage is obliged to that other to reverse the enrichment' (Article 1:101(1)). A person is deemed enriched by

---

[46] C von Bar, E Clive and H Schulte-Nölke et al (eds), *Principles, Definitions and Model Rules of European Private Law: Draft Common Frame of Reference (DCFR)*, Outline Edition (Munich, Sellier, 2009) 7; Communication from the Commission to the European Parliament and the Council of 15 March 2003—A more coherent European contract law—An action plan [2003] OJ C/063.

[47] C von Bar, E Clive and H Schulte-Nölke et al (eds), *Principles, Definitions and Model Rules of European Private Law: Draft Common Frame of Reference (DCFR)*, Interim Outline Edition (Munich, Sellier, 2008); von Bar, Clive and Schulte-Nölke, *Principles, Definitions and Model Rules of European Private Law* (n 46); von Bar and Swann (n 2).

[48] von Bar and Swann (n 2) 91–92.

(a) 'an increase in assets or a decrease in liabilities' or (c) 'use of another's assets' (Article 3:101(1)). Correspondingly, a person is disadvantaged by (a) 'a decrease in assets or an increase in liabilities' or (c) 'another's use of that person's assets' (Article 3:102(1)). The Draft also lists cases where enrichment is particularly deemed attributable to another's disadvantage. Cases such as when (a) 'an asset of that other is transferred to the enriched person by that other' or (c) 'the enriched person uses that other's asset, especially where the enriched person infringes the disadvantaged person's rights or legally protected interests' (Article 4:101).

These rules are then followed by Articles governing reversals of enrichments which have general applicability. The default remedy is returning 'the asset' itself (Article 5:101(1)). As the DCFR authors expressly state, the 'starting proposition is that the enriched person is required to transfer the asset to the disadvantaged person (paragraph 1)). A transfer in *specie* is thus the primary response of the DCFR law of unjustified enrichment'.[49] In cases of inability to reverse, an unreasonable effort or expense to do so, or if the enrichment 'does not consist of a transferable asset', the objective market value of the enrichment is owed and should be paid to the disadvantaged person (Article 5:101(2)–(3); Article 5:102(1)). According to Article 5:104, reversal of the asset or its value 'extends to the fruits and use of the enrichment' which may exceed or be below the economic saving the enriched person has had from his wrongful endeavour. This and the mental state of the enriched (eg, bad faith) affect the extent of recovery pertaining to fruits and use (Article 5:104(1)–(2)). The said Articles are then followed by a chapter on defences (Article 6) and another regarding 'Relation to other legal rules' in which the concurrent character of the claim is detailed (Article 7:102).

As explicitly stated in the DCFR, English 'has been the working language for all the Groups responsible for formulating the model rules'.[50] Interestingly the articulation of the behavioural aspect of the case is mostly ethically neutral. Neutral verbs ('obtain', 'use') are used to describe a person's behaviour, principally the enriched. Using the word 'obtains', the DCFR sets no requirement for a *wrongful* enrichment. It is irrelevant 'whether the enrichment is wrongful or not', or how the asset reaches the hands of the enriched, whether by his own act or a third party's.[51] The rules seem to waive any unethical charge of this

---

[49] ibid 445.

[50] von Bar, Clive and Schulte-Nölke, *Principles, Definitions and Model Rules of European Private Law* (n 46) 48.

[51] von Bar and Swann (n 2) 186–87; C Wendehorst, 'The Draft Principles of European Unjustified Enrichment Law Prepared by the Study Group on a European Civil Code: A Comment' (2006) 7 *CC ERA Forum* 244, 256.

protagonist's behaviour and focus instead on the asset component of the case. Additional verbs used (ie, 'increase', 'decrease', 'transferred') are mostly asset-related.

The mental status of the enriched (eg, good faith, bad faith) provided for in several Articles, for example, Articles 5:101(4)–(5), 5:102(2) and 5:104(2), is mostly immaterial for a right to unjustified enrichment. Actually, his wrongful behaviour is also alien to the enquiry at this stage. The psychological aspect is mainly confined to the remedial stage and to certain claims of defence (chapters 5 and 6). The weight is alternatively shifted to the disadvantaged person who, in general, needs to consent freely and without error to the enrichment (Article 2:101(1)(b)). Wrongful forms of conduct such as fraud, coercion, threats, associated with the enriched or a third party are not expressly attached to those protagonists, but are questions of the quality of the disadvantaged person's consent or performance (Article 2:103). These again re-emphasise the shift of focus to the disadvantaged persons.

The asset element seems to set the scene right. In fact, the enrichment, the disadvantage and the attribution, all lie with the *asset* component. The enrichment and disadvantage are determined in terms of change in assets (as opposed, for instance, to change in value) (Articles 3:101(1)(a), 3:102(1)(a)) and/or use of assets (Articles 3:101(1)(c), 3:102(1)(c)). Particular instances of attribution are stated in terms of an asset that is transferred between the parties (Article 4:101(a)) and in terms of a use of the asset made by the enriched person (Article 4:101(c)). Also in rules governing 'reversal of enrichment' (chapter 5), the *asset* is placed at the centre of division between transferable enrichments (Article 5:101) and non-transferable ones (Article 5:102).

As regards the meaning of the term *asset*, the DCFR authors explicate what they call 'an unstated criterion'. An asset, they state, 'must in some manner be recognised as "belonging" to one party'. It is an item 'to which an element of protected exclusivity attaches'.[52] This definition indicates that an asset is not only the item as it stands alone, rather it is a special bond between a person and that item, or to avoid William Blackstone's terminology (ie, property as 'that sole and despotic dominion which one man claims and exercises over the external things of the world'),[53] it is 'a legally defined relationship between persons with respect to an object' which basically works to exclude others from a resource.[54]

---

[52] ibid 345 (von Bar and Swann).
[53] W Blackstone, *Commentaries on the Laws of England*, vol 2 (Chicago, University of Chicago Press, 1979) 1–15.
[54] M Davies, *Property: Meanings, Histories, Theories* (New York, Routledge-Cavendish, 2007) 13, 18.

TRACING EXEMPLARS

A very noticeable exemplarity in European rules is waiving the need for a wrongful behaviour element on the part of the enriched person to establish a valid legal claim. It is usually not an immediate concern whether the enriched person's act is wrongful or not, or how the enrichment reaches his hands, whether by his own action or by a third party's. In so doing, the rules temporarily dismiss the unethical charge of this protagonist's behaviour and focus instead on another component of the case, namely the asset. Action descriptions utilised are usually asset-related. They mainly concern changes in the asset itself, to it, or in the identity of its holder. It is possible to figuratively argue that the rules project a scene consisting of two chronological, albeit static, images with a certain time-lapse between them. The first image depicts an initial stage where a person is an owner of an asset. The second image portrays a subsequent stage where ownership is already challenged by another, and needs to be reinstituted. Minimum conduct on the part of the enriched person is employed to swap between the two images. In fact, the shift from one stage, or image, to another seems to call for no wrongful behaviour. The pre- and post-images are the main fulcrum of the legal structure while the enrichment process and the behavioural aspect of the enriched person are of less concern, at least at the outset.

The psychological dimension of the enriched, for example, his good or bad faith, is also immaterial for the establishment of the legal claim. Since the wrongful conduct is not examined at an initial stage, it is often the case that questions of will, fault, innocence, intent, negligence, knowledge or ignorance of the facts are confined to later stages of examination like the remedial stage. However, there too, only a one-tier examination of the mental state is usually in order. The mental status enquiry is often confined to enrichment-related questions and does not necessarily extend to wrong-related ones as is the case with two-tier examination noticeable in Anglo-American laws. It is also apparent that the mental attitude usually affects the kind and amount of the reversal remedy, rather than the right for the remedy itself.

A proprietary wrongful enrichment in the European context is often a case where the enriched person infringes a protected proprietary interest of another. The scope of such infringement is often undefined. As a matter of fact, both unauthorised obtainments and illegal ones are implicitly sufficient. The first group consists of enrichments which lack proper consent by the interest-holder, and the second one gathers enrichments forbidden by law or contrary to a juridical act or court order. But as a matter of law, such distinctions are beside the point. The rules presuppose that all enrichments are unjustified including wrong-based ones unless justified by consent or some other legal or contractual grounds. And given that any appropriations or use of a proprietary interest is unjustified by default, it follows that all questions of mental attitude associated with such behaviour are chiefly irrelevant.

This default structure is explicated for instance in the renowned decision of *Masdar (UK) Ltd v Commission of the European Communities*. There, the European Court of Justice states:

> Actions for unjust enrichment do not fall under the rules governing noncontractual liability in the strict sense, which, to be invoked, require a number of conditions to be satisfied, relating to the unlawfulness of the conduct imputed to the Community, the fact of the damage alleged and the existence of a causal link between that conduct and the damage complained of ... They differ from actions brought under those rules *in that they do not require proof of unlawful conduct—indeed, of any form of conduct at all—on the part of the defendant*, but merely proof of enrichment on the part of the defendant for which there is no valid legal basis and of impoverishment on the part of the applicant which is linked to that enrichment.[55]

It seems that many European continental laws shift the weight in a wrongful enrichment scene to the interest-holder who basically needs to consent to the obtainment or use of his interest. Such rules care largely for the autonomy of this protagonist. In fact, this person does not need the protection of anti-wrong laws like delict law. He is well protected by the legal presumption that all obtainments, active or passive, direct or indirect, are unjustified. Inspected carefully, the centre of the projected scene appears to be the *asset* component. The *asset* component proves to be a bold exemplar. It is set as the basis for other elements of the case, both at terminological, construction and dynamics levels. This is visible, for example, in the enrichment and impoverishment components of the case which may involve a change in assets, a use of assets or a transition of assets from hand to hand. It is also noticeable in the remedial stage. Thus, the type and traits of the asset involved (eg, mobility or the possibility to be consumed) often impacts the type of restitution invoked (eg, return in kind or in monetary value). The remedy provided for by default is often the reversal of the asset *in specie*. Collateral benefits are also asset-related (eg, fruits or use) when articulated.[56]

This exemplar suggests that the primary measure of restitution in these rules is formed on the premise of restoration and reinstitution, rather than rectification of a wrongful behaviour. The aim is to restore the benefit or transfer it back to its holder. The rules are mostly asset-oriented rather than action-oriented. Action is relegated by default to a lower position,

---

[55] Case C-47/07 *Masdar (UK) Ltd v Commission of the European Communities* [2008] ECR I-9761, para 49 (emphasis added).

[56] cp Art 1 European Convention on Human Rights (Rome, 4 November 1950); *Kushoglu v Bulgaria* App no 48191/99 [2007] ECHR 375, paras 47–51.

and the asset element is underscored. If a given allocation of resources is challenged the law intervenes to restore the original status quo. The rules ask not *how* unjustified enrichment occurred but *where* it lies now. And as far as property-related wrongful enrichment cases are concerned, the term *enrichment* in the pair *unjustified enrichment* mostly denotes an (unjustified) asset, rather than an (unjustified) action.

ASSESSMENT

An intriguing question would be whether the analysis has fallen prey to 'circular reasoning' (*circulus in demonstrando*).[57] It is a logical fallacy which indicates that the study concludes what it sets as initial assumption.[58] An ostensible circularity here may be discerning *property* as exemplar when the case at hand is nothing other than *property* appropriation or exploitation. This claim, however, is *non-sequitur*. One should not confuse facts with the normative perception of them or assume a necessary overlap between the two. American law is one example. The rules as we will see in a later chapter are not asset-oriented but action-oriented and their reference to property is played down. The Ottoman Civil Code, also discussed later, is another example. That Code does not refer or hinge on *mulk* (ﻣﻠﻚ, property) which is the linguistic and doctrinal equivalent to property. It uses and regulates a unique concept termed *māl* (ﻣﺎﻝ, wealth) which is anything human nature is prone to save for time of need.

Another issue is relegating the action component exemplar. This exemplarity could be an offshoot of the unjustified enrichment model, followed by many civil law jurisdictions. A misplaced benefit is deemed unjustified unless a valid ground is provided to this shift of wealth. It is thus plausible to argue that the said exemplar is a simple reiteration of a widely acknowledged character of civil law model. This argument, which doubts the added-value of the analysis reaffirms the accuracy of the exemplar to the benefit of the cultural explication in the following chapter. Nevertheless, it falls short of comprehending the full intricacy of poetical reading of law as offered here. The intention is to highlight exemplarity of dry normative constructions which communicate central concerns of the law's perception. These discerned exemplars are drawn as thematic sketches of human scenes which would subsequently facilitate correlative cultural explanations. Such a process is often ignored in doctrinal reading of law.

An ostensible antithesis of these two exemplars is perhaps France. French history provides a fertile source of insights into pan-European

---

[57] cp N Asfour, 'Book Review: The Measure of Injury: Race, Gender and Tort Law' (2011) 7 *Law, Culture and the Humanities* 142, 144.

[58] B Bennett, *Logically Fallacious* (Subury, eBookIt, 2012) 89.

culture but French law, at the outset at least, barely complies with the discerned exemplars. It treats cases of property appropriation and exploitation as delict rather than unjustified enrichment.[59] Delict law is typically not asset-oriented. The general provision for delictual liability is contained in Article 1382 of the *Code Napoléon* which provides: 'Toutfait quelconque de l'homme, qui cause à autrui un dommage, oblige celui par la faute duquel il est arrive, a le réparer' ('Any act whatever of man which causes damages to another obliges him by whose fault it occurred to make reparation').[60] The provision embraces a clear behavioural perception highlighting the wrongful act of the enriched, his fault and the damage he caused.

This observation, however, is inconclusive of French current law. Although a delict hinges on damage and fault, tortuous liability has in fact increasingly shaken off its ethical aspect. Questions of damage and fault were expansively interpreted by the French Cour de cassation which was willing to establish the presence of damage on mere infringement of the right to *propriété* or *possession*.[61] This expansive interpretation made it possible for the Court to take into account the gain reaped when assessing compensation.[62] These alterations seem to reflect a wider trend in French delict law. The latter is drawing closer to a 'risk-based' liability model and further from a 'fault-based' one. Moral accountability has recently been paving the way for a new legal idea of accepting liability for one's own actions. This trend has materialised in an increasing number of wrongs hinging on strict liability and ethical-neutrality.[63]

These asset-orientations are hardly alien to the *Code Napoléon*. The latter was described as 'a breviary for owners'. Ownership was conceived as the 'centrepiece' of the Code and 'the immanent spirit of the legislation'.[64] In fact, two out of three books of the Code were originally devoted to *propriété* (property). Both chapters on delict and quasi-contract are covered by book III which deals with *Des différentes manières dont on acquiert*

---

[59] von Bar and Swann (n 2) 152; S Whittaker, 'The Law of Obligations' in J Bell, S Byron and S Whittaker (eds), *Principles of French Law* (Oxford, Oxford University Press, 2008) 294, 417–52.

[60] *The French Civil Code*, trans J Crabb (Littleton, Rothman, 1995) 252.

[61] Cass req 6 March 1934, DP 1937, I, 17, note *Blaevoet* ('holding that an infringement of the owner's *droit de possession* will suffice for a finding of *dommages-intérêts*, even if there is no proof of actual damage') cited in von Bar and Swann (n 2) 153.

[62] CA Paris 4 January 1988, D 1989 som. 92, note Amson cited in von Bar and Swann (n 2) 152–53; G Viney, 'Tort Liability' in G Bermann and E Picard (eds), *Introduction to French Law* (AH Alphen aan den Rijn, Kluwer Law International, 2009); Whittaker, 'The Law of Obligations' (n 58) 360–416.

[63] E Steiner, *French Law: A Comparative Approach* (Oxford, Oxford University Press, 2010) 344.

[64] J Halperin, *Le Code Civil* (Dalloz, 1996) cited in Steiner (n 63) 377; J Halperin, *The French Civil Code*, trans Tony Weir (New York, UCL, 2006) 37.

la propriété (different ways to acquire property). As Eva Steiner accurately notes, 'the central focus in French law is on the nature and characteristics of the right of ownership'.[65] Property underlies the whole regime of rights and obligations. It is defined in absolute manner (Article 544). According to Articles 12 and 17 of the Declaration of the Rights of Man and the Citizen 1789, property is deemed as a *naturel et imprescriptible* (natural and imprescriptible) and *inviolable et sacré* (inviolable and sacred) right of man.

This focus on property is manifest also in possessory remedies provided by the Civil Code. Many Articles provide both owners and possessors with proper actions to protect interference with their possession (eg, Articles 815, 2278–79).[66] The question remaining, however, concerns unjustified enrichment and how it is dealt with in French law. Until recently the *Code Napoléon* did not have a general provision for unjustified enrichment. It provided provisions on benevolent intervention in another's affairs (*gestion d'affaires d'autrui*) (Articles 1372–75) and undue payment (*repetition de l'indu*) (Articles 1376–81). Scholars, however, suggested that these are only special instances of a more general principle of unjustified enrichment. This view was approved by the *Cour de cassation* in the famous *Boudier* case of 1892.[67] The Court accepted the rule on grounds of equity and the *actio de in rem verso* as received in France. By so doing, it established a new source of civil liability. The new rule was expounded, restricted and refined in later decisions[68] until promulgated very recently as Article 1303 in the new reform of contract law. Unsurprisingly Article 1303-1 provides that enrichment is unjustified if it neither stems from fulfilling an obligation nor from a conferral of a gratuitous benefit.[69] This structure reaffirms, though imperfectly, the old civilian model of enrichment without ground. It re-emphasises the protected domain of the disadvantage and relegates, at the outset at least, the wrongful behaviour of the enriched.

Another concern which begets discussion is the principle of subsidiarity adhered to by some jurisdictions, notably France and Italy. The gist of the principle is to allow an unjustified enrichment claim only if other claims are unavailable and only to the extent such claim is not expressly precluded. This means that the cases at hand may actually be handled by other fields, notably delict law. Delict law typically does not adhere to the

---

[65] Steiner (n 63) 378.

[66] ibid 379. L Aynès, 'Property Law' in G Bermann and E Picard (eds), *Introduction to French Law* (AH Alphen aan den Rijn, Kluwer Law International, 2009).

[67] Req 15 Jun 1892, S 1893.281.

[68] Especially Civ 12 May 1914, S 1918.1.41 cited in von Bar and Swann (n 2) 96.

[69] Ordonnance no 2016-131 of 10 February 2016. *The New Provisions* of the *Code Civil*, trans J Cartwright, B Fauvarque-Cosson and S Whittaker, available at: www.textes.justice.gouv.fr/ art_pix/THE-LAW-OF-CONTRACT-2-5-16.pdf.

exemplar highlighted. It seems, however, that in many systems applying the principle, unjustified enrichment is perceived as a gap-filler[70] or a residual claim providing remedy when no other claim is available. John Dawson describes this as 'an adequacy test' which reserves 'the action for cases where no adequate alternative remedy' is allowed. Indeed, unjustified enrichment should not be used to evade legislative policies promoted by other areas of law.[71] But this role converts the claim to a facilitator of justice. Allowing or barring the claim would hinge on the desire to insure an equitable result. It places it with a 'higher legal order' which monitors and corrects regular statutes.[72]

It is perhaps this 'corrective role'[73] of subsidiarity which draws the unjustified enrichment claim closer to people's view of justice and equity as grounded in cultural perceptions.[74] This means that the ancillary character of unjustified enrichment does not devalue it as a source of cultural insights. On the contrary, it upgrades its role and importance as a fertile source of cultural and social attitudes. This indicates that unjustified enrichment rules should be examined even when they are not practically at work. Subordinating the claim simply strengthens its connection with people's shared pool of meanings, values and attitudes which we often call culture.

---

[70] von Bar and Swann (n 2) 96.

[71] Dawson (n 5) 106.

[72] L Smith, 'Property, Subsidiarity, and Unjust Enrichment' in D Johnston and R Zimmermann (eds), *Unjustified Enrichment: Key Issues in Comparative Perspective* (Cambridge, Cambridge University Press, 2004) 611.

[73] ibid 610–11.

[74] See generally G Jasso, 'Culture and the Sense of Justice: A Comprehensive Framework for Analysis' (2005) 36(1) *Journal of Cross-Cultural Psychology* 14.

3

European Culture

AN INTRODUCTORY NOTE

ONE OF THE dominant routes to intelligibility in archeology is placing an inspected object within 'a sequence'. Aided by stratigraphy, the study of rock layers, the apprehension of the object occurs with respect to the layer in which it was found and layers laid down before and after it. 'Sequence' and 'change' in the properties of that object, for example, 'materials', 'shape', style and 'decoration' are significant sources of archeological lucidity.[1] Law is like such an object. As a man-made artefact of a given time and place, its intelligibility lies with temporal layers of cultural discourses which give it force and meaning, and equally so, with the transformations of law and culture over time.

In line with a thematic approach, this chapter investigates the themes of wealth along Europe's history. It attempts to map three key phases in the perception of wealth, each providing different patterns of thought for European law to utilise. The period covered is a very long one. It extends from medieval times to the present day. Needless to say, any divisions, including the one offered, cannot do justice to the complexities and diversities of European thought during such a lengthy period. Nevertheless, in order to discuss a vast mass of materials, it is fruitful to seek, and at times prudently construct, those overarching generalities that indispensably hide complications and internal conflicts. This process works to facilitate a better grasp of the major outlines of European perceptions of wealth and related themes. Furthermore, it sharpens our understanding of socio-cultural meanings and values embedded in the law.

IS THERE A *EUROPEAN* CULTURE?

Perhaps one of the most intriguing questions of this chapter is whether there is indeed a *European* culture. This question is frequently discussed

---

[1] P Bahn and B Tidy, *Archaeology: A Very Short Introduction* (Oxford, Oxford University Press, 2000) 17, 18.

vis-a-vis cultural diversity. The latter is supposed to have an inverse impact on the former, or at least this is how the matter is often approached.[2] The common view is that one culture necessarily comes at the expense of another, and terms such as 'homogeny' and 'heterogeneity' are extensively employed to discuss this question. We tackle slogans like 'united in diversity' or statements such as 'national cultures are too heterogeneous to speak of a continent-wide culture'.[3] But this contrastive approach of either/or is highly problematic. It tends to miss the intricacy of the social and cultural conditions.

Basically, a person's social and cultural spheres comprise of many circles and groups in which she is part or member, for example, Jewish, Asian, woman, academic, married, senior citizen, etc. Each circle or group proposes its own set of meanings and values to grasp and interpret a person's life experience. The sum of these sets of meanings combined and internalised constitutes the social or cultural whole of a person. These sets of meanings may be interdependent or congruent. They may spark inter-tensions. But since a person's identity is indivisible, tensions often lead to elevations rather than self-antagonism or exclusions.[4] An approach which wholly or partially circumvents a certain set of meanings at the expense of another is regrettably reductive and unnecessary.

Pertaining to *European* culture, a special report by the European Commission on European Cultural Values explains that 'in the public mind there are different levels of culture which both overlap and co-exist'. On one level, there is the national culture, on another there is the European.[5] Being Austrian and European is not an either/or question but embraces both. Seeking the *European* is a matter of delineation not measurement or extent. It is a task of outlining and tracing a *European* set of meanings and values produced and disseminated by a shared history and common heritage. This approach preserves the richness of concurrent meaning systems. It evades superfluous circumventions as well as monocular perceptions of culture.

Discerning the *European* evokes the embedded social aptitude for defining the self in relation to the *Other*. To be able to make a meaningful proclamation on European culture is also to be able to set it apart from a non-European one.[6] It is a common view that Europe is culturally

---

[2] EC (2007) *European Cultural Values Report* (September 2007, Special Eurobarometer 278) 63 available at: ec.europa.eu/public_opinion/archives/ebs/ebs_278_en.pdf (ECVR).

[3] ibid 63–68.

[4] M Mautner, *Mishpat yi Tarbut* (*Law and Culture*) (Ramat-Gan, Bar-Ilan University Press, 2008) 35–37, 249–255; EC, *ECVR* (n 2) 69; G Hofstede, GJ Hofstede and M Minkov, *Cultures and Organizations: Software for the Mind* (New York, McGraw-Hill, 2010) 17.

[5] ibid (*ECVR*) 69.

[6] A Murphy, T Jordan-Bychkov and B Jordan, *The European Culture Area: A Systematic Geography* (Lanham, MD, Rowman & Littlefield, 2009) 10, 22.

'distinct from the other parts' of the so called 'West'. It shares a higher extent of aggregated culture which gives it a sense of a distinct whole. John McCormick, for instance, identifies *Europeanism* with the 'common values, preferences, predilections, and propensities across Europe's communities, nations, and states' which set it apart from other nations and peoples of the world.[7]

Many official European Union documents rest on a delineation approach.[8] Article 167 of the Treaty on the Functioning of the European Union, for example, urges the promotion of cultural diversity. Nevertheless, it stresses the need to bring 'the common cultural heritage' of Europeans 'to the fore'.[9] This heritage rests, inter alia, on acknowledgment of the 'culture and history of the European peoples' (Article 167(2) opt 1). In fact, many decisions and instruments of the Union bodies endeavour to promote a *European* culture. Decision 1855/2006/EC establishing the Cultural Programme (2007–13), for example, seeks to strengthen the awareness of 'the common European cultural heritage' as shared by the peoples of Europe.[10]

Citing the Italian actor Dario Fo, the European Agenda for Culture in a Globalising World states that 'even before Europe was united in an economic level or was conceived at the level of economic interests and trade, it was culture that united all the countries of Europe'.[11] In the same realm, the cultural policy of the European Union urges the 'strengthening and expanding' of the 'European model of society built on a set of values common to all European societies'.[12]

To conclude this point, *European* culture is nothing other than the system of meanings and values inherited and transmitted by the long-shared history and expected future of the European continent, notably 'Greco-Roman heritage', 'Christian values', the 'Renaissance', 'religious reformations', the 'Enlightenment', 'industrialism', the 'French Revolution', 'secularism' and 'diversity'.[13] With this shared past in mind, the following sections attempt to map the distinctive perceptions of wealth and related themes as traced across Europe's cultural history starting with the Christian Middle Ages until the current day.

---

[7] J McCormick, *Europeanism* (Oxford, Oxford University Press, 2010) 2.

[8] cp *ECVR* (n 2) 69.

[9] Treaty on the Functioning of the European Union [2010] OJ C83/49.

[10] European Parliament and Council Decision 1855/2006/EC establishing the Culture Programme (2007 to 2013) [2006] OJ L372/1, s 1.

[11] COM (EC) of 10 May 2007 on a European agenda for culture in a globalizing world [2007] SEC 570, s 1.

[12] McCormick (n 7) 4.

[13] Optem, *The Europeans, Culture and Cultural Values, Qualitative Study* (June 2006) 35; *ECVR* (n 2) 63; R Ostergren and M Le Bossé, *The Europeans: A Geography of People, Culture, and Environment* (New York, Guilford, 2011) 9–21.

WEALTH AS LABOUR, MORALITY AND SOCIAL PROPERTIES

'The earth is the Lord's and the fullness thereof, the world and those who dwell therein', so says King David in one of the poems of Psalms.[14] The notion of God as the creator and owner of all is prevailing in the Scriptures. It is only expected that this perception gains a dominant position in the *mentalités collectives* of Europeans in the Christian Middle Ages.[15] In fact Christian perceptions formed much of what medieval people came to live and experience throughout their lives. Peasants, serfs, nobles, lords and kings, all were greatly influenced by the religious comprehension of life and existence. Life was perceived as a temporal stage, and church as the only ladder to Heaven. Churches, cathedrals and basilicas were built to convey this message very clearly. Their art and architects, predominantly Romanesque and Gothic, represented the solidity of idealistic faith and the venerable position which the Church was held in the social cognition of medieval man.

At the time, the medieval concept of wrongful enrichment was deeply influenced by people's religious world-view (or *episteme* to follow Foucault)[16] and their distinct perceptions of wealth, property and labour. These themes are hardly comprehensible without reference to basic medieval notions of the human person, nature and the spatial dimension. Following the example of other scholars who similarly could not keep their enthusiasm for art under wraps,[17] I wish to explain the intricacy of these notions by examining commonplace medieval artwork. To that end, I chose two paintings depicting the Madonna and Child enthroned. One is by Cimabue dating from 1280–90. The other is by Segna di Bonaventura dated 1316.

Examining these paintings, we would not fail to observe the painters' deep commitment to Christian themes. The magisterial and central role of Mary and Jesus the child is nothing but obvious. A further observation, however, yields itself to the careful beholder. All figures portrayed in the paintings look similar. They seem dismantled of any individuality. All seem to follow a basic drawing design. Their facial expressions are fundamentally indistinguishable. Their age, gender and height are far from vibrant. Instead, they seem to elevate the image of the group at the expense of the individuals. This observation begs an explanation.

---

[14] Psalms 24:1.

[15] M Howell and W Prevenier, *From Reliable Sources: An Introduction to Historical Methods* (Ithaca, NY, Cornell University Press, 2001) 15.

[16] cp M Foucault, *The Archaeology of Knowledge* (London, Routledge, 2002) 211; S Mills, *Discourse* (London, Routledge, 1997) 50–51.

[17] A Gurevich, *Categories of Medieval Culture*, trans G Campbell (London, Routledge & Kegan Paul, 1985) 6; J Rifkin, *The European Dream*, Kindle edn (New York, Penguin, 2004) locations 1913–27.

In *The Civilization of Renaissance in Italy*, Jakob Burckhardt argues that the medieval person's self-conscious is profoundly different from the one we recognise today. A medieval person, he notes, is conscious of herself mainly through general categories such as family or people and mainly as a member of a bigger group. Her subjectivity is confined to the 'spiritual'.[18] The concept of human ego and awareness of what sets her apart from her group has not emerged by then.[19] Thus, a medieval person's portrayal is often construed outside-in rather than the other way around. She is Joan from Geneva, daughter of Girard, wife of Amadeus. This is, for example, how a medieval person would be introduced. Traits of subjective character addressing questions like who I am, how I feel, how I perceive myself now and in years to come, were mostly alien questions to the medieval mind.

A medieval poem would illustrate this point vividly. 'Hildebrandslied' is a famous heroic poem written in Old High German and believed to be part of Germanic tribes' literary tradition of the ninth century. It narrates the story of two great warriors, Hildebrand and Hudabrand, who meet in combat each for his army. Ignorant of their blood ties, Hildebrand asks young Hudabrand for his father's name and place of origin. Hudabrand reveals he heard he was abandoned by his father Hildebrand when still a child, and that his father became a famous warrior for King Dietrich. Hildebrand immediately recognises his own son and offers Hudabrand friendship with a band of golden rings he unties from his arm. Hudabrand, however, rejects the gift accusing his match of deception and the two end up fighting courageously. The poem tells that the warriors clash in combat and their shields are smashed by their weapons.[20]

Reading the stanzas of the poem, one does not fail to notice the absence of introspective narration. No psychological perception of the unfolding events is shared with the reader. In fact, the two warriors tend to be stereotyped. Their depiction reproduces type models rather than actual men. Distinctiveness is present only through collective adherences such as warriors, men of the East, sailors, etc. Both heroes fall to a pattern of behaviour that foretells their doom, as if their steps and fate are predetermined. While able with a couple of words to reveal his true identity and avoid the tragic end, Hildebrand can see no alternative but to face his destiny, to kill his own son or to be killed by him. They fight heroically, their shields shatter and they both seem to perish for glory. Both heroes are there to serve a greater cause. Their individuality is moulded

---

[18] J Burckhardt, *The Civilization of the Renaissance in Italy*, trans S Middlemore (London, Penguin, 1990) 98–99, fn 32.

[19] A Gurevich, *The Origins of European Individualism*, trans K Judelson (Oxford, Blackwell, 1995) 4–6.

[20] 'Hildebrandslied', trans F Wood (Chicago, University of Chicago Press, 1914).

by group perceptions, and subordinated to collective ends like courage and heroism. This literary path serves to illustrate a human conception of which individuality is still a project in the making.

Many studies have disputed the precise time individuality took shape and the processes it entailed. The fulcrum lies, however, not in the disputed subjects but in the shared assertions. Be it Burckhardt's sudden emergence of individuality in Italy's fifteenth-century Renaissance,[21] Colin Morris's gradual process of self-awareness by the late-eleventh mid-twelfth centuries,[22] or Aaron Gurevich's discovery of individuality traces in the early centuries of the Middle Ages,[23] it is widely agreed that individuality is a matter of cultural reconfiguration and not some physiological capriole.[24] Like any cultural tradition touring a vast piece of land, individuality could not obliterate prior traditions all at once or all across the continent. To that end, a good way is to discern a medieval concept of the human person, and subsequently differentiate it from other configurations of the concept, notably that of the Renaissance.

Reverting to Cimabue's and Bonaventura's paintings examined earlier, a further insight stands out. Like typical medieval paintings, the two artworks seem to lack human perception or what technically is termed a 'linear perception'. Figures contained are drawn flat and mostly vertical. Their body parts lack proportion or any correct human anatomy. Landscapes and nature are ignored altogether.[25] The whole images seem two-dimensional, with no depth or volume depicted. Instead, they embrace a reverse perspective. As if the painting stares at the viewer rather than the other way around. The images seem to expand along the horizon rather than contract as normally expected.[26]

These characteristics are neither accidental nor purely technical. They reflect a unique cultural perception of life and the human being. In medieval eyes, Earth is a temporary stage bestowed by God on humans who need to prepare for eternity. God is the sole owner of all and the true centre of the universe. It is through His eyes that all things and figures are observed. In inverse perspective, George Pattison asserts, the observer is not the actual beholder of the image, but is herself the object observed. This is, Pattison explains, 'a manifestation of the eschatological world, the redeemed and deified world, the divine life itself, reaching out into the

---

[21] Burckhardt (n 18).

[22] C Morris, *The Discovery of the Individual: 1050–1200* (Toronto, University of Toronto Press, 2004).

[23] Gurevich, *The Origins of European Individualism* (n 19).

[24] ibid 5.

[25] Gurevich, Categories of Medieval Culture (n 17) 5–6; Rifkin (n 17) Location 1917.

[26] J Kolvicki, *On Images: Their Structure and Content* (Oxford, Oxford University Press, 2009) 102, 103.

world of the "spectator"'.[27] According to Gurevich, medieval portrayals of the spatial dimension are, in fact, Christian 'symbolic interpretation of the world'.[28]

Remarkably, it is the absence of individuality and realism, as we understand them today, that allows us to approach medieval artwork for insights into medieval culture. Medieval artists had to follow 'fixed laws which could not be broken at the dictates of individual imagination'.[29] The artist perceived himself a reproducer of commonplace notions and shared ideas. This is similarly the case with various medieval literary genres, as we saw earlier. Clichés are broadly employed and reproduced.[30] This use of conventionality is hardly accidental. It implies a disinterest in the distinctiveness of earthly life. Instead, people's focus is directed elsewhere.

Medievalists' focus was lent to the supreme and invisible rather than the worldly and material. For them, nature was primarily a means to understand the Divine.[31] Medievalists 'came into contact with physical reality by way of mystical and pseudoscientific abstractions'.[32] Their attitude to nature was determined mostly by religious moulds. They did not sharply distinguish between humans and nature. Nature was perceived as 'God's creation'.[33] It had not yet been objectified or 'alienated'. Human beings were integral consumers of nature, rather than resource managers or external masters.[34]

This medieval episteme nurtured a unique perception of wealth which was firstly a matter of religious ethics. A person's wealth was indispensably tied to her worldly conduct and pursuit of eternal life. Wealth was construed in light of the Scripture and one's longing for salvation. It was not perceived as an end but as a means to insure decent living, each according to her social class and adhered traditions.[35] Accruing of wealth beyond one's need was considered a sin.[36] It stood in contrast to honour and nobility, two of the most highly regarded traits in medieval society. A rich merchant who raised her money and possessions through illicit practices was considered a disreputable and highly suspicious person.[37] More generally, the accumulation of profit as such was even morally problematic and could constitute a stumbling block for seekers of eternity.

[27] G Pattison, *Art, Modernity and Faith: Restoring the Image* (Norwich, SCM, 1998) 130.
[28] Gurevich, *Categories of Medieval Culture* (n 17) 35.
[29] E Mâle, *Religious Art in France of the Thirteenth Century* (Mineola, NY, Dover, 2012) 1.
[30] Gurevich, *Categories of Medieval Culture* (n 17) 37–38, 62.
[31] ibid 8–9, 35–36.
[32] J Le Goff and J Barrow, *Medieval Civilization 400–1500* (Oxford, Blackwell, 1991) 138.
[33] Rifkin (n 17) location 2196.
[34] Gurevich, *Categories of Medieval Culture* (n 17) 45, 54–55, 57, 59, 64.
[35] ibid 9, 215.
[36] T Aquinas, *Summa theologica* (Public Domain, 1485) Q 118, Arts 1–2 available at: www.sacred-texts.com/chr/aquinas/summa/sum374.htm.
[37] Gurevich, *Categories of Medieval Culture* (n 17) 172, 249.

In contrast, voluntary poverty or poverty at will was favoured for all true followers of Christ. A standard icon of the medieval attitude to temporal wealth was the widely circulated vita of St Francis. St Francis, the son of a wealthy merchant, made a strong statement about wealth when he publicly renounced worldly treasures for the sake of heavenly ones. St Francis abandoned his family's possessions by stripping himself publicly of clothes and handing them to his father.[38] Though this story illustrates the medieval distrust of wealth and materiality, it fosters a radical attitude that was widespread back then. In fact, the question of poverty and spirituality stood in the middle of fierce debate between the Franciscans and Pope John XXII regarding Christ's total poverty. While Jesus and his apostles were indisputably models for imitation, it remained controversial whether asceticism and total rejection of worldly possessions were needed for spiritual deliverance or not.[39]

But wealth was not only tied to spiritual ethics, it was also indivisible from one's societal properties. At many stages, medieval society was also a feudal one. In a feudal society, each person is born into a certain social class and is expected to behave accordingly. A person could be a lord, a knight, a priest, a peasant, a craftsman, a blacksmith or a guild member. Each role accentuated a specific position in a somewhat rigid social hierarchy. It denoted that person's proximity to God, the top of the hierarchy. A social status communicated that person's position as well as her personal traits and moral perfection.[40] The higher one goes, the more morally noble she is perceived.

Property, especially land, was intertwined with one's societal place. Property did not follow a model of exclusive ownership, but that of a collectively held resource. 'Things' explains Jeremy Rifkin 'were not owned outright or exclusively by anyone, but rather shared in various ways under the conditions and terms established by a rigid code of proprietary obligations'.[41] Land granted by a king to a feudal lord is subsequently held by a social chain 'from the king down through tenants and subtenants to the peasants who tilled it'. All, says Richard Schlatter, 'had a certain dominion over it, but no one had an absolute lordship over it'.[42]

The medieval concept of dominion, argues Charles McIlwain, is a pool of entitlements arranged in a hierarchic order and exercised over the

---

[38] P Robinson 'St Francis of Assisi', *The Catholic Encyclopedia* (1909) available at: www.newadvent.org/cathen/06221a.htm.

[39] P Garnsey, *Thinking about Property: From Antiquity to the Age of Revolution* (Cambridge, Cambridge University Press, 2007) 85.

[40] Gurevich, *Categories of Medieval Culture* (n 17) 56, 70, 172, 198, 214–15, 236, 254–57.

[41] Rifkin (n 17) location 2667.

[42] R Schlatter, *Private Property: The History of an Idea* (New York, Russell & Russell, 1973) 64.

same valuable according to one's rank of power or right.[43] This model of property has not drawn a line between labour and property as a means of living. Property was not yet alienated from a person's daily labour, but was part of it. Whether labour was applied directly to the resource or indirectly through subordinate agents, it was indivisible to the power to exercise dominion over that object. Dominion and labour maintained a reciprocal bond. Dominion legitimised the cultivation and farming of a land. The latter justified dominion, especially as far as unsettled or open lands were concerned.[44]

In his discussion of the medieval Roman law of unjustified enrichment, Jan Hallebeek explains that in medieval eyes 'not every advantage in life may be regarded as gained in a proper way. Some profits are unnatural or the result of an infringement of natural order'.[45] Labour in line with Christian ethics and one's social stratum were the natural way to make a living. According to Julian Vitullo and Diane Wolfthal, medieval 'monetary practices' were perpetually weighed against the spiritual and the natural.[46] Wrongful gain defied both. It was the fruit of two deadly sins: avarice and pride. Avarice, the insatiable desire for wealth, was considered the 'root of all sins'.[47] Pride was the iconic sin of Beelzebub who wanted to raise above the stars of God and enthrone himself as the Devine contra to natural order. Both sins produced a vicious circle 'in which sinners at once distance themselves from God (pride) and instead focus on worldly goods (avarice)'.[48]

Usura (Usury) was perceived the archetype of wrongful gain.[49] It was both unnatural and contrary to God's commandments. In the Inferno canticle of the *Divine Comedy*, Virgil, Dante's guide in Gehenna explains the sinfulness of usury. It was an offence against *la divina bontade* (God's goodness). It ran against the course of nature and *dal divino 'ntelletto* (the divine intellect). The latter commands humans to earn their bread in toil. Usurers, however, despised nature and sought their own pleasures, but were eventually forced to crouch on hot sand with heavy moneybags

---

[43] D Pels, *Property and Power in Social Theory: A Study in Intellectual Rivalry* (London, Routledge, 1998) 23–24.

[44] Gurevich, *Categories of Medieval Culture* (n 17) 56, 70, 172, 198, 214–15, 236, 254–57.

[45] J Hallebeek, 'Developments of Mediaeval Roman Law' in E Schrage (ed), *Unjust Enrichment: The Comparative Legal History of the Law of Restitution* (Berlin, Duncker & Humblot, 1995) 59.

[46] J Vitullo and D Wolfthal, 'Introduction' in J Vitullo and D Wolfthal (eds), *Money, Morality, and Culture in Late Medieval and Early Modern Europe* (Surrey, Ashgate, 2010) 1.

[47] Aquinas (n 36) 1st pt of 2nd pt, Q 84.

[48] Vitullo and Wolfthal, 'Introduction' (n 46) 2.

[49] J Appleby, *The Relentless Revolution: A History of Capitalism*, Kindle edn (New York, Norton, 2010) locations 1689–94.

around their necks in retribution. The *Comedy* further stripped them of their names marking the loss of their identities due to their sinful gain.[50]

On a social level, wrongful interest openly raised through money lending was considered *infamy facti* (infamy of fact). It testified the dishonest, immoral and treacherous characters of the person involved. The biblical figure of Judas, considered Christ's betrayer and the embodiment of avarice, became the prototype of usurers and wrongful economic behaviour. He represented material greed, egotism and ignorance of the Christian faith.[51] He was dialectically opposed to the biblical figure, Mary Magdalene, who portrayed a pious perception of wealth, anointing Jesus's feet with expensive ointment made from pure nard and wiping it with her own hair,[52] thus choosing spiritual salvation over worldly goods.[53] Mary's deed was detested by Judas who set his avaricious eyes on the ointment wishing he could have appropriated it to himself.[54]

As Gurevich puts it, wrongful wealth in medieval perception was not so much bound 'by its dimensions, as by the aims pursued by its owners and the means they used to get their hands on it'. A person's wealth was an integral part of one's social position. A person who seeks wealth per se sparks great distrust. Labour was the chief route to profit. Deviation from that route ran against faith and nature. Wrongful enrichment was an issue of conduct, religiosity and social dishonour. Illicit, opportunistic and unnatural economic practices such as usury were highly problematic and severely shameful. Avarice, cupidity and greed were believed to be at the root of such disgraceful deeds. They did not only disclose evil motives, but also revealed the (un)spiritual condition of the accumulator.[55]

WEALTH AS A PERSON'S EARTHLY DOMINION, PROPERTY AND POSSESSION

These medieval attitudes towards wealth and profit soon paved the way for more reasoned ones. The seeds of human individuality started to break free from former conventions. Humans commenced a reassessment of their place in the universe and eventually changed long-cherished postulates. They upgraded their position in the world and gradually perceived

---

[50] A Dante, *Divine Comedy* (Hollywood, Simon & Brown, 2013) 64–67, 92–96 ('Inferno' XI: 94–111) ('Inferno' XVII: 46–57).

[51] G Todeschini, 'The Incivility of Judas: "Manifest" Usury as a Metaphor for the "Infamy of Fact" (*infamia facti*)' in J Vitullo and D Wolfthal (eds), *Money, Morality, and Culture in Late Medieval and Early Modern Europe* (Surrey, Ashgate, 2010) 33–34, 42–43.

[52] John 12:3.

[53] Todeschini (n 51) 38.

[54] John 12: 4–6.

[55] Gurevich, *Categories of Medieval Culture* (n 17) 242.

themselves as life's 'new point of reference'.[56] Traditional ties to so-called natural order were increasingly shaken. Human awareness was morphing inwards. A new concept of Self was being born, one that accentuates a person's psyche and persona and distinguishes them from those of other kin members. The post-medieval person began to construct her earthly domain, her own material kingdom.

This new perception correlated with a great discovery in the art world. It was the linear perspective, a technique which facilitated the transition to Renaissance art. First demonstrated by none other than Brunelleschi himself,[57] the new technique presumes a human observer who examines the painting from one fixed point with objects contracting proportionally along her visual horizon. This discovery was considered a shift to a more anthropocentric attitude to the world and one's surroundings. The old bond with nature was being substituted by a more alienated one. God's creation is being subordinated to human will literally. Humans turn their eyes towards nature and see a wealth of resources ready to be deployed to their advantage. It is the creatures' own view which now grasps and evaluates the world rather than that of the Scriptures. The Renaissance perception enthrones the human person as the new ruler of her earthly domain.[58]

A clear expression of this perception is the rise of material 'acquisitiveness'. In her acclaimed book tracing the historical roots of modern 'material consumerism', Lisa Jardine argues that two of the dominant traits of the Renaissance person are 'acquisitiveness' and 'possession'. Through a methodical study of the material culture of the Renaissance and post-medieval era, she explains how people came to enjoy wealth through a 'superfluity of material possessions', and how 'mercantilism' and 'acquisitiveness' ruled the *mentalités collectives* of those eras. Property and possession, she explains, were increasingly celebrated per se. The functionality of the possessed objects was more and more side-lined. Admiration of valuables, gemstones, extravagant clothes and com-modities began to reform people's conception of wealth both in terms of quantity and quality.[59]

Property and possession were increasingly testifiers of a person's wealth and worth. It advertised social superiority and economic prosper-ity. To be 'magnificent' in the early fifteenth century, Jardine points out, is to be 'someone with the means to acquire all those coveted possessions

---

[56] ibid 34.

[57] S Edgerton, *The Renaissance Rediscovery of Linear Perspective* (New York, Basic Books, 1975) 3. See, eg, Raphael's 'The School of Athens' (1509–1511).

[58] Burckhardt (n 18) 185, 192, 195; Gurevich, *Categories of Medieval Culture* (n 17) 54, 86, 90; Rifkin (n 17) 2036–2195.

[59] L Jardine, *Worldly Goods: A New History of the Renaissance* (London, Macmillan, 1996) 12, 15, 17, 33–34, 69.

which expanding trade made available'. Giovanni Bellini's portrait of *Doge Leonardo Loredan* (1501) and Jan van Eyck's *Arnolfini Marriage* (1434) are two excellent examples of this statement. Elucidating the latter, Jardine argues, it is 'not a record of a pair of individuals; it is a celebration of ownership—of pride in possessions from wife to pet, to bed-hangings and brass work'. All these belongings are there to manifest the wealth and worth of the wedded merchant.[60]

The appreciation of material possessions, however, did not add up to the old constraints of spirituality, labour and societal properties. These medieval chains were increasingly left out and many of the values and attitudes formerly cherished were fading out. The new concept of wealth was more process blind. Social attention was shifting away from questions of deeds and compliance, embracing instead an outcome-focused concept. What one owned mattered more than how the gain was made. But this morphed perception of wealth provoked a tangible tension with former ones. Though it seemed silent on questions of ethical conduct and old societal prescriptions, it was more and more obvious that the new concept of wealth was, in fact, attempting to silence previous attitudes.

A good example of this tension is the rise and decline of the Humiliati order (1201–1571). The Humiliati was a religious order which made no commitment to asceticism. They were experienced traders openly cherishing material possessions. Increasingly, however, members of the order were unable to bring along their economic practices together with their religious vows and the order was eventually dissolved by Pope Pius V. Julia Miller and Laurie Taylor-Mitchell, who study the order's history, argue that in part, this case accentuated a wider cultural tension between material affluence and 'traditional church teachings that condemned wealth and its accumulation'. This conflict was also mirrored in many paintings produced for the Humiliati Church. The paintings often depicted devout religious themes alongside manifestations of wealth and extravagance such as gold, jewels, silken clothes and majestic decorations.[61]

According to Juliano Vitullo and Diane Wolfthal, Europeans at the time 'struggled with complex ethical issues, which were rooted in the apparent contradiction between the Christian ideals of poverty and charity, on the one hand, and the pervasive role of money and desire to accumulate wealth, on the other hand'.[62] These tensions marked the shift of weight in

---

[60] ibid 15, 18–19, 21, 64, 71–72, 93, 123–24.

[61] J Miller and L Taylor-Mitchell, 'To Honor God and Enrich Florence in Things Spiritual and Temporal: Piety, Commerce, and Art in the Humiliati Order' in J Vitullo and D Wolfthal (eds), *Money, Morality, and Culture in Late Medieval and Early Modern Europe* (Surrey, Ashgate, 2010) 129, 138–39.

[62] J Vitullo and D Wolfthal, 'Trading Values: Negotiating Masculinity in Late Medieval and Early Modern Europe' in J Vitullo and D Wolfthal (eds), *Money, Morality, and Culture in Late Medieval and Early Modern Europe* (Surrey, Ashgate, 2010) 155.

public attitudes to wealth. The outcome-focused definition of wealth was taking over the previous conduct-focused one. Culture was rephrasing its postulates about wealth and wealth accumulation. The questions about the route to profit were gradually substituted by an interest in a person's current dominion and material belongings.

But Christian ideals were not all together neglected. European culture was largely still a Christian one. It had to find its way out of traditional and ethical deadlocks. Conceptual reconfigurations were utilised to that end. Merchants, for example, 'did not simply ignore religious concerns regarding their activities'. They 'found ways to adapt to them and assuage lingering doubts'.[63] Terms formerly associated with ill-perceived practices were gradually rephrased to silence ethical doubts. Money lenders were distinguished from usurers and 'healthy' interest from usury.[64] The Church ban on interest from loans persisted, but many techniques were invented to bypass the prohibition. One such technique was offered by Johann Eck, a professor at the University of Ingolstadt, who turned the loan into a risk-bearing investment sold at profit by the lender. Such techniques meant to detach usury from its religious connotation and place it in a more tolerant sphere.[65]

Traditional constraints on wealth accumulation stimulated new forms of thought. Creative endeavours were embarked upon to balance two competing philosophies: the Christian and the proto-capitalist.[66] Religiosity and labour as the paradigmatic paths to permissible gain were taking more moderate proportions. Property and material possession were empowered. This new balance was reflected also in painting practices. Carlo Crivelli's *Annunciation with St Emidius* (1486) is a good example. The Virgin, archangel Gabriel and St Emidius are vocal religious themes. But their voice in the painting is no longer vibrant. It is now immersed in a material world of commodities and belongings.[67] The medieval role these figures fulfilled diminished and took on a more worldly proportion. The central role is now shifting to the themes of earthly dominion, corporeal wealth and belongings.

Remarkably, this new trope invaded church teaching as well. Following the heat of the poverty debate, Pope John XXII released an abrupt encyclical, *Cum Inter Nonnullos* (November 1323),[68] in which he directly

---

[63] L Kaelber, 'Max Weber and Usury: Implications for Historical Research' in L Armstrong, I Elbl and M Elbl (eds), *Money, Markets and Trade in Late Medieval Europe: Essays in Honour of John HA Munro* (Leiden, Koninklijke Brill NV, 2007) 59, 69.

[64] Vitullo and Wolfthal, 'Trading Values' (n 62) 155–56.

[65] Jardine (n 59) 102, 327–30.

[66] Vitullo and Wolfthal, 'Introducton' (n 46) 4.

[67] Jardine (n 59) 8–9.

[68] Pope John XXII, *Cum Inter Nonnullos* (12 November 1323) available at: www.franciscan-archive.org/bullarium/qinn-e.html.

condemned and declared 'erroneous and heretical' the Franciscan view of Christ's asceticism. Wealth, the Pope stressed, was not wrong or unjust per se. It was the way people used it that made it so.[69] Wealth instead promised to bring in positive revenues once circulating within Christian communities. It could serve the needy and the poor, families and relatives. It could also serve society and the common good.[70]

This call added to a general mood which increasingly projected wealth in a more positive light. Wealth was now perceived as a cause of social and economic prosperity. Wealth had all the means to fend off unchristian practices such as 'sterility', 'hoarding' and 'prodigality'. Many humanists of that era stressed the social importance of wealth. They cast it as precondition of Christian ethics, notably compassion and philanthropy.[71] Poverty, in contrast, was linked to dishonour. In his work *De Avaritia* (1428), the Italian scholar and later Florentine Chancellor, Poggio Bracciolini (1380–1459), argues that avarice could in fact depict Christian qualities. Avarice is a natural trait essential for any community. Great cities were literally constructed on the avarice of past members. A conceptual distinction should, however, be drawn between 'avarice' and 'sheer lust for money'. While the latter must be denounced, avarice and the love of money, he says, is the basis for all the good in the world.[72]

Peculiarly enough the question of spiritual salvation itself could not avoid the magical touch of wealth. On the eve of the Lutheran Reformation, the Catholic Church began to sell papal indulgences. These were printed sheets containing a personal guarantee by the Pope that purchasers were remitted from their past, and sometimes future, sins. This practice became an important 'source of income' for the Church and many of the latter's projects, for example, rebuilding St Peter's Basilica in Rome, were financed this way.[73] Wealth, says Ian Moulton, had the power to attain worldly and religious virtues. Everything 'has a price'.[74] Financial gains of the era stripped away former allegations of wrongfulness. Wealth was wrong only in as far as it challenged its own essence. A wrongful enrichment was a challenge to one's earthly domain and material possessions. It was a question of deprivation of property and less so of an ill-gotten gain.

Earlier perceptions of religiosity and social properties were interpolated and came second to new trends in wrongful wealth conceptions.

---

[69] Garnsey (n 39) 85–87, 103.

[70] eg Vitullo and Wolfthal, 'Trading Values' (n 62) 167.

[71] ibid 156–57, 159.

[72] A Proulx Lang, 'Poggio Bracciolini's De Avaitia: A Study in Fifteenth Century Florentine Attitudes Toward Avarice and Usury' (MA thesis, Montreal, Sir George Williams University, 1973) 51, 91, 97; ibid 159.

[73] Jardine (n 59) 335–37.

[74] I Moulton, 'Whores as Shopkeepers: Money and Sexuality in Aretino's *Ragionamenti*' in J Vitullo and D Wolfthal (eds), *Money, Morality, and Culture in Late Medieval and Early Modern Europe* (Surrey, Ashgate, 2010) 71, 75.

Impermissible attainment of wealth became a property issue rather than a conduct one. The wealth-as-outcome notion refuted the wealth-as-process one. Dispossession substituted misconduct and profiteering. Questions of morality and ill-behaviour were increasingly dismissed. Tropes of secularity reconceptualised the subject. Traditional wrongs like theft and deception were still criminal and severely punishable. A wrongful wealth, however, was mostly a secularly conceived challenge to one's established dominion and possessions.

WEALTH AS CAPITAL AND RIGHTS

Centuries later, a more modern concept of wealth was forming. It was significantly alien to social merits and ethical contexts. It signified the rise of capital or that impersonal economic power ownable just like actual property.[75] The new concept was nurtured by major changes that were taking place in society and commerce, some claim in the seventeenth and eighteenth centuries, others in the fuller fledged form of nineteenth-century industrial capitalism.[76] Factories, steam power and hardworking labourers signalled the begining of a 'new era',[77] where urbanisation, commodification, division of labour, developed trade practices and improved means of production were increasingly dominating the scene.[78]

Traditional attitudes perceived labour as an integral part of wealth. This perception was mostly eradicated by the new concept of wealth-as-capital. The new concept drew a clear line between wealth and labour. In fact, capital antagonised labour turning it into a sheer 'commodity' offered for a set price on the market. Workers would 'sell' their toil to capitalists, owners of the means of production, in exchange for predetermined wages. The resulting process, as Karl Marx terms it, was a 'mass proletarianisation' or 'the complete commodification of labour power'. This condition intensified as harsher competition shredded the markets and higher levels of efficiency and productivity were called for.[79]

Capitalism, says Marx, deformed former social structures turning both property and labourer into commodities. Capitalists became potential 'exploiters' of subordinated labourers who were treated as finite resources at the formers' disposal. Wealth increasingly fostered connotations of political power and social submission. It created 'a working class that

---

[75] Gurevich, *Categories of Medieval Culture* (n 17) 215, 255.
[76] E Wood, *The Origin of Capitalism: A Longer View* (New York, Verso, 2002) 3–4.
[77] Appleby (n 49) locations 2594–96, 2596–601, 2601–04; ibid 43 (Wood).
[78] Wood (n 76) 15, 20.
[79] ibid 2–3, 7, 97, 143–44; R Tawney, *Religion and the Rise of Capitalism* (New Jersey, NJ, Transaction Publishers, 2008) 43, 44.

was completely market-dependent and completely vulnerable to market disciplines'.[80] Wealth objectified every part of the economic world turning it into a mere asset at the hands of capitalists.[81] Wealth-as-capital was not just a matter of numbers and economics. It was imbued with tacit socio-political powers. It marked the beginning of the reign of capitalism.

Henri Pirenne defines capitalism as 'the tendency to the steady accumulation of wealth'.[82] According to Jack Goody, it is 'a regime based on the continuous accumulation of capital'.[83] Richard Tawney puts it differently. He explains it as the rise of the 'creed' of the individual. The capitalist, the latter argues, became the 'absolute master of his own', he pursues 'his pecuniary advantage, unrestrained by any obligation to postpone his own profit to the well-being of his neighbours'. This concept of wealth shattered previous structures of society, notably the medieval one, which was more organic with each person filling her role according to preset codes of the social hierarchy.[84] Wealth is increasingly deprived of its collective traits, focusing solely on the individual owner and her capital. It was the final nail in the coffin of wealth's ethical dimension.

The dispassion for previous attitudes to wealth was substituted for a new passion. It was the pursuit of wealth in a calculated and rational way.[85] In Goody's terms it was the 'development of a form of rationality based on the calculation of the means–end relationship'.[86] Julian Vitullo and Diane Wolfthal explained this as a growth of wealth in 'a methodical fashion'. The capitalist loathed and abandoned 'physical labor and manual tasks', and 'learned to strategize and manipulate the abstract fictions of the monetary economy'.[87] Popular culture utilised sexuality and prostitution as proper metaphors for capital and capital exchange. In similar fashion, what was once 'private and intimate' has become a mere commodity to be 'bought and sold' on the market.[88]

Resting on Goethe's *Faust* and Shakespeare's *Timon of Athens*, Marx emphasises the social disorder effected by the new perception of wealth. Capital, he says, empowers and transforms a person into her opposite. The ugly can have the 'most beautiful of women'. The lame can have 'twenty-four feet'. The brainless can 'buy clever people for himself' and

---

[80] Wood (n 76) 143–44; ibid 43, 44 (Tawney).
[81] K Marx, *Early Writings* (Harmondsworth, Penguin, 1975) 317–18; S Munzer, *A Theory of Property* (Cambridge, Cambridge University Press, 1990) 157–158.
[82] H Pirenne, *Belgian Democracy: Its Early History*, trans J Saunders (Kitchener, Batoche Books, 2004) 20.
[83] J Goody, *Capitalism and Modernity: The Great Debate* (Cambridge, Polity, 2004) 4.
[84] Tawney (78) 97, 146.
[85] Vitullo and Wolfthal, 'Introduction' (n 46) 3.
[86] Goody (n 82) 2.
[87] Vitullo and Wolfthal, 'Introduction' (n 46) 3.
[88] Moulton (n 73) 71, 72.

control them. The 'bad, dishonest, unscrupulous, stupid' can turn into a noble and highly regarded person.[89] This wealth removes 'traditional categories of hierarchy and status' and like a 'whore', 'facilitates the satisfaction of all human desires'.[90] Wealth-as-capital became, Marx argues, the 'antithesis' of labour. From a highly valued trait and a cherished way to make a living, labour became a hallmark of societal subordination and political abuse. Labour depicted the distorted and diminished servant of the new capitalist era.[91]

Traditional norms of society were abandoned. Nobility came with novelty rather than inheritance. Society was reformed by the creative mind and the pursuit of profit. The drive for money, once considered 'vulgar', was the power which facilitated the rise of the middle class. These were the bourgeoisie who owned wealth and plenty of it. They reacted to market growth by developing specialties in the work and production processes, later to be known as the 'division of labor'.[92] According to Marxist accounts of the so-called 'bourgeois revolution', members of this class utilised capitalism to liberate both itself and lower classes from what is left of feudalism and the feudal order of society.[93]

In his central work, *Lineages of the Absolutist State*, Perry Anderson explains the political revolt against former bonds of feudalism. He argues that feudal lords presented 'fragmented state power'. They abused their administrative and social powers to control lower reliant classes to their benefit. With the introduction of capitalism and the single authority of the state, these ties were debilitated. The newly deliberated classes built factories and embraced innovative means of production amid the consistently growing markets, introducing a new and probably more fragile social order.[94]

It was not long before the bourgeoisies revolted against former notions of property, especially feudal ones, demanding to secure their capital.[95] Originally, Roman law provided for *dominium* or absolute ownership. Feudal society introduced a more collective notion of 'conditional property' where entitlements held by different persons can be extracted from the same object. By the late twelfth century, feudal law made a distinction between *dominium directum*, namely a feudal lord's right to dispose of his property (mainly of land), and *dominium utile* which is the right

---

[89] K Marx and F Engels, *The Economic and Philosophic Manuscripts of 1844 and the Communist Manifesto*, trans M Milligan (New York, Prometheus Books, 1988) 136–39; ibid 75–76.

[90] Moulton (n 74) 76.

[91] Marx and Engels (n 88) 85–88.

[92] Appleby (n 49) locations 1496–501, 1501–06; Wood (n 76) 14, 62.

[93] Marx and Engels (n 88) Ch 1.

[94] P Anderson, *Lineages of the Absolutist State* (London, Verso, 1974) 19, 22–23; Wood (n 76) 44–45.

[95] Gurevich, *Categories of Medieval Culture* (n 17) 154.

of reliant persons to live on the premises and extract its benefits.[96] Feudal law also introduced the concept of 'seisen', which went half way between 'ownership' and 'possession'. It signified a formal 'investiture' which both entitled and obliged a person to administer a land for the benefit and service of her lord.[97]

But the gradual transition to capitalism revived the call for absolute ownership. The market of commodities needed to secure rights and tailor property in the shape of their individual holders. It was the time for 'clear-cut notions of absolute property' as Anderson puts it. Former notions of property rights rooted in conceptions of labour and societal properties had to go. They were eventually replaced by new, more absolute and more individualised ones. These changes correlated with other legal, reforms notably the rationalisation of evidence rules and the professionalising of adjudication. According to Anderson, these changes 'answered to vital interests of the commercial and manufacturing bourgeoisie'.[93]

The societal transformations complemented a new phase in the cultural history of Europe. Modes of wealth accumulation that were originally wrong and 'distasteful' became highly beneficial for a capitalist market. What was formerly usury turned to a prosperity enhancer.[99] Ill-perceived professions like moneydealers, bankers, moneylenders, and tax-collectors, formerly the four 'evangelists of Lucifer' according to one Dutch proverb, were now legitimate occupations regulated by the state for the sake of society and economic wealth.[100] The 'culture of capitalism' succeeded former cultures.[101] It announced wealth as the chief 'axis' upon which all life activities would dwell.[102]

The law of the state worked to secure wealth and personal liberty. In fact, property was increasingly interwoven with discourses of political rights. In his *Treatise on Political Economy*, the French classical economist, Jean-Baptiste Say (1767–1832), notes the importance of politics as the chief guarantee of property rights. 'The property a man has in his own industry, is violated, whenever he is forbidden the free exercise of his faculties and talents' he says. It is only when property is a 'reality' and a 'right' secured by law, 'can the sources of production, namely, land, capital, and industry, attain their utmost degree of fecundity'. The right of property, he concludes is 'the most powerful of all encouragements to the

---

[96] Anderson (n 94) 25.
[97] E Smith, *Commercial Real Estate: Listing Properties* (Chicago, IL, Dearborn, 2002) 83; ibid.
[98] Anderson (n 94) 25–26.
[99] Appleby (n 49) locations 1700–01.
[100] J Murray 'The Devil's Evangelists? Moneychangers in Flemish Urban Society' in J Vitullo and D Wolfthal (eds), *Money, Morality, and Culture in Late Medieval and Early Modern Europe* (Surrey, Ashgate, 2010) 53, 58–59.
[101] Appleby (n 49) locations 2037–38, 2038–39.
[102] Wood (n 76) 36–37.

multiplication of wealth'. Only when law and politics strive to preserve stability can prosperity be attained.[103]

Civic rights were not the sole bedrock of wealth. Property itself was increasingly perceived as an 'established natural right' and a guarantee of personal liberty.[104] The idea had its roots in the writings of Enlightenment thinkers who refuted religious beliefs and enthroned humans as ultimate rulers and beneficiaries of their earthly domain.[105] Natural rights were 'rights that ought to be recognised in all societies' since they were vital to 'the fulfilment of some basic human needs and purposes'.[106] Many of these rights developed to become human rights like the rights to life, dignity, liberty and movement. Likewise, property and the right to possess wealth were deemed natural rights which ought not to be affected by the passage of time or change of venue. Property was deemed a natural right. But it was also the other way around. Natural rights were themselves rooted in the proprietary concept of dominium.

In his *Natural Rights Theories: Their Origin and Development*, Richard Tuck traces the reciprocal tie between rights and dominium in early medieval thought. 'Anyone who has a *ius* in something' he points out, 'has *dominium* over it; and anyone who has a *ius* to the use of something, has *dominium* over it'. Having a *ius*, he notes, meant having dominium along with all 'its implications of control and mastery'.[107] Michel Villey traces the roots of the natural right idea in medieval glossators' analysis of rights which persistently discussed them in the frame of dominium.[108] At any rate, it seems indisputable that dominium had a vital role in the development of the idea of natural rights.

As already mentioned, property was a pledge to many basic rights. It was increasingly tied to rights like human dignity, life and liberty. According to Peter Garnsey, it was not long before property became 'worthy company for the right to life itself'.[109] Property offered self-determination and better movability, hence, greater liberty for right-holders. It protected owners from the intrusions and whims of others as well as extending their power to control their life and environment. According to Rifkin, 'the

---

[103] J Say, *A Treatise on Political Economy, or, the Production, Distribution, and Consumption of Wealth* (New York, Cosimo, 2007) 127.

[104] Garnsey (n 39) 204.

[105] R van Caenegem, *An Historical Introduction to Private Law*, trans D Johnston (Cambridge, Cambridge University Press, 2003) 127.

[106] B Tierney, *The Idea of Natural Rights: Studies on Natural Rights, Natural Law, and Church Law 1150–1625* (Cambridge, Wm B Werdmans, 2001) 5.

[107] R Tuck, *Natural Rights Theory: Their Origin and Development* (Cambridge, Cambridge University Press, 1979) 5.

[108] Tierney (n 106) 19.

[109] Garnsey (n 39) 204.

greater the accumulation of property and wealth, the larger the extension of one's domain and sphere of influence in the world'.[110]

This vital role of property materialised in the French *Déclaration des droits de l'homme et du citoyen* (Declaration of the Rights of Man and the Citizen) issued 1789 during the French Revolution by the Assemblée nationale constituante (national constitutional assembly). In Article 2, the Declaration provides that the aim of all political association is to preserve '*des droits naturels et imprescriptibles de l'homme*' ('the natural and imprescriptible rights of man') which are liberty, property, security and resistance to oppression. In Article 17, it also states that property is '*un droit inviolable et sacré*' ('inviolable and sacred right') that no one can be deprived of, unless under strict conditions.[111] 'Property is human liberty exercised over physical nature' explicated Raymond-Théodore Troplong (1795–1869), a known jurist of that era.[112]

Modern political regimes were founded on the notion of private sphere and the protection of one's property and personal wealth. This was the case with a growing number of European states. But many of these states eventually had to restrain the tropes of capitalism and embrace segments of a' welfare state' model. Following communism and socialist ideologies which deemed privately held wealth a central cause for societal discrimination against a captive working class, European states made a trade-off. A 'private property regime' says Rifkin, 'would be upheld in return for a promise that some of the excesses of unbridled market capitalism would be redistributed, in the form of government social benefits'.[113]

OBSERVING EUROPEAN LAW AND CULTURE

Europe's love affair with art is anything but invisible. In his modern classic *Ways of Seeing*, art critic John Berger describes the visual language of oil paintings produced between post-Renaissance and modern times, spanning roughly between 1500 and 1900. He says: 'oil painting, before it was anything else, was a celebration of private property. As an art-form it derived from the principle that you are what you have'.[114] Perhaps this observation epitomises the modern history of Europe and the central role of property or assets in the perception of wealth. The person–object bond

---

[110]   Rifkin (n 17) locations 2860–917.
[111]   E Steiner, *French Law: A Comparative Approach* (Oxford, Oxford University Press, 2010) 383; Garnsey (n 39) 205.
[112]   J Savage, 'From American Democracy to French Empire: Race and the Law in Tocqueville's Liberalism' in N Persram (ed), *Postcolonialism and Political Theory* (Lanham, MD, Lexington Books, 2007) 76, 91, fn 35.
[113]   Rifkin (n 17) locations 2860–917, 2918–968.
[114]   J Berger, *Ways of Seeing* (London, Penguin Modern Classics, 2009) 139.

which excludes others from appropriating or utilising what one owns or has, is a rooted postulate of European culture. It seems part of what Michel Foucault in *The Archeology of Knowledge* understood as *discursive structures*. These are the moulds 'within which culture formulates its ideas', sets the limits of discourses and determines how reality is perceived and interpreted.[115]

The legal discourses which formulated wrongful enrichment law across a long time until the present day were cultivated by cultural perceptions which venerated ownership and possessions. Former perceptions, mostly medieval, which personified and ethicised wealth were fading away. A new perception which detached wealth from religious morality and social merits, moulding instead an alienated concept of wealth, was taking over. It is with these major changes that law itself started to shift the poetical weight from the wrongdoer and her misconduct to the disadvantaged person, her property and belongings.

The disadvantaged person and her assets were increasingly emphasised in legal doctrine at the expense of the enriched person's wrongful behaviour. The wrongful enrichment question metamorphosed into a misplaced wealth one. More and more it was a matter of deprivation and dispossession of one's wealth rather than an issue of ill-behaviour or wrongful utilisation. Wrongful enrichment denoted a challenge to one's earthly domain and nearly sacred bond with her possessions and wealth. It was a bond-less enrichment. The normative perspective stresses this cultural perception and accentuates it in many aspects.

Chronologically examined, the discourses of wealth seem to draw the lines of normative legitimacy. In the medieval era wealth meant labour, religiosity and social merits. Crossing those lines was profiteering, a sin and a challenge to the social order. In the Renaissance and early modern era, wealth meant one's domain, property and belongings. Encroaching on the wealth of a person meant challenging her domain, and depriving her of her belongings and possessions. This later perception was only sharpened with the ongoing discourse of property as a basic right and as capital.[116] Wealth drew highly protective lines around one's capital, natural rights and private legal sphere. Crossing these lines were clearly wrong.

These cultural changes were imitated to various extents by legal discourses of wrongful enrichment. Originally the rules highlighted the

---

[115] Foucault (n 16) 21–71; Mills (n 16) 45–46, 50–51.

[116] A Gambaro, 'Western Property Law' in M Bussani and F Werro (eds), *European Private Law: A Handbook* (Berne, Stämpfli, 2009) 47, 55; A Clarke and P Kohler, *Property Law: Commentary and Materials* (Cambridge, Cambridge University Press, 2006) 297; J Merryman, *The Civil Law Tradition: An Introduction to the Legal Systems of Europe and Latin America* (Stanford, CA, Stanford University Press, 2007) 18–20.

enriched person and her ill-conduct but later on they were increasingly restructured around the disadvantaged one and her property. Examining current laws, one could put the occurrence depicted in the following terms: initially, a possessing and rightful person dominates her own private sphere. Subsequently, her domain is challenged by another triggering a legal response. The law steps in to restore the former balance and put the disadvantaged person back to her former position. In this light, restitution works to restore and reinstate. It restores what was taken and reinstates the person back as queen of her legal sphere.

4

American Law

THE FATHERS OF AMERICAN RESTITUTION LAW

IT MAY BE somewhat hyperbolic to equate Anglo-American common law with James Joyce's *Finnegans Wake*, one of the most challenging reads of modern literary works. Prospective readers of the novel are 'warned again and again that it is so' by the 'jostling crowd of explicators' asserting, each, his own sketch of the novel. Some years following its publication, Joseph Campbell, a professor of mythology and literature, aided by Henry Robinson, wrote *A Skeleton Key to Finnegans Wake* which attempted an outline of the basic course of action while elucidating the complex web of images and hints instated in the rich world of the novel. The objective was to clear up the vagueness and uncertainty as to what *Finnegans Wake* actually delivered.[1]

Though dramatic in a way, this equation of common law and literary craft is not unprecedented. In his highly celebrated *Law's Empire*, Ronald Dworkin explains the grounds, principles and working modes of common law. Resting on case law as a key locomotive of the Anglo-American tradition, Dworkin equates it with an ongoing enterprise of 'chain novel', where 'a group of novelists writes a novel *seriatism*. Each novelist in the chain interprets the chapters he has been given in order to write a new chapter, which is then added to what the next novelist receives, and so on'.[2] These are the judges, who develop and nurture a distinctive legal tradition, 'reasoning closely from case to case and building a body of law that binds subsequent judges, through the doctrine of *stare decisis*, to decide similar cases similarly', earning them the title of 'culture heroes, even parental figures' as John Merryman puts it.[3]

These novelists, to proceed with Dworkin's metaphor, 'aim jointly to create, so far as they can, a single unified novel that is the best it can be'.

---

[1] J Joyce, *Finnegans Wake* (New York, Penguin Books, 1999); E Knowlton, *Joyce, Joyceans, and the Rhetoric of Citation* (Gainesville, FL, University Press of Florida, 1998) 3; J Campbell and H Robinson, *A Skeleton to Finnegans Wake: Unlocking James Joyce's Masterwork* (Novato, CA, New World Library, 2005).

[2] R Dworkin, *Law's Empire* (Cambridge, MA, Harvard University Press, 1986) 229.

[3] J Merryman, *The Civil Law Tradition: An Introduction to the Legal Systems of Europe and Latin America* (Stanford, CA, Stanford University Press, 2007) 34.

Each novelist, or 'Hercules' to quote Dworkin yet again, must 'take up some view about the novel in progress, some working theory about its characters, plot, genre, theme, and point, in order to decide what counts as continuing it and not as beginning anew'.[4] Acknowledging the growing role of legislation alongside adjudication, it remains the case that judges in common law systems retain remarkable power, though within certain confines, to apply and interpret statutes with comparably great discretion.[5] This prudent liberty insures flexibility and dynamism allowing greater and faster adaptation of law to the ever-changing conditions of life.

The said traits, however, come with a price tag. The growing mass of court decisions and statute interpretations issued by America's different jurisdictions and complex chains of instances on a pragmatic case-by-case basis, inevitably produced legal contradictions and normative uncertainties. In fact, this was one of the two catalysts identified by the American Law Institute (ALI) to 'Restate' the law at the beginning of the twentieth century. Draper Lewis, the first Director of the Institute, stated that the objective of the Restatement was 'to present an orderly statement of the general common law of the United States' including both judicial decisions and statute interpretations and applications.[6]

Ironically, it was a sense of 'legal patriotism', the second catalyst to 'Restate', that introduced a continental mechanism system to American law. Founded on the premise of 'a general dissatisfaction with the administration of justice',[7] the ALI sought to combat legal uncertainty and complexity by promoting 'the clarification and simplification of the law' as officially stated in the Institute's establishing charter of 1923.[8] Alarmed by the chances of a forced desertion of the American 'common law system' and 'the adoption in its place of rigid legislative codes' as Lewis put it, the Restatement, it was argued, constituted the long-awaited 'factor' to prevent the American law from falling into a continental pattern.[9]

Yet, the prudent examination of pertinent cases to extract the 'black letter law', a chief method in the craft of Restating, ultimately endorsed a continental-like tactic of 'legal science'. It eventually introduced European traits of coherency, legal abstractionism, and systemisation.[10]

---

[4] See Dworkin (n 4) at 229, 230, 239.

[5] Merryman (n 3).

[6] ALI, *Restatement of the Law of Restitution: Quasi Contracts and Constructive Trusts* (Washington DC, West Group, 1937) ix (Rest 1st).

[7] ALI, *The Report of the Committee on the Establishment of a Permanent Organization for the Improvement of the Law* (Washington DC, ALI, 1973).

[8] ALI, Founding Charter (23 February 1923) available at: www.ali.org/doc/charter.pdf.

[9] ALI, *Restatement of the Law of Restitution* (1937) (n 6) ix.

[10] cf D Rendleman, 'Restating Restitution: The Restatement Process and its Critics' (2008) 65 *Washington and Lee Law Review* 933, 935.

'It smells of the lamp' as Merryman figuratively puts it,[11] or as Lance Liebman, the Director of the Institute openly admits over 70 years later (in 2011), 'this was American *codification* as practiced by the ALI'.[12]

Whether it was a counter-trend to the increasing influence of legal realism and sociological jurisprudence, both of which rejected formalistic and mechanical approaches to law,[13] or an expected fruition of the 'case method' for teaching law, ie, outlining cases which explain the law, as introduced by Christopher Langdell at Harvard Law School in the late nineteenth century,[14] it seems that the idea of Restating the law accepted a wind of change which characterised the American 1920s and 1930s, an era known for its intellectual, social and cultural challenge to former convictions, and of its aspiration to forge a new modern society.[15]

Within a decade following its establishment, the ALI serially published (what later would be called the *First*) Restatements. It published Restatements in Contract Law (1932), Agency Law (1933), Torts Law (1934), Conflicts of Laws and Law of Trusts (1935) and Property Law (1936). The work on the Restatement of Restitution Law was undertaken in 1933, with the appointment by the Council of Warren Seavey and Austin Scott, both of Harvard Law School, as Reporters, ie, the executive body of the ALI. The Reporters were 'responsible to the Council for the preparation of all drafts, preliminary, tentative and proposed final'. To advise and work closely with the Reporters, a committee of experts mostly of academic background was selected. The produced drafts were discussed and amended periodically by the Council and eventually presented to the Institute at the annual meetings in 1935 and 1936 leading to the adoption and publication of an official draft of the Restatement on Restitution law in 1937.[16]

While this project, grandiose and innovative in many respects, was figuratively speaking the first chapter of America's modern law of restitution, the introductory part was definitely written by William A Keener. Keener, a dean and law professor at Columbia College, realised that various cases such as mistaken payments, acquisitive torts, benefit conferrals and certain instances of contract, often treated under different heads,

---

[11] Merryman (n 3) 66–67.

[12] ALI, *Restatement of the Law of Restitution and Unjust Enrichment*, vol I (Washington DC, American Law Institute, 2011) xiii (emphasis added) (Rest 3rd vol I); cp A Burrows, *A Restatement of the English Law of Unjust Enrichment* (Oxford, Oxford University Press, 2012).

[13] B Leiter, 'American Legal Realism' in M Golding and W Edmundson (eds), *The Blackwell Guide to the Philosophy of Law and Legal Theory* (Oxford, Blackwell, 2005) 50; R Pound, 'Sociology of Law and Sociological Jurisprudence' (1943) 5(1) *University of Toronto Law Journal* 1, 5.

[14] T Sweeney, 'English Judges and Roman Jurists: The Civilian Learning behind England's First Case Law' (2012) 84(4) *Temple Law Review* 827, 856; Merryman (n 3) 66–67, 79.

[15] P Boyer, *American History: A Very Short Introduction*, Kindle edn (Oxford, Oxford University Press, 2012) location 1431.

[16] Rest 1st (n 6) x–xii.

had something in common: they all resorted to quasi-contract for redress and thus begged the discernment of an integrated theory. In his *Treatise on the Law of Quasi-Contracts* published in 1893, he however expressed deep discontent with English treatment of the subject and encouraged a more rational and fiction-free approach. Quasi-contract is not a contract, he argued. It is a civil obligation imposed by law and frequently resting on 'the doctrine that a man shall not be allowed to enrich himself unjustly at the expense of another'. Unlike an actual contract, he observed, it had nothing to do with the parties' intentions but with 'what in equity and good conscience' had to be done.[17]

Twenty years later in 1913, Frederic C Woodward, professor at Leland Stanford Junior University, published his book *The Law of Quasi Contracts*. While acknowledging Keener's 'salutary' contribution to the clarification of the subject, the need, as he put it, was for 'a further analysis and classification of quasi contractual obligations'. Woodward was more determinate in his argument that all non-contractual obligations in quasi-contract should be treated as resting solely on unjust enrichment. These are cases which refer to 'the receipt of a benefit the retention of which is unjust', to use his own words.[18] Woodward did not deviate that much from the major classifications outlined by Keener. Noticeable, however, is the fact that he brought to the fore of his book the mistaken payment group which is often treated as a paradigm case of unjust enrichment.

Nevertheless, it was the Restatement which eventually introduced a systematic and principled approach to this area of law. Liability in various cases of quasi-contract rested on unifying principles, it asserted. A person is held accountable to another for benefits unjustly obtained. He neither ought to profit from his wrongdoing nor from any officious confers he makes. And where such accountability lies, restitution of the misplaced benefit should be invoked. These principles were not rules, the Restatement stressed. They are 'too indefinite' to be literally embraced and too general to be indistinctly applied.[19] It was only by meticulous work that the Restatement successfully introduced the different rules applied in each group of cases.

These initiatives had a significant impact on the American law of restitution. They morphed old materials into a highly cohesive product which strongly affected both case law and scholarly treatment of the subject. Quasi-contract was steadily losing its charm to the more persuasive theory of restitution and unjust enrichment. The latter was working

---

[17] W Keener, *A Treatise on the Law of Quasi-Contract* (New York, Baker, Voorhis and Company, 1893) 19–20.

[18] F Woodward, *The Law of Quasi Contracts* (Boston, MA, Little, Brown and Company, 1913) vii, 2.

[19] Rest 1st (n 6) 11–23.

wonders not only in rationalising the law, but also in weakening the judiciary's reliance on English authority. The so-called 'restitution law' offered American case law a chance to break free from centuries-old precedents which no longer made sense to modern jurists. American law grasped this offer tightly and it was not long before restitution law took its rightful position next to contract and tort law as the third source of civil obligation.

AMERICAN LAW

The following section attempts to chart the central tenets of American restitution law pertaining to cases of intentional wrongful exploitation or appropriation of tangible property. It commences with a historical overview of American law as applied from the late nineteenth century onwards. This point in time corresponds, roughly, with the publishing of Keener's treatise and is widely considered the embryonic stage at which the modern law of restitution began to form. The overview, however, is confined to basic segments of the law which provide adequate grounds for the subsequent analysis. Another subsection reports current law as traced in recent authority. And the last deals with the pertinent rules of the Restatements. The latter task is undertaken in recognition of the indispensable role the Restatements have had in describing and prescribing the law of restitution. It is fairly acknowledged that the Restatements provided, and continue to provide, an indispensable source for legal development in the United States.

Historical Overview

In his treatise, Keener attempts to set things right. He persuasively challenges English commentators who identify quasi-contracts with implied contracts. The latter, he asserts, are 'true contracts', the former are not. They are 'not a contract at all'. Any analogy between the two is merely 'superficial'. True contracts stem from the will and intentions of the parties, whether expressed or inferred from actual facts. Contracts which beget inference are consensual obligations taken by the parties implicitly and can be discerned from their utterances and behaviour. These contracts are 'implied in fact'. A quasi-contract, however, is not a meeting of minds. It is only a legal form imposed on the case by the court to adapt it to a different remedy. It is a contract 'implied in law'.[20]

With the help of fiction, common law judges were able to introduce an old contract law redress to a new right in tort. It was like sewing a patch of

---

[20] Keener (n 17) 6–8.

new cloth onto an old garment. Despite the lack of the basic requisites of contract, it was feasible for judges to invoke a contractual remedy in a tort case if the plaintiff was willing to dispense with the tortuous act and resort to a fictitious construction. The victim needed simply to indicate that he assented to the illegal act, and the court would then assume that the tortfeasor promised to pay the victim for the benefit reaped by his wrongful action. For Keener, it was 'idle to speak of the possibility of contract' here, 'where there is not even the suggestion of a meeting of minds'.[21] For the court, however, this fiction was a strong hook on which it was possible to hang a pseudo-version of contract and call for a contractual redress.

According to this doctrine, referred to as 'waiver of tort', instead of seeking compensation for the loss suffered, a tort victim is able to 'waive' the tort and sue in an action of assumpsit to recover the benefit gained by the tortfeasor. This simple construct of law provides the first and basic archetypal compound of modern restitution law for wrongs. It is wrong-focused. It rests on the tortuous action of the wrongdoer to provoke a response. A benefit accruing to the enriched is not barred unless hingeing on a wrongful basis. In Keener's words, 'unless the defendant is guilty of some wrong, the plaintiff can establish no cause of action against him'. Namely, bringing an action in assumpsit does not revoke the need to prove a tortuous act.

Originally, a plaintiff in assumpsit needed to indicate prior dealing (*negotium*) by the parties. Modern contract law would refer to this aspect as 'privity'. An action in assumpsit could prevail only if privity was established. This request was moderated in the late sixteenth century when the English case of *Tottenham v Bedingfield* (1572) held that privity could be established ex post. Later, it was also possible to establish privity in the face of facts. In the English case of *Lamine v Dorrell* (1705), the Court of King's Bench readily stated that 'when the act that is done is in its nature tortuous, it is hard to turn that into a contract, and against the reason of assumpsits'. Despite this, the Court had no problem allowing fictitious contractual privity. It held that 'the plaintiff may dispense with the wrong, and suppose the sale made by his consent, and bring an action for the money they were sold for, as money received to his use'.[22]

In *Watson v Stever* (1872) this did not happen. In that case, Stever sued Watson in assumpsit for the value of converted logs. Watson, who formerly denied any right of the plaintiff to the said logs or any such right to be paid their value, refuted the claim. He claimed the logs were bought from third parties. In this case, the Supreme Court of Michigan was not

---

[21] ibid 8, 14–15, 24, 159.
[22] *Tottenham v Bedingfield* [1572] B & M 295; *Lamine v Dorrell* [1705] 92 ER 303; P Birks, 'Restitution for Wrongs' in E Schrage (ed), *Unjust Enrichment: The Comparative Legal History of the Law of Restitution* (Berlin, Duncker & Humblot, 1995) 183–85.

willing to apply the fiction of consent reasoning that the law will not imply a promise 'where the circumstances repel all implication of a promise in fact'. This was a surprising statement by the Court and reminds us of the child's cry of 'But he has nothing on at all' in Hans Christian Anderson's 'The Emperor's New Clothes'.[23] At any rate, this was an uncalled-for conclusion as the plaintiff did not prove conversion which was a precondition for allowing waiver of tort.[24]

A more paternalistic view was held in *Norden v Jones* (1873). Norden sued Jones to recover a sum due in book account. Jones counterclaimed that Norden allowed his cattle to graze without permission in Jones's pasture. Examining the case, the Supreme Court of Wisconsin stressed mainly two pragmatic reasons for allowing Jones to waive the tort and countersue in assumpsit. First, it was the need to look 'to the substantial ends of justice' rather than be trapped in sheer technicalities. Second, suing in assumpsit constituted no prejudice to Norden. On the contrary, it waived Jones's right to damages, granted Norden a right to set-off, and saved him the embarrassment and the potential imprisonment that came with a regular plea in tort. Citing English authority, the Court noted that the plaintiff 'merely waives his *claim to damages* for a wrong' (emphasis added) rather than waiving the claim to the tort itself.[25]

The wrong factor was thus indispensable in quasi-contract cases of torts. But this factor was not the only fulcrum of these cases. Another factor was the issue of profiting. A plaintiff in a waiver of tort had to establish that the tortfeasor derived a 'profit in the commission of the wrong'.[26] In *Tightmeyer v Mongold* (1878), for example, Mongold grew corn and potato crops which were unintentionally damaged by the livestock of Tightmeyer. Mongold's action to waive the tort was denied. The Supreme Court of Kansas held that although a tort was established the plaintiff failed to show any 'benefit received' by the defendant.[27] It is interesting to note that the Court resorted to the term 'benefit' rather than 'profit' to state its decision. In fact, benefit was more commonly used to describe the enrichment of the defendant in assumpsit even when profit could have been a more accurate term in many tort cases.

Profit, as George E Palmer remarks, is generally assumed to be the 'gains realised through the use of the thing' rather than 'the basis of the value immediately received by the defendant'.[28] It is an economic value which is

---

[23] H Andersen, *Eventyr fortalte for Børn* III (Copenhagen, Reitzel, 1837) (*Fairy Tales Told for Children*).

[24] *Watson v Stever* [1872] 25 Mich 386.

[25] *Norden v Jones* [1873] 33 Wis 600, 608.

[26] Keener (n 17) 160, 162.

[27] *Tightmeyer v Mongold* [1878] 20 Kan 90, 91–92; ibid 162 (*Keener*).

[28] G Palmer, *The Law of Restitution*, vol 1 (New York, Little, Brown and Company, 1978) 159.

not part of the original benefit received but accrued to the enriched owing, for example, to profitable sale or expert handling of the benefit. The first Restatement of Restitution Law used profit in this sense intermittently perhaps most plainly in its third underlying principle of restitution law. The principle provided for in Article 3 and titled 'Tortious Acquisition of a Benefit' states: 'a person is not permitted to *profit* by his own wrong at the expense of another' (emphasis added). This did not yet indicate any deliberate conceptual distinction on the part of the Restatement.

It is perhaps the equitable remedy of account of profits which bequeathed the notion of *profit* to the modern law of restitution for wrongs. Originally account render was an action in common law. It was the only means by which common law could settle disputed accounts of money. The action would be brought against receivers, guardians and custodians, but in practice it was rarely used. Due to the complex and expensive process of auditing and disputing each item in the records, especially before juries, this action was increasingly obsolete and plaintiffs had to resort to equity for remedy. Equity courts would usually assume jurisdiction in four cases: cases of fiduciary relation, especially action brought by beneficiaries against trustees; cases of mutual accounts by both parties; complicated circumstances when, for instance, many transactions were made and a remedy in law would be inaccurate or inconvenient; and when account was to supplement an injunction.[29]

Account of profits was one such account usually invoked in cases of profitable breach of fiduciary duty. Typical cases involved suits by principles against agents who received secret commissions, bribes or other profits made in ostensibly authorised transactions. Other typical cases were suits against co-partners who derived unapproved benefits from the name, property or business of the partnership. This equitable remedy rested on the principle that if a person owed a duty to act in another's best interest, he was obliged to hand in any benefit he illicitly reaped in his position as fiduciary. Predictably, this remedy did not hinge on any loss to the plaintiff. The latter did not need to establish impoverishment. It sufficed to prove obtainment of a benefit in breach of duty to attain the remedy even if the benefit did not formerly belong to the plaintiff. The remedy was regularly a pecuniary one ordering the fiduciary to disgorge his illicit profits, though in cases of embezzled chattels the plaintiff might elect to recover *in specie* or in monetary value.[30] Any such order could be supported by constructive trust, or equitable lien to insure recovery.

---

[29] J Eaton, *Handbook of Equity Jurisprudence* (St Paul, MN, West, 1923) 479–82; D Brownie, *Ashburner's Principles of Equity* (London, Butterworth & Co, 1933) 349.
[30] ibid 322–23, 327–28 (Brownie).

Account of Profits constituted the second pillar in modern restitution law for wrongs, and in many respects it fashioned it both at conceptual and reasoning levels. Though benefit was the standard term, profit both as a label for net proceeds after deducting a plaintiff's expenses and as a verb denoting the illicit making of profit, was used in decisions granting Account of Profits. Describing the defendant as making a profit from his wrong was usually a powerful reason by itself to grant remedy. Thus, for example, in *Head v Porter* (1895), a case of patent infringement, the circuit court held that a wrongdoer should disgorge the profits he made 'as it would be inequitable that he should make a profit out of his own wrong'. 'Profit' here was again broadly defined as 'the gains or savings made by the wrongdoer by the invasion of the complainant's property right'.[31]

This ethical line of justification for restitution in fact utilised the Latin maxim of *Commodum ex injuria sua nemo habere debet* (no one should profit from his wrong).[32] It denigrated wrongful profit-making, and courts often used it to stress the immoral charge of the defendant's behaviour and justify their decisions. It was not long before wrongful profiting established itself as a key principle of the American modern law of restitution for wrongs, one which underlies cases for account of profits and cases in waiver of torts. According to Palmer, until the early nineteenth century profit in the narrow sense was often recoverable in equity, and not in assumpsit. A profit was recoverable though no impoverishment or economic loss was caused to the disadvantaged person. It was sufficient that the profit was attributable to the invasion of the property interest. And though wilfulness on the part of the enriched was not required to establish a breach of fiduciary duty in a suit for account of profits, it was often essential in property-related waiver of tort cases as recovery of profit was deemed harsher than recovery of the benefit in the narrow sense.[33]

The case of *Olwell v NYE & Nissen* (1946),[34] one of frequently discussed cases in literature,[35] is a good example of these conceptual and doctrinal transformations. In this case, the plaintiff brought an action in assumpsit to recover the reasonable value of unauthorised use of his egg-washing machine by the defendant. Due to a shortage of workers after the outbreak of the Second World War, the defendant put the machine originally stored at his premises to use in his plant for nearly four years. The trial court allowed recovery, asserting that 'the tort of conversion could be

---

[31] *Head v Porter* [1895] 70 F 498, 501.

[32] F Stimson, *Glossary of Technical Terms, Phrases, and Maxims of the Common Law* (Boston, MA, Little, Brown and Company, 1881) 63.

[33] Palmer (n 28) 133, 135, 138, 159–60.

[34] *Olwell v Nye & Nissen* [1946] 173 P 2d 652.

[35] See, eg, H Dagan, *The Law and Ethics of Restitution* (Cambridge, Cambridge University Press, 2004) 210.

"waived" and suit brought in quasi-contract, upon a contract implied in law, to recover, as restitution, the profits which inured' to the defendant 'as a result of its wrongful use of the machine'.[36]

On appeal, the Supreme Court of Washington affirmed the judgment with some procedural modifications. It reasoned that 'in cases where the defendant tortfeasor has benefited by his wrong, the plaintiff may elect to "waive the tort" and bring an action in assumpsit for restitution'. The Court used primarily action terminology to construct and explain its stand. It described the behaviour as 'wrongful operation', 'wrongful invasion' and 'admittedly wrongful' 'use'. The Court distinguished cases of converting benefits in the narrow sense (where the value received equals the value lost) from the deemed more 'frequent' cases of unequal subtraction where resolution vested in the wrongfulness of the defendant's behaviour. In these cases, the Court held that 'the measure of restitution is determined with reference to the tortiousness of the defendant's conduct'. If the wrongdoer 'was consciously tortious in acquiring the benefit he is also deprived of any profit derived from his subsequent dealing with it'.[37]

Palmer summarised this line of cases stating that 'under the common-law decisions, restitution of profits always will be granted against an intentional wrongdoer, provided the profits are the product of a wrongful taking or other interference with the injured party's legally protected interest'. Allowing recovery of profits in actions at law was not, however, exclusive to these wilful torts. Courts were also willing to allow equal remedy against innocent wrongdoers in certain commercial torts like infringement of patent and copyright. Like wilful cases, these too were deemed deserving of harsher redress.[38] One difference between the two, however, is that quashing profits for a defendant in intentional torts would work to eliminate the incentive for potential tortfeasors to break the law in the first place. This is not equally true for negligent or innocent wrongdoers.[39]

Profit was a catalyst for another significant transformation in this area of law. It provoked a split in the all-inclusive term of restitution. Thus, besides 'restitution', a term denoting *giving back* something the plaintiff had before, the term 'disgorgement' was being increasingly utilised. Disgorgement is deemed a more accurate term, as it described the *giving up* of profits, rather than the *conferring back* of something originally held by the plaintiff. The term was rarely used by the fathers of modern restitution law, Keener and Woodward. The term was, however, already in use, inter alia, in equity cases. For example, in *Carborundum Co v Electric Smelting*

[36] *Olwell* (n 34) 652–53.
[37] ibid 652–54.
[38] Palmer (n 28) 163–65; For a case allowing the same remedy against an innocent wrongdoer in commercial torts see, eg, *De Acosta v Brown* [1944] 146 F 2d 408.
[39] ALI, *Restatement of the Law of Restitution and Unjust Enrichment* (n 12) 22 Reporter Note.

& Aluminum Co (1913), a case of patent infringement, the Court stated as one principle of equity that the 'wrongdoer be compelled to *disgorge* his ill-gotten gains'.[40] Years later, however, the term succeeded to establish its position in the area of wilful wrongful enrichments as a whole.[41]

Profiting, especially intentionally, was increasingly perceived as an ear-mark of restitution for wrongs. This was one of the reasons Peter Birks chose the famous case of *Edwards v Lee's Administrator* (1936), better known as the Great Onyx Cave case, as exemplar of the area. In this case, the defendant discovered a cave with rock crystal formations under his land which by extensive work he turned to a successful tourist site. The site ultimately secured a stream of steady entrance fees sufficient to cover operation costs and yield a good profit. The plaintiff claimed that part of the cave invaded his land, and brought an action for account of profit. A survey of the cave determined that nearly one-third of the cave was under the plaintiff's land. Consequently, the circuit court granted the plain-tiff a proportionate share of the net proceeds realised by the defendant.

On appeal, the Kentucky Court of Appeals, which considered the case *sui generis* and resorted to the so-called 'fundamental principles and anal-ogies' asserted that the defendant was 'guilty' of 'willful' and 'repeated trespass'. And though 'rental value' was the typical yardstick for recovery, the Court chose 'net profits' as the proper basis for recovery. The Court added that 'the unjust enrichment of the wrongdoer is the gist of the right to bring an action ex contractu' and that 'a wrongdoer shall not be permit-ted to make a profit from his own wrong'.[42] Peter Birks considered this case exemplary due to two main reasons. The first was that the action rested on pure disgorgement of profits, namely where the plaintiff suf-fered no corresponding loss. This, Birks, argued brought no risk of analytic confusion with compensation. The second reason is that profit was unmis-takably attributed to the plaintiff's wrongful action rather than any other cause.[43] With this latter reason, Birks was stressing that disgorgement rested on wrong and not on unjust enrichment as a cause of action.

Another outstanding characteristic of restitution for wrongs law is that money was largely the basic measure of recovery. As already mentioned this was the case in equitable account for profits, but it was also true for actions at law. Originally a debt claim was brought in *indebitatus assumpsit* (promise for being indebted). A claim for debt had to rest on a recognised ground which the plaintiff had to state in his plea. A claim could rest for example on a count of 'goods sold and delivered', 'work done' or 'money

---

[40] *Carborundum Co v Electric Smelting & Aluminum Co* [1913] 203 F 976, 985.
[41] eg Rest 3rd vol I (n 12) Art 3.
[42] *Edwards v Lee's Adm'r* [1936] 96 SW 2d 1028, 1030–32.
[43] Birks, 'Restitution for Wrongs' (n 22) 172–73.

had and received', with the last one being most useful in restitution cases, since it did not need a former request by the plaintiff to be successful. Thus, for example, if a defendant converts a chattel belonging to the plaintiff and sells it, the plaintiff is able to waive the tort and sue in assumpsit for money had and received. The law would then presume that the plaintiff agreed to the trade of his goods, and is therefore entitled to the actual money received, as if in trust for his uses.[44]

Classic authority, notably *Jones v Hoar* (1827),[45] held that recovery was subject to proof of actual money received. Thus, for example, if the defendant received partial or no money against the sale, only partial or no money would be recovered.[46] American courts of the eighteenth century were divided on the question whether recovery would be allowed if the converted chattel was not sold but retained, consumed or delivered to a third party.[47] Some courts were willing to extend applicability and allow recovery on the basis of reason, equity and fairness.[48] For example, in *Osborn v Bell* (1848),[49] the New York Supreme Court held that 'where the goods have been applied to the use of the wrongdoer, it may not be unreasonable, and certainly not unjust, to imply a promise to pay for them'.[50] Other courts were reluctant to allow recovery due to former precedents.[51]

The gates, however, were increasingly open and more courts were willing to allow pecuniary redress. In *Felder v Reeth* (1929),[52] for example, the appellants brought an action to recover money for goods sold to Reeth. Reeth admitted the purchase but counterclaimed alleging that he bought certain hydraulic mining machines which the appellants wrongfully converted to their use, and thus owe him the machines value as 'goods sold and delivered'. The court allowed his claim rejecting former precedents on the issue and holding that if a property owner could waive and consent both to conversion and sale, there would be no logical reason why he would not be able to do that solely to conversion and recover the market value of the chattel. Such outcome was not confined to asset value but also extended to reasonable rent. Thus, for example, in *Jansen v Dolan* (1911), Jansen sued Dolan for breach of contract. Dolan counterclaimed alleging

---

[44] Keener (n 17) 166, 170–171; *Knapp v Hobbs* [1871] 50 NH 476; *Young v Marshall* [1831] 8 Bing 43; *Hill v Davis* [1826] 3 NH 384; J Baker 'The Use of Assumpsit for Restitutionary Money Claims 1600–1800' in E Schrage (ed), *Unjust Enrichment: The Comparative Legal History of the Law of Restitution* (Berlin, Duncker & Humblot, 1995) 35, 49.

[45] *Jones v Hoar* [1827] 22 Mass 285.

[46] Keener (n 17) 173; *Rand v Nesmith* [1873] 61 Me 111, 111, 113.

[47] ibid 193 (Keener).

[48] *Starr Cash Company v Reinhardt* [1892] 20 NY Supp 872.

[49] *Osborn v Bell* [1848] 5 Denio 370 in J Scott (ed), *Cases of Quasi-Contract* (New York, Baker, Voorhis and Company, 1905) 93.

[50] ibid 95. See also *Norden* (n 25).

[51] Keener (n 17) 193–95; eg *Jones* (n 45).

[52] *Felder v Reeth* [1929] 34 F 2d 744.

that Jansen deprived her of using her horse wagon and a set of harnesses and thus owed her reasonable rent for the time her chattel was retained against her will. Her action was allowed. The court held that Jansen's right to waive the tort and claim reasonable rent 'is not to be questioned'.[53]

In the case of land exploitation which did not entail any removal of substance like timber or soil, classic authority disallowed restitution for reasonable value of use. For example, in *Adsit v Kaufman* (1903) the plaintiff sued to recover reasonable rent from the defendant who exploited the land without permission. The defendant admitted the plaintiff's ownership but claimed he rented the lot from a third party who had possession of the land at the time. The Court of Appeals affirmed the lower court's decision asserting that 'an action in the nature of assumpsit, for the use and occupation of real estate, will never lie where there has been no relation of contract between the parties, and where the possession … is tortuous and makes a defendant a tresspasser'.[54] This decision can be explained by the general disinclination to adjudicate title disputes in an action of assumpsit which is supposed to be a simple and straightforward action for money recovery.

Nevertheless, land owners could still sue for reasonable rent in an action of trespass for *mesne* profits usually brought after a successful termination of an ejectment action.[55] In *Worthington v Hiss* (1889) the court explained the law on this point holding that

> it is well settled, that in an action to recover *mesne profits*, the plaintiff must show in the best way he can, what these profits are, and there are two modes of doing so … He may either prove the profits actually received, or the annual rental value of the land. … The latter is the mode usually adopted.[56]

Some states, like New Jersey, California and Washington allowed recovery of reasonable rent under express statutes. Thus, in land exploitation, similar to cases of converted chattels whether sold or retained, money recovery was available often by default.[57]

Current law

In principle, the tortious action continued to be an indispensable basis for a restitution claim in the cases under discussion. In *Allegheny General Hospital v Philip Morris* (2000), for example, the Court of Appeals for

---

[53] *Jansen v Dolan* [1911] 157 Mo App 32, 35.
[54] *Adsit v Kaufman* [1903] 121 F 355, 356.
[55] eg *Wallace v Berdell* [1885] 101 NY 13; *Shell Petroleum Corp v Scully* [1934] 71 F 2d 772.
[56] *Worthington v Hiss* [1889] 70 Md 172, 185.
[57] Palmer (n 28) 75 especially fn 6, 76–77, 136, 157–58.

the Third Circuit decided that an unjust enrichment claim based on tort would not be allowed if the tort cause of action had been dismissed. The complaint was brought by several hospitals against tobacco companies, alleging, inter alia, that the latter had unjustly benefited by the health services of hospitals provided for nonpaying patients with tobacco-related diseases. The District Court rejected the claim holding that an unjust enrichment claim in a 'tort setting' is 'essentially another way of stating a traditional tort claim' and once the tort was dismissed, there is 'no justification' to allow an unjust enrichment claim. The Court of Appeals affirmed this reasoning.[58] On the one hand, this precedent reinforces the tortious basis of restitution for wrongs; on the other, it could have been more accurate terminologically to state that 'restitution' as a remedy would not be allowed when the tort cause of action was dismissed.

The said Court depended on the former case of *Steamfitters Local Union No 420 Welfare Fund v Philip Morris* (1999) which perceived a claim in restitution as a reiteration of a tort claim. The source of this equation was a note made in the First Restatement of Restitution holding that restitution in these settings were brought to correct imperfections in tort remedies.[59] In essence, the Restatement said the exact opposite. It argued that restitution in these settings was a different and separate base of liability. It was 'a quasi-contractual action in which the wrong by the defendant is only incidental to his unjust enrichment'. Imperfections in tort-based claims, such as shorter period of limitation, second-rate position in bankruptcy cases, termination at death of injurer, made it more advantageous to seek a new base of liability: the quasi-contractual one. As far as the Restatement First had in mind, restitution was not a restatement of tort claim but a new heading under which tort sufferers could sue back what legally belonged to them. On a functional level, however, the Restatement insisted that a conduct deemed wrongful under tort law was indispensable for a restitution claim,[60] reinforcing the dicephalic model of certain wrongs.

The duality of remedial response corresponded to the two contrasting perspectives of a wealth shift. A wealth shift is often concurrently a harm and a gain depending on whose perspective one is taking, the disadvantaged person or the enriched. Restitution was indeed restating the damage in this sense, but only imperfectly. A shift of wealth does not necessarily entail a loss. This was a conceptual crack which led to a fuller split between

---

[58] *Allegheny General Hospital v Philip Morris, Inc* [2000] 228 F 3d 429, 447; see also *Steamfitters Local Union No 420 Welfare Fund v Philip Morris, Inc* [1999] 171 F 3d 912; *Grand Union Supermarkets of the Virgin Islands, Inc v Lockhart Realty Inc* [2012] 493 F App'x 248, 254; Against: *Employer Teamsters-Local Nos 175/505 Health & Welfare Trust Fund v Bristol Myers Squibb Co* [2013] 969 F Supp 2d 463, 471.
[59] ibid 936 (*Steamfitters*).
[60] Rest 1st (n 6) 523–24, 526.

restitution and compensation. In *Saunders v Kline* (1977) for example, a medical researcher sued another alleging that the latter unjustly credited himself with the first identification of an antidepressant drug earning himself a $10,000 honorarium though the discovery was in fact a fruit of the plaintiff's research. The trial court dismissed the claim for restitution reasoning, inter alia, that the plaintiff may not have received the research award. On appeal, the New York Supreme Court reversed and remanded holding that loss is not a 'necessary element' of a restitution claim.[61]

The view that a restitution action does not require a proof of loss was the dominant view in conversion cases as well. In *John A Artukovich & Sons v Reliance Truck* (1980), the plaintiff leased a crane for use in a construction site. The lessee hired the defendant to transport the crane from one site to another. The latter used the crane, without permission, to fulfil a business obligation it had with a third party. The plaintiff sued. The trial court awarded compensation and punitive damages. The Court of Appeal reduced damages to expenses actually incurred by the plaintiff. Unsatisfied with the result, the plaintiff appealed to the Supreme Court of Arizona which held that the plaintiff suffered no loss since it had no right to use the crane during the lease period. The plaintiff was, however, entitled to restitution for the benefit accruing to the defendant by the unauthorised use of the crane. In principle, the Court held that there was no requirement that the plaintiff suffered a 'loss corresponding to the defendant's gain' to establish a restitution claim.[62]

In *Stone v East Coast Swappers* (2014) the Superior Court of Connecticut elucidated these precedents holding that 'while the plaintiff does not always need to suffer a loss, the plaintiff still must have a superior equitable entitlement to whatever asset resulted in the defendant's gain'.[63] It follows that interference with a proprietary entitlement is by itself sufficient to establish a restitution claim regardless of actual or presumed loss suffered. Thus, for instance, it was important for the Restatement Third of Restitution to omit the words 'at the expense of another' in section 3 on wrongful gain. The section originally stated that 'a person is not permitted to profit by his own wrong at the expense of another'. The purpose of the omission, according to Reporter Andrew Kull, is to clarify that restitution of such gain would clearly be available 'in cases where the plaintiff has suffered an interference with protected interests but no measurable loss whatsoever'.[64] These authorities relegate the loss component as far as restitution is concerned. Nevertheless, they continue to articulate the indispensability of the wrongful act in these claims.

---

[61] *Saunders v Kline* [1977] 55 AD 2d 887, 888.
[62] *John A Artukovich & Sons, Inc v Reliance Truck Co* [1980] 126 Ariz 246, 248.
[63] *Stone v East Coast Swappers* [2014] 2014 WL 5286864, 4.
[64] ALI, *Restatement of the Law of Restitution and Unjust Enrichment* (n 12) 26.

The economic loss doctrine offers a confirming expression of this position. Under Florida law, for example, the economic loss rule bars recovery in certain torts for pure economic damages. Since loss was mostly alien to restitution, the rule was expectedly held inapplicable in an action for restitution. The latter 'sounds in quasi-contract, not tort', it was reasoned.[65] The persisting alienation of the loss component in restitution claims brought about a second important split-up. This time in the all-encompassing term of restitution. While restitution clearly denotes the handing back of a benefit originally held by the plaintiff, it does not accurately describe the handing up of a benefit which the plaintiff has not formerly had. It is the sort of benefit which does not correspond to an equal loss or any loss whatsoever. It was inexact to speak of restitution in the sense of restoring something to its original state or holder to describe the remedy in these cases, and a more precise term was called for.

The new conceptual assignee was the term 'disgorgement'. The use of this term did not only signal the birth of a remedy but that of a new paradigm. While the general paradigm of restitution for wrongs indicates a wrongful misplacement of wealth which calls for restitution, the new paradigm denotes making a profit originating in a wrong to another and calling for disgorgement. To illustrate the difference, let us say I take your truck without your permission. Under the general paradigm, restitution makes me return your truck and probably pay you reasonable rent. Under the new paradigm, I get paid good money to load and transfer a business cargo using the appropriated truck. Disgorgement obliges me to hand you the extra cash I earned from this work or some portion of it. This said, it is yet unsettled how disgorgement is justifiable. Handing up something to the plaintiff which was not his in the first place was going the extra mile. And as such, it called for good grounds. Restitution law located these grounds mostly in the type of protected interest involved (eg, patents) or the mental attitude of the wrongdoer.

In tangible property cases, disgorgement was mostly justified by the intentional action of the enriched party. A person should not profit by his wilful wrong. Disgorgement would address any illicit profit made in deliberate wrongdoing. Disgorging profits is expected to disincentivise a conscious wrongdoer by annulling the illicit profit he reaped from another's protected interest.[66] These grounds provided both the gist of the disgorgement paradigm and the moral force to justify it. Section 3 of both Restatements underlined the rise of the new paradigm. Though the phrasing of section 3 is identical in the two Restatements except for

---

[65] *ThunderWave, Inc v Carnival Corp* [1997] 954 F Supp 1562, 1566.
[66] ALI, *Restatement of the Law of Restitution and Unjust Enrichment*, vol II (Washington DC, American Law Institute, 2011) 32, 36 (Rest 3rd vol II).

'at the expense of another' omitted in the Restatement Third, each section had a different paradigm in mind. Section 3 of the Restatement First titled 'tortious acquisition of a benefit' and elaborated in chapter 7 of the said Restatement targeted the general paradigm of restitution for wrongs. Section 3 of the Restatement Third aimed at the more specific paradigm of disgorgement and accentuated the liability to disgorge profits by a deliberate wrongdoer.

Thus, profit and wrongdoing ceased to be sheer technical terms. Profits, ill-gotten and wrongfully made, carried the justification for both restitution and disgorgement. They were increasingly utilised as performing terms with explanatory force accentuating the ethical blame of wrongful profiting and inviting wider use of ethically focused terminology to allow remedy. In *Cross v Berg Lumber* (2000), for example, a motor grader owner contracted with a third party to deliver logs to a certain sawmill. The latter used it without permission to grade access roads to one ranch owner. The grading was done negligently causing damage to the ranch. Subsequently the ranch owner requested use of the grader to repair the damage and was allowed to do so, but eventually refused to return the grader to its lawful owner. The owner sued for tortious conversion and replevin and was awarded damages including restitution and the return of the grader. The defendant appealed and the case was brought before the Supreme Court of Wyoming.[67]

Affirming the trial court decision, the Supreme Court emphasised the firm link of restitution with the idea of justice and 'the prevention of injustice'. Restitution was explained as a remedy available for the 'injured party' or the 'victim' to recover benefits made through 'wrongful invasion'. The backbone of the rules, the Court held was 'the moral obligation arising out of unjust enrichment to the tortfeasor'. 'An intending tortfeasor' the Court said, 'should not be prompted to speculate that his profits might exceed the injured party's losses, thus encouraging commission of the tort'. 'He should expect to be dealt with harshly' the Court remarked. Describing the facts as a 'wilfully deceptive misconduct' that 'should be discouraged', the Court held that application of the 'unjust enrichment remedy' (later referred to as an 'important tool to remedy wrongdoing') was 'appropriate' to offset the incentive for the profit-driven wrongful conduct.[68]

As mentioned earlier, courts' disinclination to allow restitution for trespass to land has increasingly changed either by express statutes (eg, Illinois and Texas law) or cases rejecting the traditional view. In *DeGrazia v Levato* (2012), for example, the DeGrazias leased a property to

---

[67] *Richard Cross v Berg Lumber Company* (2000) 7 P 3d 922, 929–30.
[68] ibid 933–38.

the Levatos. The lessees operated a restaurant and bar which was chiefly frequented by fans of a Chicago professional baseball team. After the lease expired, the tenants refused to vacate and continued to occupy the premises. The owners sued and were granted rent for the post-contractual period. The court held that 'use and occupancy awards are authorized' under Illinois law because 'a lessor's obligation to pay rent continues as a matter of law'.[69]

Maintaining a similar stand but reaching a different outcome is *Villarreal v Grant Geophysical* (2004). In this case, the owners of mineral estates brought an action against two survey companies alleging that they conducted seismic testing without permission, and were therefore liable in tort for trespass or in assumpsit for the reasonable value of use. The District Court granted motion for summary judgment holding that absent actual trespass or injury to land, no tort was committed. The landowners appealed but were rejected. The Texas Court of Appeals held that while Texas law allows appellants to waive the claim for trespass and sue in assumpsit for reasonable rent, no geophysical trespass was committed in this case since 'occupation' of land demanded actual physical invasion, and no such invasion was present here.[70]

The standard remedy of restitution continues to be pecuniary. Though the amount of restitution varies depending on the specific circumstances of each case, money judgment persists to be the principal method of recovery in most cases. A monetary remedy would often be available regardless of the way liability in restitution arose and of the type of benefit involved. In *Land Grantors in Henderson v United States* (2009), for example, the Court of Federal Claims discussed money as the default choice of recovery also in cases where the benefit received is explicitly a non-monetary one. Endorsing the different methods of valuation offered by the Restatement, the Court cited Dan Dobbs's words that the exact amount of restitution would eventually reflect 'the substantive law purpose that calls for restitution'.[71]

RESTATEMENTS OF RESTITUTION

The characteristics highlighted in the previous subsections are equally observed in the Restatements of Restitution Law. The indispensability of the wrongful action for the discussed paradigm of restitution and

---

[69] *DeGrazia v Levato* [2012] IL App (1st) 111549-U.
[70] *Villarreal v Grant Geophysical, Inc* [2004] 136 SW 3d 265, 269. Against: *Jantzen Beach Associates v Jantzen Dynamic Corporation* [2005] 115 P 3d 943, 945–48.
[71] *Land Grantors in Henderson v United States* [2009] 86 Fed Cl 35, 38.

that of disgorgement are clearly noted in all Restatements. Section 3 of Restatements First and Third exhibits the underlying principle that no one should profit by his wrong. An attempt at an inclusive version which combines both unjust and wrongful enrichment principles was made by the Restatement Second (Tentative Draft no 1). Section 1 of the said Restatement stated that 'a person who receives a benefit by reason of infringement of another person's interest, or of loss suffered by the other, owes restitution to him in the manner and amount necessary to prevent unjust enrichment'. Section 4 of the same draft targets additional cases of benefits received by duty-violators irrespective of the fact whether such conduct was wrongful to the disadvantaged.

The said principles are concretised in following sections. Chapter 7 of the Restatement First addresses the different types of tortious enrichment. Section 128 sets the duty of restitution for wrongful dealing with movable property markedly conversion. The Restatement endorses the classic stand which disallows restitution in land appropriation cases. Section 129(1) and section 129(2) (assuming title dispute) channel trespasses and wrongful dispossessions of land to tort law routes depriving the victim of a right to restitution. These sections, however, allow restitution in cases of tortious grazing of domestic animals upon land (without a claim of right) and certain cases of eminent domain. Section 129(3) grants restitution in cases of tortious cutting and possession of 'anything in or upon the land' without a claim of right. Sections 130 and 131 offer restitution for tortious acquisition, retaining and termination of 'a title to land, chattels, or choses in action' of another.

Comparably, the Restatement Third addresses these cases in chapter 5. Section 40 gathers tortious dealing with both movable and immovable property. The section regulates conversion and also trespass, thus taking the new view which allows restitution in land appropriation cases. The section provides that 'a person who obtains a benefit by an act of trespass or conversion, by comparable interference with other protected interests in tangible property, or in consequence of such an act by another, is liable in restitution to the victim of the wrong'. Section 44 is a residual rule applicable in cases not covered by other specific sections, markedly sections 40–43. It regulates, inter alia, cases of 'conscious interference with a claimant's legally protected interests'. Section 44(2) asserts that such interference includes 'conduct that is tortious' or one that is violating and 'constitutes an actionable wrong to the claimant'.

In his well-researched paper on restitution for wrongs and the Restatement Third (at the time, Tentative Draft no 5), James Rogers regrets, inter alia, the position taken by the Restatement in this area which 'does not create a cause of action where the claimant would otherwise have none'. He argues that 'the contribution of the law of restitution … is more than to provide an additional remedy for conduct that is judged wrongful under the law of tort or other law'.[72] Equating restitution law to Cinderella, who after decades of being 'overshadowed by its stepsisters tort and contract', was finally 'invited to the ball', Rogers points out his fear that 'in the area of restitution for wrongs' the Restatement Draft 'pushes Cinderella back to the garret, to languish in the shadow of her stepsister, the law of tort'.[73]

To meet some of Rogers' objections, certain amendments to the Tentative Draft were made at the time.[74] Section 40 (in its draft version) was interpolated to extend the scope of its 'wrongful conduct'. A wrongful conduct may consequently be marked as such also by laws other than torts. The amended version adds that a benefit may be obtained by 'interference with other protected interests in tangible property' (in any law) and not solely by an act of 'trespass or conversion' (of tort law) as formerly articulated. The section was, thus, broadened to cover also non-tortious, albeit recognised, causes of actions. Nevertheless, it remains the case, as the Kull notes, that 'if the statute that makes the challenged conduct wrongful confers no private right of action, a would-be plaintiff may not circumvent this legislative omission by styling his action one for unjust enrichment instead of damages'.[75] It is thus the aim of the Restatement that without a non-restitution law marking the conduct as wrongful and providing a cause of action, one may not invoke restitution *in this area* as an independent cause of action.[76]

On terminological and justificatory levels, section 3 uses censuring language. It describes a person who commits a 'wrong' and seeks to 'profit'. This language is expounded by further sections which label the enriched person as a 'wrongdoer' (at times a 'conscious' one) (Restatement Third, sections 44(1) and 51(3)). His actions are described in terms of 'trespass', 'conversion', 'interference', 'misconduct', 'wrong' and his profit is 'wrongfully' and 'tortiously' obtained (Restatement Third, sections 3, 40, 44, 49(4) and 51; Restatement First, sections 3, 128–31). His 'conduct' or 'act' (Restatement Third, sections 40 and 44(2)) 'violates' and is labelled 'tortious' (Restatement Third, section 44(2); Restatement First, sections 3 and 128–31). It is conceived as 'profit' and 'gain' driven (Restatement Third, sections 3 and 49(4); Restatement First, section 3). On the other end, we find the disadvantaged person who is described as a 'victim' (Restatement Third, section 40) and at times is also demoted and absent (Restatement Third, section 3).

---

[72] J Rogers, 'Restitution for Wrongs and the Restatement (Third) of the Law of Restitution' (2007) 42 *Wake Forest Law Review* 55, 62–63; Rest 3rd vol II (n 66) 77.

[73] ibid 55 (Rogers).

[74] Rest 3rd vol II (n 66) 14.

[75] ibid 85; *cf* Steamfitters (n 58) 936.

[76] *cf* D Laycock, 'The Scope and Significance of Restitution' (1989) 67 *Texas Law Review* 1277, 1286, fns 52–53.

As to remedies, chapter 8 of the Restatement First provides detailed rules of recovery. It sets monetary restitution as the standard remedy of restitution. Section 151 applies to conscious wrongdoing, namely improper acquisition, retention or disposition of property. It provides that the 'measure of recovery for the benefit received' is basically 'the value' of the appropriated asset. Sections 156 and 157 extend restitution to cover interest, direct products of the misplaced benefit and the value of use. Equitable remedies, notably constructive trust and lien are provided for in chapter 9 (sections 160 and 161), tracing and following rules are mostly regulated in chapter 13 (eg, sections 202, 205 and 214).

In similar manner, the Restatement Third addresses remedies in chapter 7. Section 49(1) sets money as the standard remedy in restitution.[77] Section 49(4) provides disgorgement of profits in wrongful enrichment cases. Restitution of 'Interest', 'use value, proceeds and consequential gains' are provided for in sections 49(5) and 53. Section 51 defines 'misconduct', 'conscious wrongdoer' and 'profit'. It also sets additional rules for restitution and disgorgement following misconduct. Constructive trust, equity lien, following and tracing rules are provided for in subsequent sections notably 55, 56, 58 and 59.

The remedial rules chiefly target advantages described as 'gain', 'profit' and 'consequential gains' meaning gains resulting from profitable actions by the enriched[78] (Restatement Third, sections 53(2)–53(3)). The pecuniary remedy is described as 'disgorgement' or 'accounting' (Restatement Third, section 51) aiming to 'strip' the enriched person 'of a wrongful gain' (Restatement Third, section 49(4)). The gain is defined as 'the net profit attributable to the underlying wrong' (Restatement Third, section 51(4)). The objective of this specific remedy is 'to eliminate profit from wrongdoing while avoiding, so far as possible, the imposition of a penalty' (Restatement Third, section 51(4)).

The main asset-based remedies such as ejectment, replevin and detinue are excluded from the Restatement of Restitution Law.[79] The Restatement First explicates this omission noting that these 'actions are primarily for damages based upon wrongs and are not merely restitutionary'. The omission actually preserves a historical distinction between tort actions and the quasi-contract action of assumpsit.[80] A more detailed explanation is provided by the Restatement Third which states that 'rights and remedies in such cases depend so immediately on property concepts that it is neither necessary nor useful to explain them by reference to the law of unjust

---

[77] Rest 3rd vol II (n 66) 177.
[78] ibid 252.
[79] Rest 1st (n 6) 19. See also *Ablah v Eyman* [1961] 365 P 2d 181, 190 and *Richard* (n 67) 934.
[80] ibid 19–20, 523 (Rest 1st); Against: Laycock (n 76) 1281.

enrichment'.[81] It is nevertheless admitted that these remedies 'correspond fully to the plain meaning' of 'restitution' and 'unjust enrichment'.[82]

TRACING EXEMPLARS

Attentive reading of the cases and Restatements reveals an interesting exemplarity both on structure and language levels. The rules propose an undeniable action orientation. As opposed to the static pictures of a property owner, at one time with and at another without, his object, cast by the European rules, the American law brings more live and dynamic pictures. It seems to care more for the action involved, how and why it is done. The main issue is the enriched person, the improper profit he seeks and the wrong committed on the way. As the protagonist of this narrative, he has actively misbehaved. He disappointed and failed expectations. His actions are wrongful and tortious. He is driven by illicit desire to make improper gain from others' wealth and property. At the other end, we have the disadvantaged person, a more marginal character. The latter is a demoted antagonist. Though victim of the chief character's behaviour, he is not always present in the scene.

American rules utilise the said exemplars to frame, describe and explain the cases under examination. The scene just described prepares the ground for the law's intervention. With the antagonist's misconduct comes the need for rectification. The proper measure to disincentive such behaviour is, at the outset, pecuniary. The question of remedy is one of money and value. As a standard, the enriched person is responsible to make restitution in money before any remedial alternative (eg, restitution in kind) is considered. Though available both inside and outside restitution law, the asset-focused measures are not brought to the fore. Instead, the rules target produced and action-related advantages. The aim is again to strip the enriched person of any ill-gotten profits attributed to his wrongful behaviour. This is how the law tends to perceive the case and this is how it tends to justify the remedy.

Unlike the European rules, the American rules are less formed on the premises of a property owner and the need to restore what was improperly taken. Instead, the rules seek first correction both of the wrong behaviour and the disapproved intention. Thus, the law of intentional wrongs becomes a tool of rectification rather than one of restoration. This understanding is explicitly acknowledged by the Restatement[83]

---

[81] Rest 3rd vol II (n 66) 176.
[82] Rest 1st (n 6) 11.
[83] ibid 7.

and case law.[84] The law openly aims to offset a bad incentive by elimi-
nating the profit realised through the wrongful behaviour. It is, thus, fair
to conclude that as far as the cases under consideration are concerned,
the term *enrichment* in *wrongful enrichment* refers first to a wrongful *action*
rather than a wrongful *asset*.

These observations correspond, though imperfectly, to a substantive
distinction noted by Douglas Laycock,[85] and later prescriptively objected
by Andrew Kull,[86] regarding the meaning of the American concept of 'restitution'. Laycock notes that the main idea of restitution bears two meanings. The first is a recovery based on unjust enrichment and measured by
the enriched person's gain which he terms 'disgorgment of unjust enrichment'. The second is 'specific restitution' denoting the return of a 'specific thing' improperly taken, and the undoing of 'disruptive transactions'
restoring 'both parties to their original position in kind'. Summing up
the Restatement's use of the word 'restitution', Laycock argues that both
senses are apparent; nevertheless the first sense remains more dominant.[87]

Addressing cases of property misappropriation and exploitation,
Laycock underlines the role each meaning plays. The first meaning, he
says, explains why profits wrongfully made are disgorged and handed
to the disadvantaged and the second meaning explains why the property
is restored to its lawful possessor. Elucidating the scope and significance
of restitution law, Laycock urges us to preserve this conceptual duality
stating that the law provides, and should provide, 'a substantive liability
based on unjust enrichment', a measure of recovery 'based on defendant's
gain instead of plaintiff's loss' and a restoration in kind of 'lost property
or its proceeds'.[88]

Opposing this view, Andrew Kull argues that restitution law should be
defined exclusively by reference to the unjust enrichment of the enriched,
and the extent to which he has gained.[89] Like Peter Birks and the English
law of restitution,[90] Kull attempts to rationalise the American law in this
field by suggesting desirable distinctions that would illuminate existing
ambiguities in terminologies and dynamics. Restitution as 'restoration
of a thing', Kull argues, bears 'no essential or even useful relation to the

---

[84] For a detailed account of the remedy, its origins and justifications see *Richard* (n 67).

[85] Laycock (n 76). James J Edelman argues that the Restatement Third 'distorts' the meaning and scope of unjust enrichment by including the 'profits-based disgorgement measure'.
See J Edelman 'Unjust Enrichment, Restitution, and Wrongs' (2000–01) 79 *Texas Law Review*
1869, 1871–72.

[86] A Kull, 'Rationalizing Restitution' (1995) 83(5) *California Law Review* 1191.

[87] Laycock (n 76) 1279–80, 1282.

[88] ibid 1280–81, 1293.

[89] See Kull (n 86) 1196.

[90] P Birks, *An Introduction to the Law of Restitution* (Oxford, Oxford University Press, 1985);
P Birks, *Unjust Enrichment* (Oxford, Oxford University Press, 2005). See also Burrows (n 12).

avoidance of unjust enrichment', and as a remedy it 'operates without regard to the defendant's enrichment'. Restitution as restoration is not related to, or part of, unjust enrichment law. Rather it is a remedial device that mostly asserts 'preexisting property entitlements' by 'putting property back into the hands of its owners'.[91]

Affirming the prescriptive nature of his contribution, Kull advises abandoning 'the futile effort to find a relation between' these 'two unrelated concepts' and adopting, instead, a clear-cut law of unjust enrichment that provides an independent basis of liability, and a remedy (mostly pecuniary) that is measured by the defendant's gain. Only this way, Kull asserts, 'we can remove the single biggest obstacle to a rationalized statement of the law of unjust enrichment'. Until then, it appears, however, that the American law of restitution as Kull argues continues 'to accept the idea that the act of restoration forms at least a subsidiary part of the law of restitution'.[92]

ASSESSMENT

The foregoing debate presents a tentative line of counter arguments. Any account of the American law of restitution for wrongs would have to consider the asset-focused elements of the law which seem to reside side by side with the action-focused ones. These elements are present both on doctrinal and terminological levels. On a doctrinal level, tracing is perhaps most outstanding. Tracing is a complex area of law rooted in equity, sometimes regarded as the third pillar of modern restitution for wrongs.[93] It provides different rules and instruments to assert the plaintiff's right to a property or its pecuniary or non-pecuniary substitutes, whether found in the wrongdoer's hands or a third party's hands. Tracing can basically empower the court to impose by law a constructive trust and grant a decree for specific recovery. It deems the property holder a trustee for the benefit of the plaintiff. Other instruments such as equitable lien to secure a monetary claim or subrogation are available too.

On a terminological level, like the action exemplarity, the asset exemplarity provides a descriptive and explanatory language for the American jurist to narrate and discuss the cases under consideration. This language basically focuses on the exploited or appropriated object. It casts the asset as a legally protected interest of the disadvantaged person with the latter being the concern of the rules. It relegates the wrongful act of the enriched person and instead opts for more ethically neutral verbs to describe his

---

[91]   Kull (n 86) 1194, 1198, 1215–17.
[92]   ibid 1194, 1198, 1214, 1219, 1222. Peter Birks regrets this stand. See P Birks, 'A Letter to America: The New Restatement of Restitution' (2003) 3(2) *Global Jurist Frontiers* 20.
[93]   Birks, 'Restitution for Wrongs' (n 22) 171.

actions. The chief player is, instead, the owner or the possessor of the said object. The gist of the law's intervention is recovering the object itself rather than any monetary replacement. The language used to frame the case and justify the remedy is very proprietary. The issue is to restore the owner back to his former position as master of the object. In Blackstonian terms, restitution simply reattaches the object to its rightful owner.

This asset exemplarity can be traced in the Restatements as well. The Restatements provide asset-focused remedies, notably constructive trust. Thus, for example, section 160 of the Restatement First and section 55 of the Restatement Third impose a constructive trust as 'a means to recover specific property from the holder of legal title, when the acquisition of title results in the unjust enrichment of the holder'.[94] Such remedial sections explicitly refer to an identifiable 'property' and 'its traceable product'. They utilise asset-focused ethically neutral verbs to describe the available recovery, such as 'convey', 'retain' and 'surrender'. The protagonist of this perspective is the disadvantaged person to whom all objects are attached.

A similar style can be found in the framing of the case and the definitions of key terms. Examples are verbs like 'obtains', 'retained', 'used', 'disposed', 'taken position' and 'severed' (Restatement Third, sections 40, 44(1); Restatement First, sections 128, 129(1), 129(3) and 130). Enrichments are said to be 'derived' (Restatement Third, section 44(3)(c)) from a protected 'interest'(s) in 'tangible property', 'chattels' or 'land' (Restatement Third, sections 40, 44; Restatement First, section 128). An example of definition is 'direct product' which is defined in the Restatement First as 'that which derived from the ownership or possession of the property' without intervention.[95]

Besides these examples, it is also possible to mention occasional decisions which hold that 'the essence of conversion is not the acquisition of property by the wrongdoer, but a wrongful deprivation of it to the owner'[96] or that 'there is no conversion until some act is done which is a denial or violation of the plaintiff's dominion over or rights in the property'.[97] These precedents make use of property-like terminology stressing the issue of sole dominion and the exercise of control over an object to the exclusion of others. A clear benefit of such use is to secure better hold of all property detachment cases while downplaying the cause and the manner in which they took place.

The aim of all former examples is to note the asset exemplarity which is also present in American law. It is not to argue that this orientation precedes the action exemplarity and definitely not that it negates it. In fact, a closer examination suggests that the action orientation is securely ahead

---

[94] Rest 3rd vol II (n 66) 305.
[95] Rest 1st (n 6) 622.
[96] eg *Variety Wholesalers, Inc v Salem Logistics Traffic Servs*, LLC [2012] 365 NC 520, 529–30.
[97] *Lake Mary Ltd Partnership v Johnston* [2001] 145 NC App 525, 532, 551.

especially as far as intentional wrongs and disgorgement are concerned. Framing and explaining these cases as a challenge to moral standards seems more appealing and rhetorically convincing to the American jurist than describing them in terms of interference with a legal institution such as property. This tendency seems to have gained speed in the last decades and is quite visible when comparisons between the two Restatements are made. A good example is perhaps the shift of meaning explained regarding section 3 of the Restatements and the steady rise of the disgorgement paradigm.

Furthermore, many of the asset-looking orientations are less operative than they seem. In practice, for example, tracing which is widely intended to grant a proprietary interest to a plaintiff in insolvency cases, will at times 'end in a simple money judgment' as Palmer notes.[98] Similarly, the asset-oriented elements defining conversion in case law seem to also have the wrongdoer's rectification in mind. While conversion is described, inter alia, as property deprivation, the aim of such definition as explicitly declared by these decisions is to justify remedy regardless of the subsequent use applied to the object or the fact that the wrongdoer derived no benefit from his actions.[99] Unlike property deprivation from an owner's standpoint (as in the European scene), American conversion is a term framed for the wrongdoer's action. It targets his conduct before anything else and it cannot be established unless 'tortious taking' or some wrongful action is proven.[100]

But let us put aside the style and content of the American rules, and question their capability to reflect a wide culture. In this realm, one could argue that case law is a collection of personal products formed by different individuals. In this sense, they rest on pure subjectivism and do not necessarily reflect a shared apprehension of the world, so the argument goes. Considering this claim from a normative standpoint, it questions the very legitimacy of the judicial craft. This is a serious charge which American legal realism had to defuse. But from a cultural standpoint, this claim is implausible since isolated subjectivism is itself impossible. As many scholars have noted, culture provides preset tendencies which affect members' cognitive processes. Any subjective output proceeds from a pool of shared meanings and conventions. Similarly, a judicial craft cannot proceed but from a societal view or some common understanding.[101]

---

[98]   Palmer (n 28) 176.

[99]   *Mace v Pyatt* [2010] 203 NC App 245.

[100]   eg *Amond v Ron York & Sons Towing* [2009] 302 SW 3d 708.

[101]   eg P Bourdieu, 'The Force of Law: Toward a Sociology of the Juridical Field', trans R Terdiman (1987) 38 *Hastings Law Journal* 805, 811; S Fish, *Is There a Text in This Class? The Authority of Interpretive Communities* (Cambridge, MA, Harvard University Press, 1980) 13–14.

5

American Culture

L ABOUR DELIVERS HUMANS from three great evils: boredom, vice and need, an old man advised Candide. Candide was a gentle young man. His early life was spent in the castle of the rich Baron of Thunder-ten-Tronckh described as a *'paradis terrestre'* (terrestrial paradise). His peaceful stay at this ostensible paradise, however, came to an end when he was expelled for kissing the baron's daughter. As the story unfolds, Candide encounters many ills which increasingly erode his innocence and personal optimism. Eventually, Candide gives up his false hope and the philosophical approach to life he was taught and leaves Europe where he sees misery and illusion. Following the old man's advice, Candide decides to find life's true meaning in the cultivation of his own home garden which is said to be placed elsewhere.[1]

Candide, Voltaire's widely studied novella, fosters a rich critique of classical Europe. The story juxtaposes two fundamentally contrasting gardens. One garden is the baronial paradise which hinges on the characters' inherited wealth and social status. Like biblical Eden and the effortless profusion that is rapidly followed by various hardships, Candide's life in the baronial paradise is heavily disturbed following his expulsion and the many problems he faces afterwards such as war, a deadly storm, and the Inquisition. The story's second garden is Candide's simple home, one which depicts a new life experience where toil through personal land cultivation provides the best possible meaning of human existence. This comparison hardly conceals the author's rejection of European traditions which has valued a person's worth on the merits of her inherited properties, notably accession and social position.[2]

Inspired by Enlightenment philosophy, Voltaire's novella urges a total societal regeneration. A person's worth should solely be determined by toil and personal effort rather than birth. In this sense, the story

---

[1] Voltaire, *Candide, ou L'optimisme* (Paris, Siréne, 1759); Voltaire, *Candide and Other Stories* (Oxford, Oxford University Press, 2008).
[2] H Mason, *European Masters: Voltaire* (London, Hutchinson, 1975) 62–63.

challenges traditional establishments which have uncritically been tagged as 'meilleur des mondes possibles' ('the best of all possible worlds'). It yearns for a new 'paradise' where one can achieve genuine success and self-realisation. These aspirations are epitomised in Candide's own assertion: 'C'est certainement le Nouveau-Monde qui est le meilleur des univers possibles' ('It is certainly the New World which is the best of all possible worlds'). Remarkably, his assertion cannot be detached from Christopher Columbus's own belief upon the discovery of the New World. The latter was convinced he had located God's biblical paradise.[3]

This chapter discusses the cultural history of the United States of America. It makes occasional references to European culture, the Enlightenment and French thinkers as critical observers of American culture.[4] As will be shortly apparent, the old man's advice to Candide is neither accidental not irrelevant. It gets to the root of American discourses of wealth and epitomises its unique vision of personal progression. The work ethic along with religious values and money shape America's notions of wealth and wrongful enrichment.

IS THERE AN *AMERICAN* CULTURE?

Whether there is an *American* culture is, unsurprisingly, the vital question to be first addressed. The United States seems so diverse that one doubts an *American* culture is at all perceptible. The enormous size of the country which means various climates, geographies and daily routines along with diversified ethnicities and spoken languages make it highly problematic to speak of any unified culture.[5] Yet, this proclamation rests on an either/or approach already challenged in previous discussion for being reductive.[6] The better approach attempts to outline the *American* set of values cherished by the majority of American people. Maryanne Datesman, JoAnn Crandell and Edward Kearny argue that in spite of linguistic and cultural diversity, a common 'sense of national identity' continues to 'bind Americans together'.[7] It is indeed possible, they assert, to trace those 'traditional, dominant cultural values', 'basic beliefs' and 'character traits' that are called *American*.[8]

---

[3] R Gray, *A History of American Literature*, Kindle edn (West Sussex, Wiley-Blackwell, 2012) location 302.

[4] eg M Evans, *America: The View from Europe* (San Francisco, CA, San Francisco Book, 1976).

[5] M Datesman, J Crandell and E Kearny, *American Ways: An Introduction to American Culture* (New York, Pearson Education, 2005) 3; N Campbell and A Kean, *American Cultural Studies: An Introduction to American Culture* (Oxford, Routledge, 2012) 3.

[6] See ch 3.

[7] Datesman, Crandell and Kearny (n 5) 8.

[8] ibid 9.

In *American Beliefs: What Keeps a Big Country and a Diverse People United*, John Harmon McElroy identifies some of these core beliefs. He argues that different behavioural 'patterns' seem to persist throughout American history signifying fixed cultural postulates of the American people as a nation. American culture, he says, holds a number of core beliefs, like the 'freedom' and 'equality', which remain unifying and consistent regardless of where and how they are expressed.[9] According to Geert Hofstede, Gert Jan Hofstede and Michael Minkov, this observation is supported on a global scale and across many cultures. Despite 'sweeping changes in practices' throughout long periods of time, they say, 'considerable stability' in values has been observed in and across all cultures examined.[10]

Remarkably, American culture often refers to itself as a 'unique' or 'exceptional' culture.[11] On an epistemological level, this very proclamation hides an implicit sense of unity among Americans. According to Donald Pease, American unity is sustained by a nationwide 'meta-narrative'. This meta-narrative epitomises various postulates, beliefs and traditions cherished by most of the American public. A 'meta-narrative', explains Pease, produces an imagined national uniqueness. Like a salient trait, it manages to conceal many ethnic, social and linguistic differences within the American people. It offers Americans an easily discernible sense of togetherness and shared fate.[12]

Asserting the *American* does not aim at marginalising differences or silencing power struggles or socio-political ones.[13] But these, too, should not invalidate or nullify the rich pool of shared meanings and values produced and cherished by Americans as a nation. In fact, it is widely accepted that in spite of excessive diversity, America succeeded in creating a cohesive character which turned different groups of migrants into a single nation. It absorbed and then immersed Americans into a grand meta-narrative cherished by the larger part of the population.[14] '*E Pluribus*

---

[9] cp McElroy's themes: Practicality, Freedom, Responsibility and Equity. See J McElroy, *American Beliefs: What Keeps a Big Country and a Diverse People United* (Chicago, IL, Ivan R Dee, 1999) 2, 4, 220.

[10] G Hofstede, GJ Hofstede and M Minkov, *Cultures and Organizations: Software for the Mind*, Kindle edn (New York, McGraw-Hill, 2010) locations 319–40.

[11] Campbell and Kean (n 5) 2.

[12] D Pease, 'National Identities, Postmodern Artifacts, and Postnational Narratives' in D Pease (ed), *National Identities and Post-Americanist Narratives* (Durham, NC, Duke University Press, 1994) 1–3; ibid 2.

[13] ibid 18 (Campbell and Kean).

[14] C Fischer, *Made in America: A Social History of American Culture and Character* (Chicago, IL, University of Chicago Press, 2010) 12; Datesman, Crandell and Kearny (n 5) 4. See also Barack Obama's 2012 victory speech stressing American unity in diversity; B Obama, victory speech following re-election (7 November 2012) available at: www.theguardian.com/world/2012/nov/07/barack-obama-speech-full-text.

Unum' ('From many, one') states the motto of the United States' official seal. It is only with such an embracive approach that one is able to evade the trap of advocating diversity as an anti-reductive argument, at the expense of a fallacious and reductive conclusion that there is no *American* culture.

WEALTH AS WORK ETHIC, RELIGIOUS VALUES AND MONEY

In his well-written analysis of the American uniqueness, Pease exposes the constructive role of national meta-narrative in making and sustaining a nation. A national meta-narrative, he argues, produces 'imaginary' ties that hold people together promoting a sense of unity and inclusion. It introduces a conceptual shift from a 'proto-national' state to a national one. The task is to spot those 'key terms in the national meta-narrative commonly understood to be descriptive of that community'.[15] Discerning those postulates is a vital precondition to obtaining a clearer sense of a people's *Volksgeist* (nation's spirit) and its cultural perceptions.

In America's case, the national meta-narrative amalgamates diverse biblical and colonialist elements. It narrates a story of the first progenitor who reaches virgin territories and is immersed by an 'exemplary national motive' defined as a holy 'errand into the wilderness'.[16] Perry Miller explains this 'errand' as a spiritual mission accepted by the Puritans, the first English settlers of America, to turn the wilderness into the biblical-inspired 'city on a hill', an ideal place of devout, hard-working and God-fearing Christians.[17]

This narrative is hardly detachable from the biblical story of the fall and banishment. After Adam defies God's ban on the tree of knowledge, and before he is expelled from Eden, the land is cursed by God and Adam is doomed to earn his day by the sweat of his brow. In toil, it is written, 'Adam shall eat of the land till the day he remerges with it'.[18] Rooted in Calvinist theology,[19] American narrative transformed what was formerly considered a verdict of damnation into a vehicle of salvation. Toil became the corrective and redeeming antagonist of sin and wrongdoing. It gained a key role in American culture and was increasingly infused in nearly all aspects of 'American social ideology'. Facilitated by puritan religious

---

[15] Pease (n 12) 1, 3, 4.
[16] ibid.
[17] P Miller, *Errand into the Wilderness* (Cambridge, MA, Harvard University Press, 2000).
[18] Genesis 3: 17–19.
[19] M Weber, The Protestant Ethic and the Spirit of Capitalism: and Other Writings (New York, Penguin, 2002).

thought, massive migrations and a tradition of a wild West, labour rapidly became a core postulate of American culture.[20]

According to Max Weber, religiosity and hard work have been inseparable elements of America's repertoire throughout history.[21] Unsurprisingly, America's perception of economic gain is deeply impacted by both themes. According to Marjorie Kornhauser, Americans 'imbue earned income with an aura of morality and virtuousness that unearned income' does not possess. 'Earned' gain, she notes, is that which is obtained by one's own hard work. America holds in high esteem those who attain wealth by their own toil and skills, and degrades those who are slothful or corrupt.[22]

Americans believe in toil as the main route to growth and prosperity. They promise equal opportunity for all. Equality, a fruit of Enlightenment philosophy, was the main facilitator for America's dearly held conviction of personal progression. Equality promised to dismantle tacit powers of stereotypes. No 'matter who you are or where you come from', assured Barak Obama, America's forty-fourth President, himself living proof of the American repertoire, personal progression is attainable for all Americans on equal footing, if they are 'willing to work hard'.[23] America's succeeding President, Donald Trump, a successful and wealthy businessman, promised in his inauguration speech to continue to work hard during his presidency and 'get the job done'.[24]

As early as the constituting Declaration of Independence, equality was perceived a 'self-evident' truth and necessary ground for many indefeasible rights, such as the rights to 'Life, Liberty and the pursuit of Happiness'.[25] Benjamin Franklin, one of the founding fathers of the American nation assured that self-contentment is attainable through 'ceaseless personal improvement' and 'making something out of oneself'.[26] Many of Franklin's proverbs stress the merits of toil and self-discipline as indispensable to the route to wealth and economic flourishing. 'Idle hands are the Devil's workshop', 'Never put off till tomorrow what can be done today',[27] 'early to bed and early to rise, makes a man healthy, wealthy

---

[20] H Applebaum, *The American Work Ethic and the Changing Work Force* (Westport, CT, Greenwood Press, 1999) x–xiii.

[21] Weber (n 19).

[22] M Kornhauser, 'The Morality of Money: American Attitudes Toward Wealth and the Income Tax' (1994) 70(1) *Indiana Law Journal* 119, 119–20.

[23] Obama (n 14).

[24] D Trump, Inauguration Speech (21 January 2017) available at: www.theguardian.com/world/2017/jan/20/donald-trump-inauguration-speech-full-text.

[25] American Congress, 'Declaration of Independence (July 4, 1776)' in P Henry, B Franklin and T Jefferson et al (eds), *15 Documents and Speeches That Built America*, Kindle edn (Seattle, WA, Amazon Digital Services, 2011) locations 442–97.

[26] J Rifkin, *The European Dream*, Kindle edn (New York, Penguin, 2004) locations 518–19.

[27] ibid locations 533–34.

and wise', 'laziness travels so slowly, that Poverty soon overtakes him' and 'at the working man's house hunger looks in but dares not enter'.[28] All Franklin's proverbs glorify hard work and the American 'self-made' person.

Franklin's proverbs were not empty slogans; they accentuated a genuine American devotion to these ideals. Comparison with post-revolutionary France illustrates this point vividly. In spite of a passionate defence of similar ideals, notably equality and personal autonomy, by the *Déclaration des droits de l'homme et du citoyen* (Declaration of the Rights of Man and of the Citizen), France of the late eighteenth century failed to follow America's example. Bitter and gory times awaited the young republic, and many of the said ideals were no more than ink on paper. This perplexing condition incited the utmost curiosity among French intellectuals to understand the causes of such a reversed outcome.[29] An enquiry to that end was carried out by Alexis de Tocqueville, a French political thinker, who visited the United States in 1831 to examine the political and social merits of American democracy.[30]

In his monograph, de Tocqueville rapidly announced equality as the 'fundamental fact' upon which all other facts rested in America. Unlike French equality which played into the hands of the 'governing powers', American equality was an inalienable virtue of 'the governed' he said. Equality shaped the entirety of people's culture, or what the terminology of the eighteenth century referred to as the 'opinions', 'sentiments' and 'practices' of the 'civil society'.[31] Interestingly, de Tocqueville identified another dissimilarity with the continent. Americans, he noted, paid very little attention to philosophy. They had 'no philosophical school of their own' and did not mind 'all the schools' debated in Europe. Instead, Americans perceived themselves as a practical nation 'living entirely for the purposes of action and not of thought'.[32]

This cultural readiness to accommodate the approaching era of industrialism is hardly different from contemporary American spirit. Outlining America's key values, Stan Nussbaum argues that Americans are 'people of action'. They dislike 'rules and regulations that prevent action'. They disdain 'authority structures' and value action as the best route to

---

[28] B Franklin, *Poor Richard's Almanack*, issues: 1735, 1737, 1756 (Philadelphia, PA, Franklin, 1734, 1737, 1756).

[29] cp J Agassi, *ha-Ni'urut ha-ḥadasha* (*The New Enlightenment*) (Ben-Shemen, Modan, 2012) 11.

[30] A de Tocqueville, *Democracy in America*, vol 1, trans H Reeve, Kindle edn (Public Domain, 1835) locations 63–76.

[31] ibid locations 177–178, 201.

[32] A de Tocqueville, *Democracy in America*, vol 2, trans H Reeve, Kindle edn (Public Domain, 1840) 3, 27.

success.[33] American culture cherishes a pragmatic approach. It favours substance over form, and ends over means. In forms, they find 'useless and inconvenient veils placed between them and the truth'. Asserting truth is an inside-out process. Truth is construed by one's own judgement rather than by external factors like traditions and prejudices. For a conviction to be true, it must rest on reason and sheer facts.[34]

Though this scientific-like approach to life enhanced intellectual and political independence from habits of the Old World, it could hardly be detached from its European roots. Francis Bacon and René Descartes, two European cogitators of the early Enlightenment, advocated the abandonment of prejudices and traditions as a necessary path to sound reasoning.[35] In his *Novum organum* (1620), Bacon argues that one needs to reject certain 'Idols' of the mind which hinder immaculate thinking. Idols like the tendency to perceive things in systems, the tendency to exaggerate positive evidence and the blind adherence to canons, are all stumbling stones in the pursuit of truthfulness.[36] Peter Urbach efficaciously defines these Idols as 'tendencies to adhere to theories uncritically or defend them dogmatically, either avoiding counter-evidence, or ignoring it when it presents itself, or finding ways around it when it cannot be ignored'.[37]

Similarly, Descartes in his *Discourse on the Method* (1637) offers scepticism as a proper means to question doubtful ideas and suggest truer ones.[38] Noting Bacon's and Descartes' approaches Joseph Agassi explains them in terms of 'radicalism', namely 'the need to start over', and 'eradicate the roots' of blindly held ideas.[39] This modus operandi of American culture, as observed by de Tocqueville and others,[40] seeks reasoned explanation for every given condition. Nothing is unexplainable, preternatural or extraordinary.[41] American culture seeks the actual and sensible not the metaphysical. It adores the reasonable and material not the dogmatic or abstract. New gratifications are always in demand. American people, says Patricia O'Toole, are perpetually looking for a 'virgin territory' in all aspects of life, 'geographic, social, economic, and

---

[33] S Nussbaum, *American Cultural Baggage: How to Recognise and Deal with it* (New York, Orbis Books, 2005) 18.

[34] de Tocqueville, *Democracy in America*, vol 2 (n 32) 3–4, 32.

[35] Agassi (n 29) 22–23.

[36] F Bacon, *Novum Organum* (*New Instrument*) trans P Urbach and J Gibson (eds) (Illinois, Open Court, 2000) book I, 46–68.

[37] ibid xix–xx.

[38] R Descartes, *Discourse on the Method of Rightly Conducting One's Reason and of Seeking Truth in the Sciences* (Charleston, SC, BiblioBazar, 2007) 32.

[39] Agassi (n 29) 22–23.

[40] See, eg, G Althen and J Bennett, *American Ways: A Cultural Guide to the United States* (Boston, MA, Intercultural, 2011).

[41] de Tocqueville, *Democracy in America*, vol 2 (n 32) 4.

intellectual'. They rapidly ditch the old and familiar seeking instead the new and gratifying.[42] Jeremy Rifkin identifies this character as a stark contrast to a European one. Americans, he says, associate success with shaking off old formats and practices. Europeans find it in preserving them.[43]

In this light, American liberty may be construed as liberty from past creeds and dogmatism. But such a statement fails to explain the fact that America is a very religious country.[44] According to recent empirical polls conducted by the World Values Survey, the majority of responding Americans believe in God and perceive Him important in their lives. About two-thirds define themselves as religious, pray on a daily or weekly basis and have confidence in churches. And more than third are active members of a church or religious organisation.[45] Furthermore, the official motto of the county is America's trust in God. A similar assertion is borne by its currency. American politics is pervaded with religious language notably 'Manichaeism' of 'good' versus 'evil'.[46]

This condition is ostensibly paradoxical. A culture which admires human reason and refutes the unintelligible is not expected to embrace religious creeds and metaphysical convictions.[47] Denis Lacorne unties this logical knot. He argues that two forces compete for America's soul. One is secular and seeks political disentanglement from religiosity and traditional creeds. The other is profoundly religious. It descends from Puritan convictions and has its roots in the Protestant Reformation.[48] This contemporary account corresponds, though imperfectly, to de Tocqueville's nineteenth century one. According to de Tocqueville, two cultural spirits can be discerned in American culture: a 'spirit of liberty' which calls, essentially, for democratic ideals and a 'spirit of religion' which is largely dogmatic and Protestant. Compared with France's condition, de Tocqueville notes that while France's equivalent spirits are hostile, American ones work jointly to achieve worldly and spiritual gains.[49]

This cultural dichotomy nurtures a unique attitude to money and wealth. Money, says Lewis Lapham, is ambivalently perceived in America. On the one hand, it is only 'a commodity (as drab as wood, or straw or cloth)' in an ethical communitarian country. On the other hand, it is a

[42] P O'Toole, *Money and Morals in America: A History* (New York, Clarkson Potter, 1998) xviii.

[43] Rifkin (n 26) location 280.

[44] D Lacorne, *Religion in America: A Political History*, trans George Holoch, Kindle edn (New York, Columbia University Press, 2011) location 144.

[45] World Values Survey Wave 6 2010–2014, available at: www.worldvaluessurvey.org/ WVSOnline.jsp; Campbell and Kean (n 5) 114; Datesman, Crandell and Kearny (n 5) 52.

[46] Lacorne (n 44) locations 143–44, 152; Rifkin (n 26) location 497.

[47] de Tocqueville, *Democracy in America*, vol 2 (n 32) 8.

[48] Lacorne (n 44) locations 101, 169, 174–79.

[49] de Tocqueville, *Democracy in America*, vol 1 (n 30) 8, 23, 38, 255.

'sacrament' in a perpetual pursuit of economic gain and personal progress. These conflicting attitudes produce constant tension. To reach a stable condition, income must adhere to ethical prescriptions. Money that is rightfully earned, notably by toil and talent, is highly respected. It enjoys a semi-sacred position in the heart of Americans. American wealth, stresses Lapham, is not only about fast vehicles, luxurious residences and trendy garments, it is about the revered position of money in the American mind and money's capability to transfigure lives.[50]

If Eastern tales invented Aladdin's magic lamp for climbing up the social ladder, America mythologised money to that end.[51] American culture narrated effective tales of 'rags to riches', of the 'self-made man' who casts off poverty and rises to wealth by unceasing action.[52] These tales pervaded America's culture industry. A notable example is *The Pursuit of Happyness* (intentionally misspelled). The film is a biographical drama based on Chris Gardner's memoir of his struggle with homelessness. Starring famous actor Will Smith, the film tells the story of Chris Gardner, a black middle-aged father who falls into extreme poverty and is forced to leave his rented apartment along with his five-year-old child. The two subsequently face a cruel life of penury and homelessness. Infused with a boundless motivation to 'fight back', Chris struggles his way up as an unpaid intern stockbroker for a respected firm and is eventually accepted for a paid job. The film powerfully portrays the so-called 'American Dream' as well as the issue of equal opportunity. Everyone can make it in America (including Chris who is Afro-American) if one is willing to try hard.

In her critical book, *Facing Up to the American Dream*, Jennifer Hochschild describes the American Dream as the 'central ideology' of America. It is not only about one's entitlement to be wealthy, but also about equal opportunity for all to materialise this privilege if they decide to do so.[53] Hochschild cites President Bill Clinton's 1993 speech before the Democratic Leadership Council as reflective of these convictions. Clinton assured Americans that if they 'work hard and play by the rules', they 'should be given a chance to go as far as' their 'God-given ability'. The American Dream promises a better life for anyone willing to engage in constant action to upgrade it. Hochschild, however, contests this promise on account of socio-ethnic barriers. She identifies the tacit

---

[50] L Lapham, *Money and Class in America: Notes and Observations on Our Civil Religion* (New York, Weidenfeld & Nicolson, 1988) 4–5, 217.

[51] N Aldrich, *Old Money: The Mythology of Wealth in America* (New York, Allworth, 1996) xiii.

[52] Gray (n 3) location 13289.

[53] J Hochschild, *Facing Up to the American Dream* (New Jersey, NJ, Princeton University Press, 1996) xvii.

'weakness' of the Dream. It lies in the 'epistemological choice' made with it. Individualistic and action-focused, the promise prioritises individuals' actions and ignores implicit social and political constraints that delimit its applicability.[54] Hochschild's account reaffirms the repeated observation that the American perception of wealth and achievement is largely an issue of perpetual action.

Action in American perception is the answer to any aspiration or need. This pragmatic attitude forges an occupation-focused population with high intra-mobility. In principle, any person can become who she wants if she strives hard and takes action. In an action-centred society, money ranks higher than property.[55] Money is mutable. It can take all forms and can remedy nearly all needs. It evades geographical and financial fixity providing the best means for individuals who are constantly in motion. If castles and churches are the materials with which Europe is built, money, notes Lapham, is the fabric of America. While societies around the world came to venerate different ideals such as kinship, honour, spirituality, or social status, America idealises that which dominates societies placing money in a semi-religious position. Lapham criticises this condition and, what he deems, America's spiritual commitment to money, accusing it of causing various ills such as criminality, economic dearth and immorality.[56] Interestingly, while polls suggest that most Americans believe avarice is a 'sin against God', they also mark Americans' strong affection for money and their warm approval of a passionate pursuit of wealth.[57]

Money in America's cultural perception deliberates humans from chains of servitude and bondage. It promises to bring a person to a state of ideal happiness[58] submersing her in all sorts of material gratifications and worldly excitements. In fact, money morphs social ties into reason-based ones. It replaces 'personal bonds with calculative instrumental ties' when it dominates the fabric of society. Money standardises social relationship and makes it both measurable and fungible.[59] Marriage is an agreement or partnership, parents are care providers and friendship can be mass-produced, or so America's culture concludes. In a deeply individualistic society, money works as a 'talisman' says Kenneth Doyle. It safeguards a person from her worries and fears of being left alone.[60]

---

[54]   ibid 18, 36.
[55]   McElroy (n 9) 64.
[56]   Lapham (n 50) 78–81, 83, 86, 200–01, 214–16, 242–43.
[57]   R Wuthnow, *God and Mammon in America* (New York, Free Press, 1994) 125–26.
[58]   ibid 134.
[59]   V Zelizer, *The Social Meaning of Money* (New Jersey, NJ, Princeton University Press, 1997) 2, 3, 6.
[60]   See generally K Doyle, *The Social Meanings of Money and Property: In Search of a Talisman* (Thousand Oaks, CA, Sage, 1999).

Material gain is integral to America's founding stage. At the time, Americans as a nation of 'action and achievements' were profoundly influenced by ideas of Enlightenment philosopher John Locke.[61] Locke argued that each person had a 'natural right' to own a thing, if she puts an effort into acquiring it. The legitimacy of this claim lies not in human-made laws but in the natural condition of scarce resources and an innate human inclination to survive.[62] According to Locke, a person's body is her property. The labour of her hands is justly hers. If she 'mixes' labour with a given object, that object rightfully becomes her own.[63] America's early attitudes to wealth were engrained with this theory. 'Americans' notes Carl Becker, 'absorbed Locke's work as a kind of political gospel'.[64] It inspired America's revolutionary war and was clearly expressed in its Declaration of Independence.[65]

In that era, Americans' settlement project was expanding west against a wild frontier. The settlers unceasingly seized new territories part unoccupied and part inhabited by native Americans. These invasions brought vast land spaces under the settlers' control and Locke's treatises provided an excellent apology for their sovereignty claims. As long as the settlers applied time, money and effort cultivating and adapting natural resources to their needs, they were able to utilise Locke's theory of property-as-invested-labour to justify their dominion and acquired right to soil.[66] Remarkably, while the French Revolution passionately supported the right to property and declared it a basic right of man,[67] America's Declaration of Independence did not take a similar stand and wilfully omitted the right to property.

Plausible explanations for this omission may be historical such as native Americans' controversial entitlement to land or human slavery. Peter Garnsey, however, suggests another cogent explanation. Following Jean-Jacques Burlamaqui's distinction between innate rights and procured rights, Garnsey argues that the right to property was of the second type

---

[61] M Foley, *American Credo: The Place of Ideas in US Politics* (New York, Oxford University Press, 2007) 57.

[62] P Garnsey, *Thinking about Property: From Antiquity to the Age of Revolution* (Cambridge, Cambridge University Press, 2007) 142–43.

[63] J Locke, *Two Treatises of Government* (Cambridge, Cambridge University Press, 1988) 287–88.

[64] C Becker, *The Declaration of Independence: A Study in the History of Political Ideas* (New York, Peter Smith, 1933) 27 cited in M Foley, *American Credo: The Place of Ideas in US Politics* (New York, Oxford University Press, 2007) 59.

[65] Agassi (n 29) 9.

[66] See generally B Arneil, *John Locke and America: The Defence of English Colonialism* (Oxford, Clarendon Press, 1996); Foley (n 61) 57–59.

[67] *Déclaration des droits de l'homme et du citoyen*, 1789, Arts 2, 17, available at: www.textes.justice.gouv.fr/textes-fondamentaux-10086/droits-de-lhomme-et-libertes-fondamentales-10087/declaration-des-droits-de-lhomme-et-du-citoyen-de-1789-10116.html.

and thus alien to a declaration of natural rights. Basically, an innate right is enjoyed regardless of any human action. A procured right, on the other hand, is enjoyed only after some human attainment process such as labour or legislative act. And since property right was traditionally tied to human action, it was not regarded an innate right and was wilfully omitted from the Declaration.[68]

Puritans attained wealth on the bases of *vacuum domicilium* (uncultivated land). They claimed ownership of supposedly unpossessed natural resources on the merits of utilising them. But their labour was not driven by selfish interests. In fact, material indulgences were harshly condemned at the time. Hard work was meant to serve a higher goal. It was a Christian ethic for God-fearing pioneers. It signified each person's faith and praise for God. Work was a sign of health and grace bestowed by the Heavens. Idleness, in contrast, was socially and spiritually degrading. Economic gain was subject to religious bans and moral prescriptions. Deceptive trade, illicit profit-making, exploiting others' belongings and economic misconduct were all denounced and punishable by colony laws. According to Patricia O'Toole, a Puritan had to subordinate her own interest to that of others.[69] An enrichment wrongfully attained was perceived a serious challenge both to one's call for spiritual devotion and to one's responsibility to care for her community's ongoing survival project.

These Puritan values persisted in America's revolution era. In fact, toil was a mark of revolt against the British monarchy and conventions. It challenged English socio-political traditions which exalted aristocracy, titles and leisure practices. Through ethical and hard labour, any person could prove his self-value and be considered for the highest positions in society. Work as an empowering trait was a direct debunk to former British codes which reserved governing positions to the upper social classes. In American eyes, diligent and honest work could turn copper into gold. Factually, it facilitated the invalidation of former royal and noble titles offering, instead, equal standing for all citizens. A person's wealth was not what she owned but what she produced. 'Property' writes Applebaum 'became associated less with the authority of its possessor and more with the labor that produced and improved it'.[70]

In their comparative study of tales, Mohan Dutta-Berman and Kenneth Doyle describe the British conception of wealth as mostly possession-focused. Wealth in British eyes, had the power to convert a person, rather than the other way around. In *Timon of Athens*, Shakespeare reflects this attitude. 'Gold? Yellow, glittering, precious gold?' Timon says, 'Thus

---

[68] Garnsey (n 62) 222–25.
[69] O'Toole (n 42) 5, 10–13.
[70] Applebaum (n 20) 51, 52, 55.

much of this, will make black white; foul, fair; wrong right; base noble; old young; coward valiant'. British tales, explain Dutta-Berman and Doyle, focus on 'the metamorphoses introduced into the lives of the protagonist by the power of wealth'. Once possessed, wealth is the 'central element in British thought'. It is a venerable force mostly detached from its form of procurement. Daniel Defoe's novel *Roxana* is a good example of this trait. Roxana attained wealth by prostitution. As a rich lady, however, she was able to liberate herself from many patriarchal chains of traditional society. 'Wealth' notes Dutta-Berman and Doyle, 'can change the life of the user, irrespective of the act that produces it'. 'Action' they stress, is 'separated from the outcome' in British culture.[71]

This perception may be fruitfully contrasted with the American. Though both cultures venerate labour to various extents, American culture traces the converting force in each American's determination to work hard and prove herself and not in wealth itself. American wealth is hardly detachable from the actions which produced it. Benjamin Franklin reminds his readers 'that time is money'. Idleness does not make money it squanders it and money brings more money. But he stresses that the 'way to wealth' depends 'chiefly' on one's own 'industry'. Like Franklin, later American leaders continued to stress the work ethic and to urge meticulous compliance with Christian ideals such as honesty, truth and equity in one's commerce and dealings.[72] Action was deeply esteemed in America, it even denied women the entitlement to inherit farms fearing the lands 'would lie fallow if there were no hands' to till them.[73]

Unlike American culture, British culture did not commend work categorically. Applebaum notes, for example, that Samuel Johnson's *Dictionary of the English Language* (1755) defined 'mechanic' as 'servile, of mean occupation'. This English attitude persisted also in the nineteenth century with the *Oxford English Dictionary* (1881) describing 'mechanic' as 'belonging to or characteristic of the lower orders; base, coarse, vulgar'. American blue-collar workers challenged these convictions. Their leaders continuously asserted that human beings were, by nature, working creatures. The slothfulness and indolence of the noble class were 'unnatural' habits that must be avoided at all cost. In fact, nobility as practised by the British removed its members from the public making them ignorant of daily life challenges, hence, ineligible to fulfil any representational or political role.[74]

---

[71] Both examples are cited in M Dutta-Bergman and K Doyle, 'Money and Meaning in India and Great Britain: Tales of Similarities and Differences' (2001) 45 *American Behavioral Scientist* 205, 207, 220–21.

[72] D Leeming and J Page, *Myths, Legends, and Folktales of America: An Anthology* (Oxford, Oxford University Press, 1999) 36–38.

[73] O'Toole (n 42) 29.

[74] Applebaum (n 20) 51–55. Both dictionaries are cited there.

These attitudes were carried well into nineteenth-century America. Toil and action continued to be the dominant track to wealth and self-realisation in American culture. De Tocqueville describes Americans of that era as 'actively in motion' steadily pursuing greatness or wealth.[75] In a similar vein, Francis Grund, noted that 'business' and 'active occupation' were passionately performed by Americans back then. Action seemed to offer them joy, self-worth and distinction.[76] For de Tocqueville it was a condition he called 'indefinite perfectibility'. A European's fate, he argued, was conceived, predestined and bound by one's social stratum and place. Americans, however, perpetually sought social equality. Each person's socio-economic condition was not fixed but tied to her own actions. And action could change one's fate. In this sense, 'ideal perfection', notes de Tocqueville, has been set as a goal to be pursued by the constant refining of one's life conditions.[77]

According to this world-view, idleness was not the antithesis of work, but that of morals and religion. It was an anti-social behaviour which predicted negative characters of a person. Examining Seymour Norton's fable 'Ten Men of Money Island' (1879), Daniel Rodgers notes that the idle person of the time was perceived as unprincipled and deceitful. He was a 'villain' acting wrongfully and inappropriately. He did not earn his living by the sweat of his brow but tried to reap what others laboured. He created 'interest, mortgages, securities, and currency contraction'. He lived as a 'tax collector' and as 'parasite' on other's earned money. He is described as the 'corruptor' and 'thief' who sought 'ill fortune' and lived on others' backs. Idleness, thus, was not an issue of inaction but of wrongful action. An idle person was not conceived only as work-shy, but more as an inherently exploiting person with socially and morally disgraceful actions.[78]

Rodgers suggests the notion of 'usefulness' to understand Americans' nineteenth-century perception of wealth. According to Rodgers, Puritan perception stressed one's vocational call to glorify God through one's labour and the 'moral superiority' of toil and earned money over slothfulness and ill-profit.[79] This perception, says Rodgers, has not perished in nineteenth-century America but morphed into the idea of 'usefulness'. A person is expected to be 'useful'. Her usefulness is not measured by reference to her own interests but more so to the good of society as a

---

[75] de Tocqueville, *Democracy in America*, vol 2 (n 32) Location 33.

[76] F Grund, *The Americans in their Moral, Social, and Political Relations*, vol II (London, Longman and Company, 1837) 1–2. Brought to attention by D Rodgers, *The Work Ethic in Industrial America, 1850–1920* (Chicago, University of Chicago Press, 1979) 5, 6. For an artistic depiction of this spirit, see Louise Emerson Rönnebeck's painting, *The Harvest* (1940).

[77] de Tocqueville, *Democracy in America*, vol 2 (n 32) 26–27.

[78] Rodgers (n 76) 210–11, 215, 219.

[79] Applebaum (n 20) x–xi.

whole. A person should contribute her output to the aggregated good of all individuals in society.[80] This is an expected attitude in an era filled with transforming discoveries and inventions, like electric light and machinery, made by individual persons to the benefit of others.[81] In cultural terms, the notion of usefulness sharpened its binary opposite in the American mind. It placed wrong and harmful conduct to others as the conceptual contrast to that of gain through toil. Thus, while wealth attained by useful conduct was highly praised,[82] accumulating wealth through wrong to others was the unacceptable opposite.

This perceptual dichotomy between gaining by benefiting another and gaining by a wrong to another bore continuing significance on America's later perceptions of wealth. America of the twentieth century witnessed fast and powerful technologies which replaced post-industrial machines. It also marked the steady growth in mass production and many revisions of labour practices. The new era had increasing faith in technology and its capability to replace human hands. These transformations beg the question whether personal action and hard work are still perceived in America as the dominant route to wealth.[83] According to Kevin Smith and Lorene Stone, in spite of these developments one's financial condition continues to be perceived as a direct outcome of one's effort and personal action. Traits such as labour, self-motivation and risk-taking are still perceived the ultimate and chief cause of wealth in America.[84]

According to Joan Huber and William Form, the 'dominant stratification ideology' in America is that society offers individuals many chances to prosper if they are willing to grasp them. It generously recompenses hard workers and punishes idle hands with penury.[85] According to James Kluegel and Eliot Smith, on an empirical level, most Americans adhere to this ideology. Americans, they note, embrace a logic called the 'logic of opportunity syllogism' which holds that opportunity 'for economic achievement based on hard work is plentiful'. Determination and persistence guarantee economic success and personal realisation. And every individual is liable to her destiny and social stratum.[86]

---

[80] Rodgers (n 76) xi, 9–10, 17.
[81] Applebaum (n 20) 63–64.
[82] See also McElroy (n 9) 157 arguing that 'Americans enculturated the belief *Every Person's Success Improves Society*'.
[83] Applebaum (n 20) 131–38.
[84] K Smith and L Stone, 'Rags, Riches and Bootstraps: Beliefs about the Causes of Wealth and Poverty' (1989) 30(1) *Sociological Quarterly* 93, 94.
[85] J Huber and W Form, *Income and Ideology: An Analysis of the American Political Formula* (New York, Free Press, 1973) 6 cited in Smith and Stone, ibid.
[86] J Kluegel and E Smith, *Beliefs About Inequality: Americans' Views of What Is and What Ought to Be* (New Jersey, NJ, Transaction Books, 2009) 5, 7, 23.

Samuel Huntington accentuated a similar idea in his 'American creed'. According to Huntington, contemporary American creed embodies certain republic ideals immersed in the national character, ideals like 'liberty', 'equality', 'individualism' and 'representative government'. This creed descended from an early American culture which stressed ideals like '*Sola scriptura*' (scripture alone), 'moralism' and 'liberalism'. The creed promotes a non-hierarchic form of governance and a personal liability to one's life condition.[87] Huntington's creed successfully exemplifies an eclectic and anti-reductive review of American core ideals which at times complement and at others compete to provide the observer with a better clue of what it is to be American.

In similar vein, Robert Bellah, Richard Madsen, William Sullivan, Ann Swidler and Steven Tipton identify four competing cultures in America. The first is a 'Biblical' culture which asserts the religious foundation of the nation and its ethical convictions. The second is a 'Republican' culture which is committed to constitutional values notably freedom and equal rights. The third is 'Expressive Individualism' which advocates autonomy and self-sustenance urging personal progress and self-realisation. The fourth is 'Utilitarianism' which solicits functionality and 'usefulness' in a person's life.[88] Connectedly, Kornhauser proposes a descriptive model she terms 'moral economic individualism' to recount America's complex attitude to wealth accumulation. The model stresses three drivers of that attitude. The first is an individualistic one which urges economic gain asserting each person's entitlement to the fruit of her work. The second is a republican drive which advocates 'equality' on multifarious levels stressing personal effort over heritage. The two former drives complement a third religious one which calls to live a pious life and to glorify the Divine through personal toil.[89]

The former account casts a harmonious synthesis of the different drives. Robert Wuthnow, however, questions the claimed cordiality of economic individualism and religiosity. Stressing the 'impossibility of serving God and Mammon' concurrently, Wuthnow examines the inner dynamics between the two drives pondering whether Americans indeed succeeded in reconciling spirituality with the pursuit of money. One possible answer, he argues, maintains an irreconcilable tension between the two attitudes with one drive simply prevailing. Another possibility miraculously unites the perceptions within a baffling harmony. A third possibility

---

[87] S Huntington, *Who Are We?: The Challenges to America's National Identity* (New York, Simon & Schuster, 2004) 41, 68.

[88] R Bellah, R Madsen and W Sullivan et al, *Habits of the Heart: Individualism and Commitment in American Life* (Berkeley, CA, University of California Press, 1996) viii–xi, 28–35.

[89] Kornhauser (n 22) 124–31.

perceives religiosity as motivating 'in some subtle way to amass worldly riches'. The fourth possibility diminishes religiosity to a state where it seldom enters the 'conscience when pocketbook issues are at stake'.[90]

According to Wuthnow, religiosity continues to have a great impact on an individual's careerist and financial choices, but it lacks the capacity to turn economic considerations upside down. Profit-making decisions continue to be reached, putting religion on temporary suspension. In a somewhat prescriptive tone, Wuthnow concludes that 'work and money are too central' for Americans 'to be divorced from values and assumption' of religious convictions.[91] His conclusion could be placed somewhere between the first two forms of dynamics identified earlier. Another conclusion which could be aligned with Wuthnow's third possibility is Max Weber's famous theory of the Protestant work ethic as a drive to capitalism.

Weber studies the impact of Protestantism on America's work ethic. He argues that America's distinctive commitment to work has been motivated by religious faith, notably Calvinist doctrine. According to this doctrine, a person's fate in the afterlife, though concealed and predetermined, could be disclosed to her by industrious pursuit of a worldly 'calling' (*berufsmäßig*). The implicit assumption is that a person will be rewarded on Earth if she obediently pursues an earthly vocation and perpetually accumulates wealth. This religiously rooted motivation is described by Weber as the 'spirit' of capitalism, which 'strives systematically for profit for its own sake'. It eventually works to create a more 'secular and materialistic culture' in America.[92]

Weber's thesis generated many critiques, with some contesting the very core of its arguments.[93] On a theological front, for instance, the thesis was accused of 'dogmatic' errors. 'Pastoral literature', it was argued, denounced the earthly pursuit of wealth[94] noting that 'it is easier for a camel to go through the eye of a needle, than for a rich man to enter into the kingdom of God'.[95] Calvinist doctrine urged 'spiritual' labour not a worldly one to attain salvation.[96] Weber counter-argued that Calvinist self-denial dogma denounced the greedy pursuit of money or putting

---

[90] Wuthnow (n 57) 2–7.

[91] ibid 9.

[92] Weber (n 19) ix–xxxi, 19.

[93] See, eg, M MacKinnon, 'The Longevity of the Thesis: A Critique of the Critics' in H Lehmann and G Roth (eds), *Weber's Protestant Ethic: Origins, Evidence, Contexts* (Cambridge, Cambridge University Press, 1995) 211; G Marshall, *In Search of the Spirit of Capitalism: An Essay on Max Weber's Protestant Ethic Thesis* (London, Hutchinson, 1982).

[94] ibid 212 (MacKinnon).

[95] Matthew 19:24.

[96] MacKinnon (n 93) 212.

wealth as an end in itself, not the pursuit of wealth per se. In fact, it placed persistence in a worldly vocation as perceptible 'proof' of divine grace and the best 'ascetic path' to salvation.[97]

On a historical front, the thesis was deemed reductive and fallacious most notably by Felix Rachfahl. Rachfahl argued that the 'spirit of capitalism' predated the Protestant Reformation and had much more powerful drives than religious ones. 'Power', 'honour' and 'financial stability' comprised more important routes to capitalism. On an 'empirical' basis, religiosity played an insignificant role in 'developed' economic countries of the era, like the Netherlands. The latter boosted capitalism before the Reformation. At the time, America only had a modest agricultural economy. Furthermore, the call to comply with religious values in economic decisions is infused also in 'Roman Catholic' doctrine but equal results were not observed in countries embracing 'Catholicism'. For Rachfahl, it was not the Protestant ethic which lead to proto-capitalism but Protestant open-mindeness towards 'new forms' of economic and societal practices which cleared traditional constraints to the capitalist project.[98]

Weber was not fond of these arguments to say the least. He argued that Catholic doctrine sustained a fierce tension between Catholic values and profit-seeking. The religious obligation to make restitution of money acquired by 'usury' is an example of this tension. The fate of the Humiliati order which intermingled religious ideals with commercial and materialistic practices is another example. While Catholicism imposed monastic life on those who pursued asceticism, Protestantism managed to reconcile religiosity with profit-seeking making one a proof and a drive to the other. Weber also argued that his thesis did not dismiss the role of personal motives in the pursuit of profit, noting that his research focused on the collective inclinations of American society at its developing stage. He added that the thesis did not attempt to expound the drives for capitalism on a global scale and wherever capitalist markets were present.[99]

On an economic front, the thesis was criticised for ignoring economic structures, like banks and finance systems, which had a decisive role in rationalising the process of money making. Critics argued that it was the developing economic systems and financial practices which boosted capitalism and not some religious doctrine. Weber replied to this criticism noting that economic and other material strands could not give rise to a 'spirit of capitalism'. Though they were essential for the maturation of

---

[97] Weber (n 19) 116–17.
[98] W Davis, '"Anticritical Last Word on The Spirit of Capitalism", by Max Weber' (1978) 83(5) *American Journal of Sociology* 1105, 1106–08; MacKinnon (n 93) 223–24.
[99] Weber (n 19) 261–62, 264, 269, 270, 290–91, 301, 303.

'capitalism', they were incapable of generating the cognitive and psychological dimensions involved.[100]

Irrespective of the actual dynamics which correlated religiosity with Americans' systematic pursuit of profit, it is evident that themes of hard work and religious values remain indispensable to any sensible analysis of America's wealth perceptions. Furthermore, even with the arguable absence of religious drives, money-making continues to be a morally shaped process. Michèle Lamont, for example, asserts that morality is a visible factor in America's workplace. It sets proper codes of conduct urging 'honesty, work ethic, personal integrity, and consideration for others'. From numerous interviews that she conducts, Lamont learns that people who defy these ethical codes are degradingly perceived as 'dishonest', 'phonies', social climbers' and having 'low-morals' among colleagues and friends.[101] Thus, values, whether religious or secular, are indispensable to America's perception of wealth.

These values have been pragmatically framed by what John McElroy called the 'law of right and wrong'. According to McElroy, since an early stage, America's culture has sustained the belief that 'there is a right and wrong' in every step of life a person takes and that 'the rightness or wrongness of an action will be revealed in its results'. For this reason, Americans are prone to read and interpret their daily life experience in terms of a binary 'right or wrong' perception.[102] Empirical polls conducted by the World Values Survey confirm this tendency. According to periodical surveys, American participants scored saliently higher that their European peers as far as their belief that there are 'clear guidelines about what is good and evil'. European nationals, on the other hand, tended to perceive 'good and evil' as mostly dependent on 'circumstances'.[103]

According to Jeremy Rifkin, Americans are predisposed to perceive world events as an endless 'battleground' between 'good and evil forces'. This dualistic view, he notes, is exemplified in many White House addresses to the American public. Thus, a decision to declare war, for example, is presented as 'a struggle of good against evil'. War against terror is a 'great crusade' and totalitarian regimes are the 'axis of evil'.[104] This Manichaean view of life in which America is constantly in battle with evil forces can be explained by Americans' self-view as 'God's

---

[100] MacKinnon (n 93) 214.

[101] M Lamont, *Money, Morals, and Manners: The Culture of the French and American Upper-Middle Class* (Chicago, University of Chicago Press, 1994) 4, 25–27.

[102] McElroy (n 9) 120–22, 124.

[103] See World Values Survey Data analysis tool waves 1981–84, 1990–94, 1995–98, 1999–2004, 2005–09, 2010–14, available at: www.worldvaluessurvey.org/WVSOnline.jsp; Rifkin (n 26) location 437.

[104] ibid locations 436–53 (Rifkin).

Chosen People'. According to Neil Campbell and Alasdair Kean, America's actions have been tightly interpreted within a religious framework, making a strong cultural nexus between political and religious views.[105]

OBSERVING AMERICAN LAW AND CULTURE

In its account of restitution law, the Restatement Third mentions three proximate causes for the exclusion of asset-based remedies like ejectment, replevin and detinue. They are described as 'historical', 'theoretical' and 'practical' explanations.[106] It is perhaps possible to add a fourth explanation of a distal nature, 'culture'. Wealth accumulation in America's perception is primarily a money-centred process. While European law utilises a possession perception of wealth and seeks to restore unjustified possessions, American law is disinclined to take a similar stand. Money in American culture is superior to possessions. It is a '*magna carta* of personal freedom', to use Georg Simmel's words. It literately deliberates from the bond of law bestowing a 'right to buy oneself out of a personal obligation'.[107] In this sense, monetary restitution is far more *American* than asset-based restitution. It pays greater tribute to America's culture.

Though at their cores America and Europe are both arguably capitalist, it is fallacious to frame their socio-economic perceptions ignoring each one's cultural and historical context. Capitalism, says Joyce Appleby, is primarily a 'cultural system' immersed in the 'laws and customs' of the place. It is shaped by the distinctive traits of the people and their collective beliefs.[108] While Europe is prone to grasp wealth in terms of property, personal attachment and private sphere, America perceives wealth as personal effort, money and morals. Money and commerce, however, come second to private property in Europe. According to Clotaire Rapaille, 'many European cultures' have a distinctive 'view of money and its function'. 'If one earns a great deal of money', she 'simply settles back on the estate, leaving the world of commerce behind'.[109]

These perceptions left their clear mark on the laws addressing wrongful enrichment in each continent. At one end, European law is more static.

---

[105] Campbell and Kean (n 5) 117–18.
[106] ALI, *Restatement of the Law of Restitution and Unjust Enrichment*, vol I (Washington DC, American Law Institute, 2011) 6.
[107] G Simmel, *The Philosophy of Money* trans T Bottomore and D Frisby (London, Routledge, 2004) 286.
[108] J Appleby, *The Relentless Revolution: A History of Capitalism*, Kindle edn (New York, Norton, 2010) locations 341, 365, 457.
[109] C Rapaille, *The Culture Code: An Ingenious Way to Understand Why People Around the World Live and Buy as They Do* (New York, Broadway, 2007) 126.

It stresses the person–asset bond seeking justification for any disentanglement. In lack of justification, the law restores the original bond. It re-
enthrones the disadvantaged person back as lady of her private domain.
American law, at the other end, is more dynamic. It focuses on the active
pursuit of money. It abstains from halting the shift of wealth from one person to another unless a contaminating action is observed. In case of such
action, the law intervenes to rectify the wrongful behaviour.

Interestingly, the action exemplarity of American law presents a
dazzling affinity to American convictions of hard work. The pursuer of
gain and her actions are the prominent concerns of both law and culture.
It suffices to read the legal principle underlying disgorgement remedy
along with the American belief in the self-made person to see an intriguing connection. The first holds that no one should benefit from her own
wrong, the second provides that a person should benefit from her own
effort.[110] In this sense, law and culture jointly produce complementing
statements about Americans' socio-legal perception. At one end there
is hard work, at the other wrongful conduct. The first is cherished and
legal, the second is denounced and illegal. America, thus, cares for the
action involved. It puts on ethical glasses to read that action. A person
who gains through wrongful conduct, calls for restitution mainly as a
process of rectification.

'Cultural Manichaeism', or what McElroy called 'the law of right and
wrong', is apparent in the legal frames offered to grasp the action involved.
A gainful action can be either right or wrong. The second category of case
is penalised to different extents by the law. In the case of wilful action,
the law works to provide a disincentive for the illicit motive. The main
question of both American law and American culture is how the enriched
person has attained her gain. In contrast, the main question epitomising
the European doctrine, at least since the Renaissance, is what happened to
the disadvantaged person and her wealth. In America, the enriched person is the leading protagonist of the scene, in Europe it is her antagonist.
Though these observations are not necessarily conclusive of the American
condition, they illuminate notable affinities between American law and
culture which ought not to be dismissed. They also elucidate the mimetic
processes of law and culture, as noted in the European context.

---

[110] McElroy (n 9) 37, 48, 227.

6

Ottoman Law

THE GENESIS OF THE *MECELLE*

SOME YEARS FOLLOWING its publication, Victor Hugo's widely read novel *Les Misérables* (1862) was translated into Ottoman Turkish. It introduced a new genre of Western literature unfamiliar to Eastern readers. Up to that time, traditional folk tales such as *Kerem and Asli* or *Mecnun Leyla* which often narrated imaginary, somewhat inflated, love stories, were the most disseminated form of fiction.[1] The new novel along with many other novels of European origin, like *Robinson Crusoe* and *The Count of Monte Cristo*, rapidly captured the minds of Ottoman intellectuals who appealed to 'the possibility of introducing into Ottoman culture the modern Western values they admired'.[2] This, however, was not what Ali Şehbaz Efendi, a jurist and member of the Ottoman Court of Cassation (*Mahkeme-i Temyiz*) had in mind when he read the novel. Reminiscing, in many senses, Judge Richard Posner's *Law and Literature: A Misunderstood Relation* (1988),[3] Şehbaz Efendi wrote, back in the 1890s, what he thought literature, and Victor Hugo's *Les Misérables* more specifically, should not offer the law of the waning Empire.[4]

Şehbaz Efendi discussed governmental initiatives to embrace European codes into its legal system. He used Hugo's novel to exemplify what he understood as a stark dissimilarity between European society and an Eastern one. As noted by Avi Robin, Efendi utilised the miseries in the novel to assert what he perceived as Europeans' typical cold-heartedness standing in contrast to Easterners' warmth and kindness. While European mercilessness could afford a poor person begging for food and sympathy and be denied both, Easterners could hardly conceive such a scene. Their

---

[1] O Okay, 'al-Adab al-Turky fī 'ṣr al-Taghrīb' ('The Turkish Literature in the Westernisation Era') in E İhsanoğlu (ed), *al-Dawlah al-'uthmānyah: Tarīkh Waḥadārah* (*The Ottoman State: History and Civilization*) vol II, trans Ş Sa'dāwy (Cairo, Maktabat al-shurūq al-Dawlyah, 2010) 116.

[2] H İnci, 'novel', *Encyclopedia of the Ottoman Empire* (2009) 439.

[3] R Posner, *Law and Literature: A Misunderstood Relation* (Cambridge, MA, Harvard University Press, 1988).

[4] A Rubin, *Ottoman Nizamiye Courts: Law and Modernity* (New York, Palgrave Macmillan, 2009) 21–22, 164.

social solidarity and solicitousness are good enough pledges that no such incident occurs, so goes Efendi's argument.[5] Yet unlike other intellectuals who used such stereotypes to oppose legal transplantations, Efendi's aim was the opposite. As Rubin explains, Efendi treated these presumed differences as a given and then developed a formalistic approach to law. He advocated the idea that law is, and should be, an 'autonomous space in society' dictated by its own rubrics, irrespective of any perceivable social or cultural context. For this reason, adopting Western legal models was a viable option despite any cultural differences.[6]

Whether Efendi's position was compatible with the Empire's aspiration for modernisation and administrative reform or not, it definitely reflected the ongoing debate on the proper measures to be taken to that end. The Ottoman aspiration for social progression (or perhaps Westernisation)[7] began to consolidate in the reign of Sultan Mahmud II (1808–39). Mahmud, who embraced an enlightened world view, took various steps to introduce a new administration capable of emulating the early modern countries of Europe. Perhaps the two most notable steps in this regard were the termination of the Yeniçeris order and the forming of the Porte. After a failed revolt and recurring war failures, Mahmud eradicated the centuries-old Ottoman soldiers known as the Yeniçeris order, instating instead modern troops which he had trained by European experts. And in an attempt to centralise his ruling powers and prevent further dissociation of Ottoman territories, he founded the Porte, the central executive government of the Empire.[8]

His break with traditional form of government reached a higher level as he meddled with the two most venerated positions in the Empire, the *Sadrazam* (sultan's vicar) and the *Seyhul-Islâm* (leader of Islam). He replaced the *Sadrazam* with 'a *başvekil'* (prime minister) and '*vekiller* (ministers)', the first a functionary of both the sultan and government, the second constituting the government itself. As to the *Seyhul-Islâm*, the highest authority of Islam he was denied any governmental powers delimiting his office to head of *Şeriat* courts. In this respect, Mahmud matched the office of *Seyhul-Islâm* with the heads of the Christian and Jewish courts

---

[5] ibid.

[6] ibid 21–22, 164.

[7] O Okay 'Dirasah Awalyah 'n al-ḥayah al-Fikryah Khilāl 'hd al-Taghrīb' ('Initial Study of the Intellectual Life in the Westernisation Era') in E İhsanoğlu (ed), *al-Dawlah al-'uthmānyah: Tarīkh Waḥadārah (The Ottoman State: History and Civilization)* vol II, trans Ṣ Saʻdāwy (Cairo, Maktabat al-shurūq al-Dawlyah, 2010) 267.

[8] N Berkes, *The Development of Secularism in Turkey* (London, Hurst & Company, 1998) 93, 97–98; K Beydilli, 'al-Dawlah al-uthmānyah min Mu'āhadat Qynarjah al-Ṣughrah ḥatta al-inhyār' ('The Ottoman State from the Treaty of Küçük Kaynarca Until the Collapse') in E İhsanoğlu (ed), *al-Dawlah al-'uthmānyah: Tarīkh Waḥadārah (The Ottoman State: History and Civilization)* vol I, trans Ṣ Saʻdāwy (Cairo, Maktabat al-shurūq al-Dawlyah, 2010) 97–100.

which basically enjoyed legal jurisdiction confined to religious, personal and familial issues of their respective communities.[9]

These reformative measures did not only ignite a democratising process of governmental institutions, but more significantly they facilitated a new concept of 'justice (*adâlet*)', mostly alien to former traditions. While the former concept of '*adâlet*' meant giving 'each his due in the interests of order and stability' and in accordance with one's 'function or state in society', the new concept denoted equity and fairness for all, regardless of ethnicity, religion or social status. It inspired legal revisions as well as fresh interpretations of old norms. Niyazi Berkes expressed this legal reformation as a catalytic interplay between '*Şeriat*' (Islamic law), '*kanûn*' (Ruler's law) and '*adâlet*'. *Şeriat*, the code of conduct bestowed by God to regulate Muslims' earthly life, '*kanûn*' (Ruler's law), the sultan's decree in matters (mostly public law) that were not handled by '*Şeriat*' and derived from legislative powers of the '*Padişah*' (sultan), and *adâlet* the new concept of 'justice',[10] were three legal concepts which offered new administrative balances that aided in the transition towards a modern, more secular and more liberal society.

By the end of Mahmud's rule and the succession of Abdul-Mecid I (1839–61), a new initiative for systematic reformation was set forth. The initiative was issued as a Sultanic Edict by Abdul-Mecid under the official title '*Hatti Şerif of Gülhane*' ('Noble Edict of the Rose Chamber') of 1839. The Edict which was widely known as the Charter of *Tanzimat* (reorganisation)[11] or the 'Gülhane Charter', called for many administrative and legal reorganisations in the Ottoman Empire. For one thing, it announced the regularisation and standardisation of areas like tax collection and army service; for another and perhaps more significantly, it voiced its first strong commitment to each person's 'security', 'honour' and 'property' in the Empire.[12]

In retrospective examination, what proves most foundational is the Charter's official amalgamation of two, mostly irreconcilable, strands: a religious traditional one and a secular progressive one. On the one hand, the Charter asserts its full confidence in the divine *Şeriat* and the

[9] ibid 93, 97–98 (Berkes); ibid (Beydilli); M Abacherli, 'Nuẓum al-Dawlah al-'uthmānyah' ('Systems of the Ottoman State') in E İhsanoğlu (ed), *al-Dawlah al-'uthmānyah: Tārīkh Waḥadārah* (*The Ottoman State: History and Civilization*) vol I, trans Ṣ Saʻdāwy (Cairo, Maktabat al-shurūq al-Dawlyah, 2010) 150, 302–03; C Findley, *Bureaucratic Reform in the Ottoman Empire: The Sublime Porte, 1789–1922* (Princeton, NJ, Princeton University Press, 1980) 140–42.

[10] ibid 94–95 (Berkes); J Starr, Law as Metaphor: From Islamic Courts to the Palace of Justice (Albany, NY, State University of New York, 1992) 21.

[11] ibid 144–45 (Berkes).

[12] E Creasy and J von Hammer-Purgstall, *History of the Ottoman Turks: From the Beginning of Their Empire to the Present Time*, vol II (London, Richard Bentley, 1856) 452–55.

honoured *kanûn* as an attested source of 'strength', 'greatness' and 'pros-perity' for the Empire and its subjects. On the other, it states that a 'succes-sion of incidents and various causes' have eroded the observance of the law, and calls for introducing a new (chiefly modern) discourse of 'equal-ity', 'liberty', 'progress' and 'welfare' if genuine socio-political changes are to be achieved. These two forces, history tells, would continue to compete for primacy in the political, economic and societal agendas of the Empire for quite a long time.[13]

At the time, the Charter signified a growing empowerment of the rational and worldly vis-à-vis the deep-rooted customary and sacred. Factually, a corpus of administrative law which was systematically pro-duced by a legislative body had increasingly encroached on *Şeriat* domains. Many economic barriers, identified with former customs and traditions, such as levies, exclusive marketing privileges and exportation bans were eventually dropped, enabling free trade with Christian Europe. The Char-ter, says Berkes, 'opened the first formal breach between the "temporal" and the "religious"'.[14] This breach signifies an increasing inclination to break with former conventions. Nevertheless, it remains highly contro-versial whether these initiatives aimed at instating Western progressive ideals or in fact had other visions in mind.

Though articulated within a genuine Ottoman context, it could hardly be overlooked that the Charter rephrased many of the Western values endorsed by the French Declaration of human and civic rights (1789), values such as human dignity, the rule of law and private property.[15] This, however, had not convinced many observers of that era who devot-edly insisted that the *Tanzimat* Charter and its successive measures aimed at putting Ottoman institutions in their original state of Islamic purity, not at modernising those institutions in the European sense.[16]

In fact, a strong tone of the *Tanzimat* romanticised former triumphs and glories of the Empire asserting that closer observance of Islamic doctrine was the best way forward. This position was well expressed by French historian Abdolonyme Ubicini who wrote early as 1856 that the concept of *Tanzimat* 'does not denote, as has been erroneously supposed, a new order of things, but, on the contrary, a regeneration or return to the ancient sys-tem, into which abuses had crept, owing to lapse of time and the usurpation

---

[13] ibid.

[14] Berkes (n 8) 132–33, 138–39, 147.

[15] S Shaw and E Kural Shaw, *History of the Ottoman Empire and Modern Turkey: Reform, Revolution, and Republic—The Rise of Modern Turkey 1808–1975*, vol II (New York, Cambridge University Press, 1997) 61.

[16] F Bailey, *British Policy and the Turkish Reform Movement: A Study in Anglo-Turkish Rela-tions, 1826–1853* (Cambridge, MA, Harvard University Press, 1942) 199–200 cited in N Berkes, *The Development of Secularism in Turkey* (London, Hurst & Company, 1998) 148.

of power by the Janissaries'.[17] This position seems supported also by a central statement of the Charter itself which asserts that: 'As these present institutions are solely intended for the regeneration of religion, Government, the nation, and the Empire, we engage to do nothing which may be opposed to them'.[18] Whatever the actual vision was, Mehmet Âkif Aydin argues that the *Tanzimat* with its mixture of Ottoman and Western legal traditions produced a confused law which 'spoiled the authentic character of Ottoman rights' turning it 'to one badly sewed dress that is patched allover'.[19]

Following dissatisfaction with the slow implementation of the Gülhane Charter, a second and more elaborate initiative was made with the announcement of the Reform firman (*Islahat Fermani*) in 1856. The new firman which is phrased in a tender, almost fatherly tone, addresses the Empire's subjects with a highly tolerant and liberal content. It explicates the sultan's 'wish' to (literally) 'make' everyone 'happy', irrespective of any social properties or religious affiliations, for 'they', he says, 'are all equal in my eyes'. The firman explicitly abolishes any class differentiations and any official use of social 'distinctions'. It reassures its commitment to each person's 'security', 'property' and 'honour', and permits the free exercise of rites and religion.[20]

The firman drops the former ban on aliens to acquire and own lands in the Empire. It also confirms 'all privileges and immunities' bestowed on religious minorities, rearranges some of their monetary, institutional and administrative matters and enables them to form their own education schemes and institutions. It sets and rearranges taxation issues, army recruitment and employment, periodical budget, credit and banking systems, and public infrastructure maintenance. The firman also abolishes 'all ill-treatment and corporal punishment or torture', and calls for a law against corruption. It erects 'mixed courts' for cross-community litigation, and promises the publication of 'a commercial and criminal code' which will be translated 'into all the languages' used in the Empire.[21]

The new firman can be fruitfully compared to the American Declaration of Independence, with both promising 'happiness' for their subjects and appealing to many ideals like equality and justice boosted by Western

---

[17] A Ubicini, *Letters on Turkey: An Account of The Religious, Political, Social, and Commercial Condition of the Ottoman Empire, Part I: Turkey and the Turks*, trans L Easthope (London, John Murray, 1856) 27–28; ibid (Berkes).

[18] Creasy and von Hammer-Purgstall (n 12) 455.

[19] M Aydin, 'al-Nuẓ um al-Qānūnyya fī al-Dawlah al-'uthmānyah' ('Legal Systems in the Ottoman State') in E İhsanoğlu (ed), *al-Dawlah al-'uthmānyah: Tārīkh Waḥadārah* (*The Ottoman State: History and Civilization*) vol I, trans Ṣ Sa'dāwy (Cairo, Maktabat al-shurūq al-Dawlyah, 2010) 519.

[20] Creasy and von Hammer-Purgstall (n 12) 456–60.

[21] ibid.

Enlightenment thinkers. A closer examination, however, reveals major ideological differences between the two documents. While both rely on a higher source (eg, Creator, sultan) to bestow certain entitlements to the people, the American Declaration adopts a clear 'rights' terminology[22] (a rubric well fitted to a Western socio-political order and ideals) asserting the actuality of 'certain unalienable Rights' that 'Governments' need to 'secure'.[23] The Ottoman Edict does not do so. It chiefly refrains from a 'rights' terminology, utilising instead what may be called an 'assurances', 'privileges' and 'immunities' language.

For example, the Ottoman Edict assures that 'all religions can be exercised freely'; that 'the security of the lives, the property, and honour' of all subjects will 'be minutely observed'; that Christian and other communities' 'privileges and immunities' are 'confirmed'; that 'the movable and immovable goods of the clergy will not be touched'; that 'a community may celebrate publicly its religious ceremonies' and so on.[24] This terminology is far from accidental. It preserves the controlling power of the sultan, and relies on his constant will (and presence) to enforce these entitlements. In this sense, the Edict represents a sort of covenant between the sultan and his people. Without the sultan as the second party to this covenant, no entitlements could be bestowed on the people.

Conversely, the American document is a 'declaration' of entitlements. It does not depend on governments to bestow entitlements but only to 'secure' what is prima facie possessed by the people. This distinction is crucial and tenacious. While the Ottoman Edict outlines certain *specified* freedoms that may be exercised under the scrutinising eyes of the ruler (eg, religious freedom), the American Declaration secures an unalienable right to an unspecified all-embracing 'Liberty'. Consequently, Americans have a right 'to pursue Happiness' according to their best judgement. Ottomans, on the other hand, are promised 'Happiness' in accordance with their ruler's best discretion.

These differences underline a structural tension that persists in many *Tanzimat* measures which on the one hand seek reformative ends inspired by Western ideologies, and on the other, preserve a restraining power to any actual change in the hands of the ruler. What this means is that Western ideals such as liberty which are originally meant to be self-evident and self-boosted, are transplanted in the Ottoman context only after they are stripped of their autonomous and regenerating essence.

---

[22] *cf* W Hohfeld, 'Fundamental Legal Conceptions as Applied in Judicial Reasoning' (1913) 23 *Yale Law Journal* 16, 28–32, 32–38, 41–42, 44–46, 52–53, 54, 55, 58–59.

[23] American Congress, 'Declaration of Independence (July 4, 1776)' in P Henry, B Franklin and T Jefferson et al (eds), *15 Documents and Speeches That Built America*, Kindle edn, (Seattle, WA, Amazon Digital Services, 2011) locations 442–97.

[24] Creasy and von Hammer-Purgstall (n 12) 457–58.

This '*Ottomanisation*' process generates an inherent tension between what seems to be a liberal and progressive content and the actual conservative dynamics that such content has to go through to see the light of day.

A similar phenomenon can be observed in one of the most important achievements of the *Tanzimat* era: the Ottoman Civil Code. The Code, widely known as the *Mecelle* or in its full official title *Mecelle-i Ahkâm-i Adliye*, is considered 'the first attempt by any Islamic state to codify part of shariah'.[25] Following promulgation of several codes in other areas, for example, the Commercial Code of 1850 and Penal Code of 1858, which borrowed extensively from equivalent Napoleonic codes, ie, *Code de commerce 1807* (Commercial Code) and *Code penal de 1810* (Penal Code), the initiative to modernise the area of private law was put on the table.[26]

While former codifications deviated to various extents from *Şeriat*, the current initiative undermined its very role as the undisputed regulator of Islamic society. It openly challenged *Şeriat*, calling to substitute it with foreign legal wisdom. This calling generated a continued debate on the proper path to 'modernise' the important field of private law. One view led by Mehmed Kabulî Paşa, devotedly supported the application of the French *Code civil 1804* (Civil Code) and to that end a committee was formed and a big portion of the Code translated. Another view led by Ahmet Cevdet Paşa, a former Şeriat scholar and a government official, held that *fiqh* (Islamic jurisprudence) was the best suitable source for any modernisation attempt of civil law. Eventually Cevdet Paşa's view conquered and he was appointed to head a committee for this purpose.[27]

From 1869 to 1876, Cevdet Paşa's committee produced and promulgated 16 books of the *Mecelle* which built on Islamic Hanafi *fiqh*, the official school of the Empire,[28] in content and resonating French codification in form. Interestingly, both qualities of this document were challenged. At one level, it was argued that the *Mecelle* was not a *civil* code in the pure private law sense.[29] Indeed, the *Mecelle* compiled additional materials such as ethical standards for judges, evidence law, civil procedural law, commercial law and partnership law. At another level, it was argued that the *Mecelle* was not a *code* in the continental sense, but a 'nonconclusive digest of existing rules of Islamic law'.[30] Avi Rubin rejects this and

---

[25] 'Mecelle', *The Oxford Dictionary of Islam* (2003) 199 (*ODI*).

[26] Aydin (n 19) 516–19.

[27] Berkes (n 8) 160–68; Rubin (n 4) 28–30.

[28] S al-Qubbaj, *Majallat al-Aḥkam al-'dlyyah: Maṣāḍiraha wa-'tharaha fī Qwanīn al-Sharq* (*Ottoman Civil Code: Its Sources and Effect on the Laws of the Islamic East*) (Ammān, Alfatḥ, 2008) 40.

[29] ibid 192. For the argument that *Mecelle* was a civil code, see *ODI* (n 25).

[30] M Khadduri and H Liebensky (eds), *Law in the Middle East* (Washington DC, The Middle East Institute, 1955) 295–96 cited in A Rubin, *Ottoman Nizamiye Courts: Law and Modernity* (New York, Palgrave Macmillan, 2009) 30, 167.

other dichotomy-based accounts. He argues that 'either' a *Şeriat* 'or' a European code approach is inappropriate to describe the *Mecelle*. For him, the *Mecelle* is 'a hybrid legal artifact', consisting of Islamic law in substance, and European schemes of legal discretion in style. The latter, he argues, imposed new notable constraints on deep-rooted traditions of the judicial task.[31]

Without dipping into the deep waters of the Gluckman–Bohannan debate on the proper way to describe institutions in cross-cultural studies,[32] it seems more sensible not to impose a Western legal concept (ie, code) on a unique Ottoman artefact to avoid definition inaccuracies. On its own terms, *Mecelle* means a periodical journal containing certain wisdom and published at regular intervals, one issue following the other.[33] In their official report, Cevdet Paşa's committee confined the reasons for writing this work to five: (1) the secular courts' ignorance of the *Şeriat* (eg, *Nizamyie* and *Temyiz* courts) and the need to prevent parallel litigations; (2) the inaccessibility of *Şeriat* to the unversed; (3) the shortage of those knowledgeable enough in *Şeriat*; (4) the 'great troubles' stemming from the use of 'European laws which are not enacted according to a Sultanic decree and cannot be the pivot of adjudication in the Ottoman empire'; and (5) the change of times and needs.[34]

The committee described the work as 'a book in *fiḳh* affairs that is accurate, easy to utilise, free of controversies, containing selected dictums, easy for everyone to read', a book which is 'highly beneficial to all *Şeriat* judges, Nizamyie courts members and administrative officials' making them 'proficient and knowledgeable in Islamic Law' and 'capable of dealing with lawsuits according to the Holly Islamic Law', thus, sparing 'the need to enact law for civil lawsuits' brought before 'Nizamyie courts'.[35]

Taken at face value, it seems that the committee had no intention of modernising the law, and definitely no intention of 'Europeanising' it. While adaptive ends were expressed, the committee stated no plan to break with former traditions and no intent to treat the effects of modern themes such as secularity, science, technology, capitalism or gender.[36] The aims, as openly stated, were mostly conservative, pragmatic and pre-emptive. This, however, neither explains the great admiration with which scholars

---

[31] Rubin (n 4) 30–31.

[32] J Conley and W O'Barr, *Just Words: Law, Language and Power* (Chicago, IL, University of Chicago Press, 2005) 98–115.

[33] al-Qubbaj (n 28) 48.

[34] Translated from report preface (1868) by *Cevdet Paşa* committee as brought in S Baz, *Sharh al-Majallah* (*Commentary on the Ottoman Civil Code*) (Beirut, Dar al-'elm lel-Jamī', 1998) 7–12.

[35] ibid.

[36] C Butler, *Modernism: A Very Short Introduction* (Oxford, Oxford University Press, 2010) 1–2.

approached the *Mecelle*, nor their insistence on its innovative (some say, reformative) qualities.[37] In a critical assessment, it seems that the *Mecelle* indeed signified an important break with former traditions. To decode this break, however, it is vital to understand the adaptive dynamics of *Şeriat* and the different track eventually taken by the *Mecelle*.

Unlike the traditional conviction prompted by the system's dependence on a fixed scripture and unalterable commandments,[38] *Şeriat* is not a sealed legal corpos 'incapable of change'; on the contrary. Resting on what Joseph Schacht calls the 'analogical method', *Şeriat* (like *Halacha*, Jewish law) develops along 'doctrinal' and 'casuist' lines. Its evolution is founded on a constant interaction with life and its change rests on perpetual 'parataxis and association'. This characteristic eventually produces a more or less net-like (rather than 'pyramidal') shape of legal corpus, with 'interpretation' (instead of enactment) as its chief locomotive towards change and adaptation.[39]

The *Mecelle* largely deviated from this path, imitating instead the path of Roman law, Post-Trent Canon law and major systems of the continental law countries.[40] Schacht calls this path the 'analytical method'. In this method, the system opts for 'the creation of logically organized legal norms in an ascending order'. It relies on legislation as a key force for changing and adapting the system, producing a normative picture that is 'arranged according to a vertical hierarchical organization'. In these respects, the *Mecelle* changed the rules of the game, and the reason for that is not incomprehensible. It stems from the need to centralise authority and to voice this change very clearly. According to Silvio Ferrari, in a 'network' model of law, 'authority is distributed in various points of the system', whereas in a 'pyramidal' one 'authority is concentrated in one single point'.[41]

The *Mecelle* signified the presence of a single authority and a more rigid, better controlled, system. It allowed 'less room for unauthorized deviations', avoiding the interpretive open-endedness associated with the traditional form of *Şeriat*. The new path of the *Mecelle* preserved a more

---

[37] See, eg, N Feldman, *The Fall and Rise of the Islamic State*, Kindle edn (New Jersey, NJ, Princeton University Press, 2008) location 1274.

[38] S Ferrari, 'Adapting Divine Law to Change: The Experience of the Roman Catholic Church (with some reference to Jewish and Islamic Law)' (2006) 28(1) *Cardozo Law Review* 53, 53, 57, 64–65.

[39] ibid.

[40] For Islamic jurisprudence '*taqnīn*' method which restated *Şeriat* in a serial, thematic and ordered way, see al-Qubbaj (n 28) 23–28.

[41] J Schacht 'Law and the State: Islamic Religious Law' in J Schacht and C Bosworth (eds), *The Legacy of Islam* (Oxford, Clarendon Press, 1974) 392, 397 cited in Ferrari, 'Adapting Divine Law to Change' The Experience of the Roman Catholic Church (with some reference to Jewish and Islamic Law)' (2006) 28(1) *Cardozo Law Review* 53, 64; Ferrari (n 39) 64–65.

unified form of development that was able to keep track of all interpretive outputs.[42] This structural alteration preserves strong monitoring powers over any drive to renovate. It debilitated bottom-up paths to progression or societal regeneration, safeguarding instead the authority's role as chief pilot of any such initiatives. This intricacy ensured that the Empire's publicised intention to introduce (Western) modern values of independent self-boosted nature (eg, equality and justice) would not run amok.

THE OTTOMAN *MECELLE*

As a legal craft of the late Ottoman era, the *Mecelle* is a fascinating document. It vividly articulates Eastern legal thought as well as many of the people's social, cultural and economic practices. Written in Ottoman Turkish, it comprises of 1851 articles organised into 16 books. It opens with a definition of *fiḳh* (Islamic jurisprudence), the scientific study of law pertaining to life aspects ('matrimonial', 'dealings' and 'penal') and the afterlife ('worship') (Article 1). The gist of these aspects is revealed in subsequent Articles which set out 99 jurisprudential principles (Articles 2–100). These principles provide the postulates of the whole document as well as reflecting the life philosophy of the *Mecelle*. The principles are written in proverbial style with notable brevity and precision. A number of principles, for instance, comprise of no more than three words (eg, Articles 56, 69) and one comprises of just two (Article 36). This style illustrates some of the impressive phrasing skills practised by Ottoman jurists.[43]

This phenomenon, which stands on the tangent line of Sharia, literary talent and fine aesthetics is called '*al-Mutūn*'. It describes *fiqh* articulated in short and concise manner. Though beautifully written like poetry and effective for memorising purposes, *al-Mutūn* has been under attack for its obvious drawback. Mustafa al-Zarqa, a renown Sharia scholar, describes *al-Mutūn* as 'collecting all topics of knowledge in narrow articulations' which jurists 'race in brevity, till these articulations reach a point of deformation or enigmas'. He picturesquely equates it to putting 'a camel in a flask'.[44] On a general level, over-brevity could indeed lead to meaning distortions which jurists have to deal with. In the case of jurisprudential principles, however, this style could actually preserve qualities essential for

---

[42] N Asfour, 'Law and Literature: Jewish and Christian Models' (2012) 6(2) *Pólemos* 263, 276–77.

[43] Against: R Eisenman, *Islamic Law in Palestine and Israel: A History of the Survival of Tanzimat in the British Mandate and Jewish State* (Leiden, Brill, 1978) 24.

[44] M al-Zarqa, *al-Madkhal al-Fiqhī al-'ām* (*General Introduction to Fiqh*) (Damascus, Dar al-Kalam, 1998) 212.

proper functioning of any principle. Principles as normative guidelines should not be exhaustive. Instead, they are expected to maintain certain flexibility, thus better adaptation capacities.

On a substance level, the principles are distinctive also in their articulation of Ottoman life experience which generally opts for the constants of reality rather than the variants. In many senses, they depict traditional, conservative and anti-progressive philosophy. They explicitly prefer the fixed and permanent over the temporal and changing. According to this world-view, life is largely bound by circumstances that reside outside the control or will of man. Human action is not the norm of life. Human intervention in the world is perceived as wearying and at times even troublesome. Collectively examined, the principles recount what may be described as a submissive and reactive, rather than proactive, portrayal of man. For example, denoting a chiefly static picture of the world, the *Mecelle* states that the 'original condition' of things is that they remain as they are (Article 5). And what is considered 'old' shall be left that way (Article 6).[45] The underlying assumption of these two principles is that by default nothing is normally expected to be changed or achieved.

Another Article provides that the original state of utilities, generally referred to as 'passing qualities', is 'nothingness' (Article 9). Namely, unless shown otherwise no such qualities, like business profit, are deemed to be obtained or possessed. Furthermore, what has been proved by the passage of time shall be ordered to stay that way (Article 10).[46] This anti-progressive, passive and risk-aversive perception is reaffirmed in the submissive depiction of man as victim of his life circumstances. Thus, what is 'dropped' or 'gone' cannot be brought back (Article 51), and staying with a given condition of life or a thing is easier than changing it or 'beginning' anew (Article 56).[47]

The *Mecelle* warns of life variants and the desire to make a change. It states that the blessing of a thing equals its resentment (Article 88). Hence, man ought to be careful and perhaps think twice before reaping the benefits of a thing, as it may carry equal troubles for him. Man is warned of rushing things. Thus, he who hastens a thing before its due time is punished with its deprivation (Article 99). If man considers taking some action, then he should bar the 'corruptive' rather than seek to reap 'benefits' (Article 30). In similar context, and perhaps reminiscing

---

[45] Art 166 defines 'old' as that whom no one knows its beginning.

[46] For disciplinary elucidations of these principles see al-Zarqa (n 44) 982, 998.

[47] A Haider, *Durar al-Ḥukkam fī-Sharḥ Majallat al-Aḥkām* (*Perils of the Rulers Explaining the Ottoman Civil Code*) vol I, trans F El-husseini (Beirut, al-Nāsher Dar al-Kutub al-'ilmyyah, 1925) 20, 23, 24, 48–49, 51.

Şehbaz Efendi's portrayal of Easterners as merciful and compassionate,[48] the *Mecelle* provides that 'hardship' calls for facilitation (Article 17). When a case is burdensome, it is permissible and even essential to show care and consideration. In like manner, necessity and need permits the forbidden (Article 21). This, however, does not legitimate unexcused empathy. What is permissible for an 'excuse' is to be barred when the excuse passes (Article 23). Nevertheless, a person is generally trustworthy, thus, the origin of talk is 'truthfulness' (Article 12). A man's word is generally trusted unless there is a reason not to do so.[49]

Subsequent Articles mostly deal with different areas of private law. The first book deals with sales and contractual obligations (Articles 101–403). The second with leases (Articles 404–611). The third with guarantees (Articles 612–72). The fourth book treats debt assignment (Articles 673–700). The fifth covers mortgage (Articles 701–61). The sixth, deposits and trusts (Articles 762–832). The seventh book regulates gifts (Articles 833–80). The eighth treats usurpation and damage (Articles 881–940). The ninth treats guardianship, coercion and pre-emption (Articles 941–1044). The tenth, partnership (Articles 1045–1448). The eleventh deals with agency (Articles 1449–1530). The twelfth with compromise and discharge of obligations and debts (Articles 1531–71). The thirteenth book treats confession (Articles 1572–1612). The fourteenth covers suits and litigation (Articles 1613–75). The fifteenth, evidence and oath (Articles 1676–1783). And the last book treats adjudication, courts and judges (Articles 1784–1851).

Wrongful enrichment is dealt with in book eight and several complementing Articles throughout the *Mecelle* (eg, Articles 95, 472, 596). Like the German BGB, the *Mecelle* provides a general principle against unjustified enrichment which states that it is impermissible for one to take the *māl* (مال) (some economic value) belonging to another without a legitimate reason (*bilā sabab maṣrū'*, بلا سبب مشروع) (Article 97). Supplementary Articles provide that it is impermissible for one to exercise control over the property of another without the latter's permission (Article 96) and also that one's demand to take control of another's property is 'void' and invalid (Article 95). It is important to note that Articles 95 and 96 are not confined to enriching actions, but serve harmful ones as well. Thus, for example, slaughtering someone's sheep or setting his cloth on fire is prohibited and similarly, a demand to do so is void and ineffective.[50]

The *Mecelle* defines cases of *māl* appropriation and exploitation in terms of usurpation (*ġaṣb*, غصب). Article 881 defines *ġaṣb* as taking possession of

---

[48] Şehbaz Efendi, 'Usul-i Muhakeme-i Cezaiye' (Manuscript, 1896, Atatürk Library) cited in A Rubin, *Ottoman Nizamiye Courts: Law and Modernity* (New York, Palgrave Macmillan, 2009) 21–22, 164.

[49] Haider, vol I (n 47) 26–27, 31–35, 37, 79–80, 87.

[50] ibid 84–86.

someone's *māl* publicly without the latter's permission. It uses the different derivatives of *ġaṣb* to describe the whole occurrence. Thus, the wrongdoer is called 'usurper' (*ġāṣib*, غاصب), the usurped *māl* is termed 'usurped' (*maġṣūb*, مغصوب) and the owner is termed 'usurped from' (*maġṣūb minhu*, مغصوب منه). The word *ġaṣb*, itself, denotes a sinful action. It carries heavy religious connotations of extortion, illegal force, disgrace, immorality and violation of someone's body or right. The *Mecelle* extends the definition of *ġaṣb* to include all cases involving dispelling an owner's right to exercise authority over his *māl* (Article 901). For example, when a man denies refunding a deposit he was entrusted with or exploits someone's beast of burden to reach a destination far more than agreed. These are cases of *ġaṣb*.[51]

The main reparatory measure for these cases is restitution of the *māl* taken (Articles 890, 892).[52] The usurped *māl* has to be returned to its owner from the same place in which it was usurped in order to dismiss civil liability (*żamān*, ضمان). Restitution in a different place, like another town or a 'scary' place (Article 894), requires the owner's approval. According to Islamic jurisprudence, *żamān* is a civil liability to make remedy. In the case of *māl*, 'it is the *māl* which needs to be delivered in place of a lost *māl*'.[53] In like manner, if the usurped *māl* is no longer available, due to consumption, damage or rottenness, *żamān* is invoked (Article 891) and the usurper is liable to make restitution in kind (Article 145), ie, to deliver a fungible item if found in the market, or to make restitution in value (Article 146) for a rare object (Article 416). If the owner refuses to take the equivalent value offered, a judge can compel him to do so (Article 895).

The owner can plea for *żamān*, if the 'qualities' of the usurped *māl* were changed by the wrongdoer. For example, if an appropriated dress was coloured by the usurper, the owner may retain the dress provided he pays for the added colour, or he may request *żamān*, here the value of the dress (Article 898).[54] If the essence of *māl* was changed, for example, from wheat to flour, *żamān* is automatically triggered and the wrongdoer has to give an equivalent of the original *māl* (Article 899).[55] It is important to note that *żamān* is not confined to restitution, but also extends to compensation. Thus, damaging a *māl* triggers *żamān* to compensate the victim, for his loss, either in kind or in value (Article 912), even when no enrichment is involved whatsoever.

---

[51]   Baz (n 34) 430.

[52]   ibid 422–23.

[53]   A el-khafīf, *al-Żamān fī al-Fiqh al-Islāmī* (*Żamān in Islamic Jurisprudence*) (Cairo, Dar el-fikr el-Arabi, 2000) 7.

[54]   Similarly, if usurped fruits shrivel, the owner can either claim them back or claim *żamān* (Art 897).

[55]   Baz (n 34) 427–29.

As to *māl*, it is not wealth or any economic value. It is defined as 'that which the human person inclines to and can be saved for the time of need, be it moveable or not' (Articles 126–27). *Māl* can only refer to rightful value or object namely one which is religiously permissible to use. Thus, for example, pork, a dead body, wine, a non-slave, witchcraft tools, fighting roosters, goddess sculptures are not considered *māl* due to various religious bans on their possession and use. *Māl* has also to be 'achieved', ie, be obtainable and within arm's reach. Thus, a fish in the sea and a bird in the sky are not considered *māl*. It also has to be 'respected', that is religiously forbidden to take without a permissible reason. Thus, for example, the treasures of the enemy are not considered respected *māl*, as they are religiously permissible to seize following victorious war.[56] Their appropriation is not considered *ġaṣb* and does not entail restitution.

Māl is not to be confused with money (*nukūd*, نقود) or property (*mülk*, ملك). Money is defined as gold and silver, be they minted or not (Article 130). Banknotes and copper coins are excluded and are mainly considered commodities, rather than exchange currencies in the modern sense.[57] As to property, it comprises of two parts: the essence, meaning the thing itself (*e'yān*, اعيان), and its utilities (*manāfi'*, منافع), namely its gainable benefits and uses (Article 125). For example, an apartment is deemed an essence, whereas its use as accommodation is considered utility. Similarly, a beast of burden is an essence, whereas its riding or loading are considered utilities. Furthermore, according to the *Mecelle*, utilities are not considered *māl* and cannot be exchanged for *māl*. This is, for instance, one reason for banning interest (ربا) in Islamic jurisprudence, as it exchanges *mâl* for nothing. In similar vein, the usurpation of utilities is not considered *ġaṣb*, and triggers no duty of restitution.[58]

Three exceptions to this last rule apply. The first is utilities drawn from a religious endowment's *māl* (*vakf*, وقف). For example, when a person uses the courtyard of a mosque to sell goods without permission, he is obliged to pay the equivalent of a user fee. The second exception is utilities drawn from a minor's *māl* (*ṣaġīr*, صغير) especially an orphan. These exceptions were provided as protective measures against what was observed as a growing encroachment on the *māl* of 'religious endowments and orphans'.[59] The third exception concerns utilities drawn from a *māl* that was explicitly prepared for use (eg, lease)[60] or utilities previously offered

---

[56] A Haider, *Durar al-Ḥukkam fī-Sharḥ Majallat al-Aḥ kām* (*Perils of the Rulers Explaining the Ottoman Civil Code*) vol II, trans F El-husseini (Beirut, al-Nāsher Dar al-Kutub al-'ilmyyah, 1925) 443–45.

[57] Haider, vol I (n 47) 101.

[58] Haider, vol II (n 56) 585; Baz (n 34) 272–73.

[59] ibid 585 (Haider).

[60] See Art 416 for a definition of 'prepared for use'.

for rent (Articles 472, 596). In the first case, a constructive contract is construed between the parties. And if this contract lacks certain validating components, it is perceived voidable and calls for payment of equivalent use value (Articles 460–62). In the second case, the unauthorised use is considered a consent of the usurper to pay the suggested rent fee and restitution is based on contract (Articles 437–38).

Another related term is additions (*zava'd*, زوائد).[61] Additions are mainly natural increases in *māl*, like the fruits of a tree, honey of bees and the wool, milk or offspring of animals. The *Mecelle* provides that the additions of a usurped *māl* belong to the owner and have to be handed to him along with the *māl* itself (Article 903). Nevertheless, additions are not considered usurped *māl* (*maġsūb*) but a deposit (*emānet*, امانت) in the hands of the usurper. Therefore, a *māl* which perishes in the latter's position calls for *żamān* in all circumstances regardless of the reason for perishing. Since additions originate in God's act, however, *żamān* is invoked only if eliminated by a direct or indirect act of the usurper. Natural perishing—again an act of God—does not provoke *żamān*. A further distinction is made by the *Mecelle* between attached additions (eg, wool) and unattached ones (eg, offspring). Attached additions which have not been (or could not be) claimed separately do not trigger *żamān*, and the owner's right to these very additions is basically secured. What naturally follows a thing, for example, an embryo in an animal's pregnancy, is considered non-detachable from that thing and cannot be legally conceived, treated or sold separately (Articles 47 and 48).[62]

The *Mecelle* also covers the case of usurping immovable property and orders its return to the rightful owner without any changes or diminishment. Otherwise, changes should be eradicated and diminishes compensated if caused by the usurper (Article 905). And last, the *Mecelle* regulates the special case of usurping from a usurper (Articles 910 and 911). It provides that the second usurper is responsible for the owner, if the *māl* is consumed or spoiled by him, but if he returns the *māl* to the first usurper he is dismissed from liability to the owner.[63]

TRACING EXEMPLARS

Attentive reading of the *Mecelle*'s treatment of property appropriation and exploitation cases reveals an interesting disposition that is reaffirmed by various commentaries.[64] The *Mecelle* seems to embrace a powerful

---

[61] Baz (n 34) 431.
[62] Haider, vol II (n 56) 500–04; ibid 419–20 (Baz).
[63] ibid 432–39 (Baz).
[64] See, eg, Haider, vol I (n 47) 59; Baz (n 34).

'accountability' attitude. The central focus of the law is not the asset or action involved per se but the human person, or more specifically his accountability record. According to this religious model, each person sustains an accountability record as early as his birth or even earlier as a human embryo. Every person needs to abide by certain preset rules if he wishes to keep a clear record. Like a person's shadow, an accountability record follows that person wherever he goes and whatever he chooses to do. This record is officially termed *zimmit* (ذمت), and it is explicitly dealt with in different parts of the *Mecelle*.

For example, it is provided that by default a person is held to have a 'clear' *zimmit* (Article 8). Thus, if a person damages the *māl* of another and the two disagree on its value, the assertion of the tortfeasor is taken to be truthful unless proved otherwise by the owner. This rule places the burden of proof on the claimant, reflecting pragmatic concerns such as the parties' evidential positions, expected incentives and nature of proof. More significantly, it asserts a basic belief that a tortfeasor does not cease to be a trustworthy person. He is entrusted to state his actual misconduct, clear his *zimmet* and avoid social censure. Other examples are debts, guarantees and bills of payment. A debt is defined as the amount of money proved to be in the *zimmit* of a person. A guarantee is metaphorically described as joining the *zimmit* of the guarantor to that of the debtor, making both persons answerable. Similarly, a bill of payment is described as the passage of *zimmit* from one person to another.[65]

Ali Haider, a regarded commentator of the *Mecelle*,[66] explains *zimmit* in terms of a covenant and trust. According to Haider, 'every person is born with a clear *zimmit* which becomes engaged afterwards according to one's dealings'. *Zimmit* implies the social disparagement which he bears if he betrays the trust invested in him. On a legal level, it accounts 'for what a person is entitled and what he is answerable'.[67] In many senses, it recalls legal capacity. The latter enables a person to engage in legal activities, to hold and exercise rights and duties, and to maintain statuses and relations with others.[68] *Zimmit*, however, is not exactly that. The accurate term for legal capacity in *fiqh* is *ahlyat* (أهلية). *Zimmet* is considered a real characteristic of the natural person, it is not only a legal apparatus. Haider equates it to a person's 'soul and self'. It denotes both a person's inherent trustworthiness as a human being and what he has been entrusted with.

---

[65] Respectively, Arts 158, 612, 618 and 673.
[66] According to Haider, his commentary was the only work officially confirmed by the Ottoman High Court of Islam; Haider, vol I (n 47) 7; al-Qubbaj (n 28) 62.
[67] ibid 22 (Haider).
[68] See, eg, S Joseph, J Schultz and M Castan, *The International Covenant on Civil and Political Rights* (Oxford, Oxford University Press, 2004) 299.

The concept has its roots in the socio-divine covenant believed to have been made by God and human beings. According to Islamic faith, God made a covenant with humans on the day of Creation. The covenant entrusted humans with their expected conduct and fates. This day is referred to as the 'Day of Covenant'.[69] *Zimmit* is a derived yield, a sort of personal record founded on the covenant according to which each person is expected to behave in order to keep the record clear and avoid divine punishment and social criticism. Mulla Khusru, an Ottoman jurist, says: *zimmit* is a 'covenant' bestowed by God on humans so they 'be eligible for rights and duties'. He proceeds 'this is the covenant which was set between Exalted God and his servants in the day of creation'.[70]

The *Mecelle* sets different types of *zimmit* clearing (*ibrā'*, ابراء) in financial issues. *Ibrā'* can be based on waiving or relinquishing the claim or right. This sort of *ibrā'* is called *isḳāṭ* (اسقاط). Another sort of *ibrā'* is named *istīfā* (استيفا). It implies the discharge of a duty, performing an obligation or fulfilling a demand. In case of debt, *ibrā'* can also be specific, namely address a specified claim, or it can be general, namely clear all claims of all sorts. To clear *zimmit*, a person must not be a minor, insane or an imbecile. He should articulate his intent in certain words and not others. He has to name the person involved. Acceptance on the part of that person is not needed to validate *ibrā'*. And in general, *ibrā'* is considered binding if no exceptional circumstances are involved such as bankruptcy.[71]

With this accountability focused philosophy in mind, it is possible to understand the complementing role of *ġaṣb* as *māl* appropriation or exploitation. *Ġaṣb* is a highly-charged term. Islam regards *ġaṣb* as a severe injustice. Terminologically, it is linked to *iġtiṣāb* (also rape), the act of violating the sanctity of another by force and subduing.[72] The Quran commands that one should not 'consume one another's wealth unjustly'.[73] It says 'You who have believed, do not consume the wealth of one another unjustly but only in mutually consented business'.[74] The Prophet cautions against such injustice urging 'Beware of injustice, for indeed injustice will be darkness on the Day of Judgment'.[75] He specifically warns of appropriating someone's *māl* without a justified cause saying: 'if anyone takes a span of land unjustly, its extent taken from seven earths will be tied

---

[69] 'ali al-Dimashqi, *Sharḥ Īmān al-Tahawi* (*Explanation of the Tahawī Faith*) (Beirut, al-Risālah, 1997) 303–17.

[70] M Khusru, *Mir'āt Asāsyyat* (*Mirror of Fundamentals*) (Istanbul, Busnawi, 1872) 321.

[71] Respectively, Arts 1536, 1552, 1537, 1538, 1539, 1561, 1567, 1568, 1571 and 1562.

[72] Haider, vol I (n 47) 440.

[73] Quran 2:188.

[74] Quran 4:29.

[75] Sahih Al-Bukhari: 2315 and Sahih Muslim: 2579 both cited in F Bahammam, *Wealth in Islam*, Kindle edn, (Birmingham, Modern Guide, 2012) locations 172–73.

round his neck on the Day of Resurrection',[76] and on another occasion, 'he whom I offered a right owned by his brother should not accept it, as I have offered him a cut of fire'.[77]

It is with these loaded connotations that the *Mecelle* constructs the case of wrongful enrichment. The *Mecelle* rubricates all the case's elements in the religious frame of *ġaṣb*.[78] When *ġaṣb* is intentional it is not only a civil wrong but also an insolent sin against God. It attaches the loathed title of *ġāṣib* (usurper) to the wrongdoer relegating other neutral descriptions. *Māl* which in definition and scope abides strict religious restrictions is referred to as *maġṣūb* (usurped) bearing the unmistakable guise of ill-gotten wealth. This is also the case with the owner. He too forsakes any possibly less intense titles and puts on that of a victim. As *maġṣūb minhu* (usurped from), the owner is publicly the bearer of great injustice and thus deserves legal assistance and care. This construction voices a clear religiously charged attitude which puts the sin of *ġaṣb* on the wrongdoer's record. He has betrayed the trust and failed the covenant.

Following *ġaṣb* the *ẓimmit* of the usurper becomes occupied. He is now expected and coerced to return the appropriated *māl* to the lawful owner. And while *żamān* as restitution in kind or value is often not invoked in cases of perishing or value diminishing of the *māl* for natural causes (eg, sudden death of an animal) in the hands of a holder, in the case of *ġaṣb*, *żamān* is fully invoked as clear payback for the wrong committed by the wrongdoer. It is with restitution that he is able to clear his record (*ẓimmit*). This punitive attitude is derived from religious commandments, such as the Koranic verses' 'assault whoever has assaulted you in the same manner with which he has assaulted you' and 'the retribution for an evil is a similar evil'.[79] It clearly states the role of religion in constructing property appropriation and exploitation cases.

Collectively perceived, the divine and social *ẓimmit* outlined, the strictly defined concepts of *māl*, *zava'd* and *manāfi'*, the religiously charged rubrics of *ġaṣb*, and the punitively practised *żamān*, all portray a vocal picture of human violation of sacred and social commandments. Ottomans are religiously, socially and legally entrusted to comply with certain rules bestowed by an ultimate power and to keep their record (*ẓimmit*) clean. Violation calls for a severe response that is motivated and shaped by religious objectives, social tenets and legal mechanisms. In this scene, God or His earthly agent is at the core of the Ottoman doctrine of *ġaṣb*. He sets the rules of the game, and He too sets the measures in case of breach. This

---

[76] Sahih Al-Bukhari: 2321 and Sahih Muslim: 1610, both cited in Bahammam, ibid.
[77] 'a al-Qarnī, *al-Fiqh al-Muyassar* (*Accessible Jurisprudence*) (Riyaḍ, Obeican, 2009) 564.
[78] See C Imber, *Ebu's-Su'ud: The Islamic Legal Tradition* (Stanford, CA, Stanford University Press, 2009) 215.
[79] Quran 2:194, 42:40 cited in el-Khafīf (n 53) 92.

paradigm resembles the institution of trusteeship. Yet, unlike a standard trust, in this sacred trust, humans are answerable trustees for God who sets the trust terms. Their conduct, be it compliance or defiance, is never understood without the Divine in mind.

ASSESSMENT

The Ottoman approach to proprietary wrongful enrichments seems compatible with the Islamic doctrine of economics and property rights. According to Muhammad Abdul-Rauf, Islamic economics 'is a moral doctrine' resting on 'religious values' of the Quran. It aims at fulfilling human needs as well as blazing their way to the afterlife. Though property is protected in Islam, Islam insists 'it is a sacred right'. The right is bound by the belief that God is the ultimate owner of all things on Earth. 'What appears to be ownership', explains Abdul-Rauf, 'is in fact a matter of trusteeship, whereby we have temporary authority to handle and benefit from property, which will change hands on death'.[80] Like a 'sacred trust', humans are expected to act responsibly and in 'compliance with Islamic principles' to retain legitimacy for their actions.[81]

Many *fiqh* scholars have been troubled with what they argue is the *Mecelle's disregard* for unjustified enrichment. According to Samer Al-Kubbaj, one of the 'faults' of the *Mecelle* is that it has not systematically dealt with this branch of law but settled for sporadic treatment of particular cases.[82] The *Mecelle's* disregard has been explained by the dismissal of unjustified enrichment as source of legal obligation in *fiqh*.[83] Conferrals of undue *māl*, even by mistake, is instead deemed as sheer donation triggering no right to restitution.[84] Subsequently, groundless enrichments are, by default, a matter of irreversible gratuity rather than a basis for legal recovery.

Abdul Razeq al-Sanhūri, a regarded *fiqh* scholar, rejects this emphatic assertion. He proposes a distinction between undue payment, unjustified enrichment and benevolent intervention in another's affairs. The first, he argues, is fully recognised, the last is deemed a gratuitous act, while unjustified enrichment is recognised only if motivated by self-interest, if

---

[80] M Abdul-Rauf, *A Muslim's Reflections on Democratic Capitalism* (Washington DC, American Enterprise Institute, 1984) 19.

[81] S Sait and H Lim, *Paper 1: Islamic Land Theories and their Application* (Nairobi, UN-HANI-TAT, 2005) 10.

[82] eg Art 1313. See also al-Qubbaj (n 28) 210–13, 315.

[83] A al-Sanhūri, *al-Waṣīṭ fī Sharḥ al-Qānūn al-Madanī* (*The Mediator in the Explanation of Civil Law*) vol I (Cairo, Dar el-Nashr lel-Jame'at Al-Masryyah, 1952) 938.

[84] al-Zarqa (n 44) 92.

caused by mingling properties of different owners indivisibly, or in case of a void contract due to incapacity.[85] This position offers a plausible middle way between two rival drives. One is the religious precept encouraging Muslims to care and vouch for each other voluntarily. The other is allowing restitution when it seems fair to do so. Al-Sanhūri's proposition attempts to strike a categorical balance between the two drives, he suggests, according to preset groups of cases. Others, however, advocate a more flexible approach. They treat unjustified enrichment as imperfect benevolence. At the heart of benevolence lies the intention to serve another. When this objective is lacking, the disadvantaged may lay a claim in unjustified enrichment, so goes the argument. This solution seems a forced one. Whether benevolent intervention in another's affairs should lead to restitution is itself a debated issue in *fiqh*. Furthermore, the two claims are dissimilar. For example, actionable benevolence is often based on some need for intervention, whereas enrichment is normally caused by the disadvantaged who usually has to suffer a loss, and restitution is normally limited to expenditures. This is not necessarily so in an unjustified enrichment claim.[86] Hence, despite the shared notion of a misplaced wealth, the two doctrines do not necessarily synchronise. It rather seems that utilising a recognised claim to foster an unrecognised one risks distorting both.

Some scholars have stressed the pluralistic character of Islamic jurisprudence. Morkus Suleiman, for example, argues that the Hanafi *Madhhab* (school of thought) on which the *Mecelle* is based recognises a general principle obliging restitution of unjustified enrichment. The latter could be 'predestined' or caused by any of the involved parties. This view is indeed supported by the *Mecelle* which explicitly states the impermissibility of taking another's *māl* without a legitimate reason (Article 97). The question remains whether *ġaṣb* is based on the idea of unjustified enrichment.[87] While it definitely can be discussed in those terms, it is viable not to flatten the doctrine in the process and lose its distinctive traits. The doctrine of *ġaṣb* carries powerful religious and cultural significances that ought not to be silenced.

Ġaṣb is a harshly condemned act rooted in Islamic faith. It is nurtured by religious texts and narratives that feed and interact with the Islamic and Ottoman experience. Though comparable to Western doctrines of wrongful enrichment, Ottoman *ġaṣb* should not be delimited to a taxonomy produced by, and for, other legal traditions. It should also be examined on

---

[85] W al-Sharqawi, *Naẓaryat al-ethra' bilā sabab taṭbīqātihā fī al-fiqh al-eslamī* (*The Theory of Unjustified Enrichment in Applications in Islamic Jurisprudence*) (Alexandria, Dar el-jami'a al-jadīda lil-nashr, 2009) 60–61.

[86] ibid.

[87] ibid 20, 201.

its own terms and rubrics to avoid obscuration of its unique cultural and historical contexts. As already discussed, Ottoman *ġaṣb* relies on a distinctive and cohesive world-view which reflects Islamic faith and practices. It stands on a developed system of rules inseparable from one's *zimmet* and personal accountability to a higher power.

But this Ottoman taxonomy which arguably sustains the gateways to cultural examination, may itself mark the absolute detachment from the masses' cultures. As pointed out by Noah Feldman, the *Mecelle* is not a product of commoners, but of 'a distinguished committee of scholars and experts'.[88] In fact, it was largely perplexing to common people. Composed by highly educated jurists and *fiqh* experts, it was written in Ottoman Turkish, 'a highly stylised version of Turkish with a considerable Arabic influence' exclusively used by the ruling class.[89] Commoners comprising chiefly of agriculturists, craftsmen and merchants spoke '*Kaba türkçe*' (rough Turkish)[90] and were mostly unlearned people. In this regard, one should ponder whether the *Mecelle* transgresses the cultural boundaries of the ruling class.

Tackling this question, it is vital to bear in mind that the *Mecelle* is not only an Ottoman artefact but an Islamic one as well. Though produced by an Ottoman elite, the *Mecelle* mimics a religious tradition which cuts across many of the masses' linguistic and societal differences. It draws heavily on Islamic ethics held and practised by vast parts of the population. Furthermore, Islam was the official religion of the Empire. It was shared by many districts regardless of ethnicity or class. The voice of Islam reached many areas of the Empire and was present in every Muslim village. Islam regulated many aspects of an Ottoman's life extending to education, customs, rituals, language and even day-to-day conduct.[91] Furthermore, shortly after its promulgation, the *Mecelle* was officially translated into Arabic and used in the Arabian Peninsula, the Levant, North Africa and the rest of the Arabic-speaking regions, thus enhancing its mobility and dissemination.

It was the diversity of the Empire's population which called for a unifying thread. According to Kia Mehrdad, the Empire consisted of 'Turks, Tatars, Hungarians, Serbs, Montenegrins, Bosnians, Albanians, Romanians, Bulgarians, Greeks, Greorgians, Circassians, Abkhazians, Armenians, Arabs, Berbers, Kurds, Jews, and many others' with each possessing 'its own unique customs and traditions'.[92] With this heterogeneity,

---

[88] Feldman (n 37) location 1292.
[89] M Kia, *Daily Life in the Ottoman Empire* (Santa Barbara, CA, Greenwood Press, 2011) 63.
[90] M Glenny, *The Balkans—Nationalism, War, and the Great Powers, 1804–1999* (New York, Penguin, 2001) 99.
[91] Kia (n 89) 112, 133, 153–61.
[92] ibid xiv.

it was imperative for the Empire to *Ottomanise* Islam to sustain a sense of unity. As will be discussed in the following chapter, the late administration utilised Islam to compose a sense of Ottoman nationality needed to relegate diversity and minimise the risk of revolts. The *Mecelle* was an important tool in that realm. It projected, boldly and clearly, a common ground for all subjects of the Empire rooted in the life and experience of the majority.

7

Ottoman Culture

POLITICISED POETICS

FOR THE OTTOMAN administration, the late nineteenth century was no time for idleness. The administration knew very well it had to take action. The regime and all its institutions were at stake. The genie of modernity was out of the bottle pledging a rosy future. The list of politically secured rights was growing longer. Education and knowledge were morphing into social and economic power. Lower classes were challenging old hierarchies. Foreign countries were extending their influence on the Empire. The spell of Western ideals was increasingly cast on Ottomans promising them better life conditions. Many regions within the Empire were disclosing their aspiration for self-determination.[1] The risk of social turbulence and political upheaval was materialising. The threat to both the stability and integrity of the Ottoman Empire was very real and the administration had to act. The need was to trace those threads that would tighten the Ottoman weave and prevent it from rupturing.

A leading strategy was to boost the monarch's legitimacy and promote a sense of unity among Ottomans. The caliphate institution was extensively deployed to that end. The appeal of the sultan's religious role as leader of Islam was alluring.[2] It was part of a systemised 'propaganda' embarked on by the administration to present the Ottoman emperor as the 'shadow of God' and the Empire as the guardian of Muslims.[3] Ironically, it was Islam defending the waning Empire and its threatened monarchy and not the other way around. Religious beliefs were blatantly used by the administration to serve its political ends. Religiosity became an instrument in the hands of the regime integrating, perfectly, with its crisis agenda. Boosted by political motives, religiosity was tactfully re-engineered to defuse the

---

[1] See generally K Karpat, *The Politicization of Islam: Reconstructing Identity, State, Faith, and Community in the Late Ottoman State* (Oxford, Oxford University Press, 2001).

[2] S Deringil, *The Well-Protected Domains: Ideology and Legitimation of Power in the Ottoman Empire 1876–1909* (London, Tauris, 2011) 55.

[3] ibid 48–49; C Findley, *The Turks in World History* (Oxford, Oxford University Press, 2005) 115.

growing threats to the Empire. Some described this political use of Islam as early versions of 'Islamism' or 'Pan-Islamism'.[4]

The codification of *Şeriat* (Islamic law) was part of the administration's crisis strategy.[5] And though the idea of codification was imported, codification did not yield an alien fruit. In fact, the Code deftly correlated with unique traits of the Ottoman society accentuating rooted traditions like 'patrimonialism' and 'social stratification'.[6] Codification politicised the religious doctrine of personal accountability correlating it with the physical world. The doctrine was brought to transcend its religious denotation and was used to fashion Ottomans' perception of life in the Empire. The religious responsibility for one's actions before God brought a corresponding notion of one's responsibility before God's temporal delegate, the sultan. The latter urged compliance with an earthly code of conduct produced by codified *Şeriat* and the distinctive socio-political conditions of life in the Empire. A person's economic behaviour was, thus, assessed by salient Ottoman themes, notably Islamic doctrine, patrimonialism and personal accountability.

WAS THERE AN *OTTOMAN* CULTURE?

Besides the various regional and ethnic cultures traceable in the Ottoman Empire, Şerif Mardin argues that two dominant cultures have been discernible. One is a so-called 'Great' culture which constitutes the habits, customs and attitudes of urban life including ruling, high and high middle classes of Ottoman society. The other is the 'Little' culture which constitutes the non-urbanised and agrarian way of life and is mostly associated with the general population. According to Mardin, a great gap separated the two cultures. And instead of merging them into one supra-culture, nineteenth-century *Tanzimat* (reorganisation) increased the gap and eventually led to the Young Turk Revolution of 1908.[7]

But this was not what the administration had in mind. It embarked on a systematised process of *Ottomanising* culture by reviving symbols, themes, customs and values of the Islamic tradition.[8] The ultimate vision was an

---

[4] See, eg, A Bissenove, 'Ottomanism, Pan-Islamism, and the Caliphate Discourse at the Turn of the 20th Century' (2004) 9(1) *Barqiyya* 2; Karpat (n 1) 15–16.

[5] Deringil 50.

[6] Ş Mardin, *Religion, Society and Modernity in Turkey* (New York, Syracuse University, 2006) 62, 68, 69, 72.

[7] ibid 33–40.

[8] Deringil (n 2) 46–47; A Ocak, 'al-Ḥayat al-Dīnyya wa al-Fikryya' ('The Religious and Intellectual Life)' in E İhsanoğlu (ed), *al-Dawlah al-'uthmānyah: Tarīkh Waḥadārah* (*The Ottoman State: History and Civilization*) vol II, trans Ş Sa'dāwy (Cairo, Maktabat al-shurūq al-Dawlyah, 2010) 153, 157.

Ottoman supra-culture rooted in a religion which appealed to most its subjects. The supra-culture, it was hoped, would pave the way to an integrated proto-national identity. Eric Hobsbawm explains 'popular proto-nationalism' as a cohesion process which promotes a shared sense of 'national patriotism' among subjects of the same sovereignty.[9] Following the example of the Austrian and Russian Empires, the Ottoman Empire sought to 'legitimate' itself both inwards and outwards by producing a shared pool of customs, attitudes and perceptions, all *Ottomanised*. The plan aimed to defuse the increasing threats of dissolution.[10]

According to June Starr, Islam played a chief role liaising the different cultures of the Empire.[11] And as Selim Deringil points out, the *Tanzimat* reformations were an excellent occasion to establish the new sense of 'Ottomanism'.[12] Islamic religion was, thus, revitalised within a politicised plan to materialise and inseminate an Ottomanised supra-culture that would integrate the majority of subjects in the Empire.[13] It is this purposely fashioned culture which could claim copyrights to the *Mecelle* as a legal document. Immersed in Islamic ethics and doctrine, the *Mecelle* materialised an important part of the political agenda of the administration to appeal to all Muslims in the Empire and unite them under the Ottoman sultan.[14]

WEALTH AS SOCIO-POLITICAL STATUS AND RELIGIOUS TRUST

Like many traditional Eastern monarchies, the Ottoman Empire was mostly a bureaucratic administration working ceaselessly to emphasise the religious role of the sultan and the undisputed legitimacy of his ruling powers.[15] Below the sultan, 'two main groups' occupied a hierarchic pyramid.[16] One was the ruling group the 'guardians',[17] personifying the sultan's sovereignty and enjoying a relatively high social status. This group consisted of several subgroups, notably officials and soldiers or the so-called 'masters of pen and sword', and also judges and *Şeriat* jurists.

[9] E Hobsbawm, *Nations and Nationalism Since 1780: Programme, Myth, Reality* (Cambridge, Cambridge University Press, 2012) 46, 73.

[10] Deringil (n 2) 44–50.

[11] J Starr, *Law as Metaphor: From Islamic Courts to the Palace of Justice* (Albany, NY, State University of New York, 1992) 5–6.

[12] Deringil (n 2) 46–47; Ocak (n 8).

[13] Hobsbawm (n 9) 46, 73.

[14] Starr (n 11) xxxiv, 3, 5.

[15] H Inalcik 'Capital Formation in the Ottoman Empire' (1969) 29(1) *Journal of Economic History* 97, 97.

[16] Bibliographic sources use the words *group* and *class* interchangeably.

[17] See, eg, Mardin (n 6) 24, 61.

The other group was the ruled which consisted of lower-class, illiterate and taxpaying people, mostly peasants, artisans and traders.[18]

In spite of this seemingly clear division, cross-group 'mobility' was possible due to loose social and residential restraints. Each subject had the legitimate right to shift to urban areas, acquire proper secular or religious education and fulfil administrative or military positions associated with the ruling group. Although upward 'mobility' would inevitably suffer the restraining effects of the ruling hegemony, stories of social climbing were not infrequent.[19] Moving in the opposite direction was also possible due to the limited right to bequeath 'wealth and status' to descendants,[20] and the power of the sultan to revoke political and economic privileges formerly granted.[21]

To understand the Ottoman model of governance, one can fruitfully juxtapose it with traditional feudalism. In feudalism, the king depended on a number of intermediaries such as lords and vassals to govern lower classes. Feudal ties were mostly personal. For example, a sub-vassal took a personal oath of honour to her direct superior, the vassal, in exchange for certain fiefs. Feudalism, thus, produced multi-tiered ties organised in a hierarchical order.[22] The Ottoman model of governance was mostly patrimonial.[23] As Mardin points out, the Ottoman sultan was deemed 'personally responsible for the welfare of his subjects'.[24] He is directly held accountable for the security and economic well-being of his subjects.

In his *Economy and Society*,[25] Weber explains patrimonialism as a mode of patriarchal authority extended to fit the scale and needs of a sizeable population. The crux of the system is to care for 'the needs of the ruler's personal household' providing nutrition, garmenture and weaponry. And to secure these supplies, the ruler exercises tight political and economic dominion over her citizens, imposing duties, collecting taxes and controlling the market. Governmental offices were usually tied to the

---

[18] H Inalcik, 'The Nature of Traditional Society: Turkey' in R Ward and D Rustow (eds), *Political Modernization in Japan and Turkey* (Princeton, NJ, Princeton University Press, 1964) 42, 44; Inalcik, 'Capital Formation in the Ottoman Empire' (n 15) 97.

[19] See, eg, D Quataert, *The Ottoman Empire, 1700–1922* (Cambridge, Cambridge University Press, 2007) 144.

[20] E Karababa, 'Approaching Non-Western Consumer Cultures from a Historical Perspective: The Case of Early Modern Ottoman Consumer Culture' (2012) 12(1) *Marketing Theory* 13, 16–17.

[21] Mardin (n 6) 61.

[22] For feudalism in Max Weber's thought, see R Bendix, *Max Weber: An Intellectual Portrait* (London, University of California Press, 1977) 360.

[23] Starr (n 11) 7; Mardin (n 6) 24–25.

[24] ibid 25 (Mardin).

[25] M Weber, *Economy and Society: An Outline of Interpretive Sociology* G Roth and C Wittich (eds) (Berkeley, CA, University of California Press, 1978).

ruler's household. They were deemed 'personal servants and personal representatives of the ruler', and were directly accountable to him. All positions and prerogatives stem from the ruler who could revoke any of these if she decides to do so.[26]

Though patrimonialism was the dominant form of governance in the Ottoman Empire, it was argued that ever since nineteenth-century reforms, if not earlier,[27] elements of neopatrimonialism were being introduced.[28] In contrast to traditional patrimonialism which rested, mainly, on the rule of one person, the modern form of governance was pillared by a formalised and extensive body of administrative officials enforcing patrimonial domination.[29] It is important to note that the bureaucratic powers of an office were not exercised as a mode of 'public service' or 'official function' but as a 'personal status' bestowed by the ruler and repealed at her will.[30] Thus, while the executive powers of the ruler were dispersed among a bureaucratic body, the ruler continued to be 'the source of legitimacy' and 'the capstone of the system'.[31]

This socio-political system forged a distinctive perception of wealth which readily correlated with the ethics and values of *Şeriat*. Wealth was traditionally understood in terms of preserving and promoting the ruler's dominance. For this reason, wealth accumulation was ceaselessly monitored by the administration. The aim was to ensure each person exhibited the traits of her social stratum and got her 'traditionally allotted share' of wealth. This economic perception was a *sine qua non* ground for the socio-political stability of the Empire[32] and a pillar on which the whole government was based.

Bahaeddin Yediyildiz explains this perception. He notes that Ottoman social ethics valued the human person considering him the 'noblest of creatures' and a profoundly sociable one. Cooperation, mutual support and reciprocity between society members were crucial to the survival of each person. According to Ottoman perception, economic prosperity is achievable only if each person is present in her 'allocated' social place serving the system in accordance with her faculties, skills and abilities. This perception is rooted in the religious belief that God allocated traits and faculties between humans, placing some in better positions than

---

[26] Bendix (n 22) 334–35.

[27] Mardin (n 6) 24–25.

[28] See, eg, C Findley, *Bureaucratic Reform in the Ottoman Empire: The Sublime Porte, 1789–1922* (New Jersey, NJ, Princeton University Press, 1980) 149, 353–54.

[29] C Clapham, *Third World Politics: An Introduction* (Madison, WI, University of Wisconsin Press, 1985) 47; G Erdmann and U Engel, 'Neopatrimonialism Reconsidered: Critical Review and Elaboration of an Elusive Concept' (2007) 45(1) *Commonwealth & Comparative Politics* 95, 105; ibid 353, fn 6 (Findley).

[30] ibid 48 (Clapham).

[31] Mardin (n 6) 25.

[32] Inalcik, 'Capital Formation in the Ottoman Empire' (n 15) 97; ibid 62 (Mardin).

others.[33] The perception was also elucidated utilising the so-called 'circle of justice' paradigm. The paradigm held that peace between subjects in the 'stately walled garden' of the world is 'ensured by justice'. Justice is ensured by *Şeriat*. The latter is protected by state sovereignty which rests on the army and the subjects' wealth. Stability among subjects is ensured by justice.[34]

To that end, the Ottoman administration kept a close track on all paths to wealth. Firm regulations were imposed on farmers, craftsmen and local traders to ensure honest dealing and restrained profit rates.[35] Subjects relied on the sultan to impose fair market prices, and the latter relied on his subjects' contentment to maintain stability. The sultan's responsibility to provide food and fair living conditions for his subjects insured the administration's durability.[36] Price ceiling (*narh*), a main instrument of market control (*hisbah*),[37] was practised by the administration, pertaining to various services and commodities. Market regulations were strictly observed and any transgression called for a prompt redress. Deceptive and overcharging practices bore severe and public penalties. Defective products and illicit profits were confiscated.[38] And wrongdoers were economically and socially punished.

Harsh retribution proved very effective in restraining wrongful enrichments.[39] Ottomans were often deemed honest traders. Exceptions were attributed to uncommon moral distortions caused by urbanised life or contact with foreigners. Writing in the early nineteenth century, for example, Charles Pertusier, one of the suite of the French Embassy at the Ottoman Porte, stressed that it is very infrequent for an Ottoman seller to overprice products. He added, however, that this observation was truer for rural areas than to the city of Istanbul where the 'intercourse with the Franks has, in some measure, altered the characteristic probity of the people'.[40]

As expected, regulations were tighter for small-scale traders than for importers and wholesale traders referred to as '*tüccar*' (also '*matrabaz*',

---

[33] Quran 43:32.

[34] B Yediyildiz, 'al-Mujtama' al-'Uthmānī' (*Ottoman Society*) in E İhsanoğlu (ed), *al-Dawlah al-'uthmānyah: Tarīkh Waḥadārah* (*The Ottoman State: History and Civilization*) vol 1, trans Ṣ Sa'dāwy (Cairo, Maktabat al-shurūq al-Dawlyah, 2010) 523, 524–26.

[35] Inalcik, 'Capital Formation in the Ottoman Empire' (n 15) 98; M Kia, *Daily Life in the Ottoman Empire* (Santa Barbara, CA, Greenwood Press, 2011) 85–86.

[36] E Boyar and K Fleet, *A Social History of Ottoman Istanbul* (Cambridge, Cambridge University Press, 2010) 158, 163, 165.

[37] Ş Pamuk, *A Monetary History of the Ottoman Empire* (Cambridge, Cambridge University Press, 2001) 13.

[38] Boyar and Fleet (n 36) 167–69.

[39] ibid 169–72.

[40] C Pertusier, *Picturesque Promenades in and near Constantinople and on the Waters of the Bosphorus* (London, Phillips, 1820) 83. Source brought to attention by Boyar and Fleet (n 36) 172.

'bazirgan'). These were mostly 'free to accumulate' money in any legal way they chose. Their wealth, however, was closely screened by different official records like the recording registry (*'sijill-defterleri'*) which documented business deals, and the 'estate' inventory (*'tereke-defterleri'*) which documented the value of a deceased's assets. And in return for the permissive trade space they were allowed, the administration took strict steps when any form of overcharging, speculative gaining or illicit trade practices was observed. In such cases, the administration did not hesitate to confiscate any portion of wealth acquired through wrongful conduct.[41]

It is worth noting that merchants' liberty to pursue wealth did not give rise to a capitalist spirit. Social malevolence towards the arrogant merchant along with various religious bans on lust for money did not allow such a spirit. Unlike Calvinist doctrine which identified wealth with God's grace and content, Islam expressly detached any link between the two.[42] Halil Inalcik argues, however, that disapproval of capitalism should not be attributed solely to 'religious' bans but more so to the 'basic social and economic structure' of Ottoman society. A spirit of capitalism, he notes, threatened to distort the socio-economic equilibriums of noncompetitive guild systems in relatively small markets. 'The competitive spirit and the profit motive' says Inalcik, 'were regarded as crimes' leading to the collapse of the whole 'system and the existing social order'.[43]

Like powerful trade unions, Ottoman 'guilds' (*'esnaf'*) regulated all aspects of craftsmanship and trade. They regulated tutoring issues, monitored the size of the guild, organised the purchase of necessary 'materials', supervised crafting methods, paid shared expenditures, stood by a member's family in times of distress, and paid funeral expenses. Guilds negotiated prices with officials and mediated relations with state administration. Guilds prevented inner and intra competition. Their system was perfectly suited to non-expanding and non-competitive markets.[44]

For this reason, guilds reinforced social hierarchies and preserved the equal distribution of wealth by maintaining their members' interdependence. A member who acquired too much wealth was expelled from the guild and considered a 'merchant'. The conceptual reframing of her profession, invited social disparage. An expelled member was often accused of price inflation, market shortages, money hoarding and deceptive trade practices. She was deemed a racketeer and her conduct illicit and speculative.[45] A guild member, notes Mehrdad Kia, 'was respected for the

---

[41] Inalcik, 'Capital Formation in the Ottoman Empire' (n 15) 98–99, 106–107.
[42] See, eg, Quran 28: 76–81 recounting God's punishment of arrogant Korah who credited himself for his unprecedented wealth instead of crediting God.
[43] Inalcik, 'Capital Formation in the Ottoman Empire' (n 15) 104–05.
[44] Kia (n 35) 84–86; ibid 105 (Inalcik).
[45] Inalcik, 'Capital Formation in the Ottoman Empire' (n 15) 105–106; Mardin (n 6) 62.

beauty and artistic quality' of her 'work' and not her 'ability to market' her 'products' and make a gain. In fact, any economic 'competition' was disapproved of and deemed disgraceful. This non-competitive spirit can be observed in the concentration of similar shops at same market sections, and in specialised shops selling one type of product rather than various types.[46]

Wealth reflected these socio-economic structures as well as the patrimonial role of the sultan. Ottoman wealth accentuated a person's social stratum and her proximity to political power. This condition was secured by a range of state policies which prevented the outbreak of capitalism.[47] Good examples of such policies are the fiscal and land governance regulations. At the time, Ottoman lands were sorted into five types. The bulk of lands were deemed *'mîrî'* (prince-related). These were agrarian lands owned by the state and held in special fief-like condition. The second type, also owned by the state, was *'metrouke'* (left). These were lands 'reserved for public or communal use, such as roads and pastures'. Another type was *'mevat'* (superfluous). This type referred to 'uncultivated' state lands outside inhabited areas. The fourth type was *'vakif'* (endowment) namely lands held in trust and serving communal and religious objectives. The last type, comprising the least often found, was *'mülk'* (owned) and referred to lands privately owned.[48]

These classifications preserved the powerful grip of the Ottoman administration on vast areas of land in the Empire. Only those who earned the trust of the administration could enjoy entitlements to the cherished resource. This condition was also salient in the 'tax farming' privilege (*'iltizam'*). As the Empire needed an efficient tax collection system to back its military and other needs, it privatised its tax collecting power and sold it to individuals for a fixed period. Private tax collectors gathered taxes and kept a portion of it for themselves. This 'fiscal device' was very profitable to both parties. It prevented, however, the development of other sources of state revenue such as trade, modernising markets and privatising lands.[49] It also defused the drive of privileged people to pursue any serious economic activity.

Industrial and mechanical advancements of the mid- to late-nineteenth century bore some changes to this condition. Nevertheless, traits of the 'traditional Ottoman system' were still dominant. 'Innovations' were merely 'new forms moulded to old shapes' stressed Ebru Boyar and Kate Fleet.[50] Privatising *mîrî* lands continued to be performed infrequently,

---

[46] Kia (n 35) 87–88.
[47] Mardin (n 6) 25.
[48] Starr (n 11) 46–47; Kia (n 35) 66.
[49] Quataert (n 19) 28–30; ibid 66–68 (Kia); ibid 47–49 (Starr); Mardin (n 6) 27–28.
[50] Boyar and Fleet (n 36) 281; ibid 70 (Mardin).

and then only when privileged persons were involved. For the administration, privatising land meant less collectible tax.[51] Furthermore, it opposed the Ottoman cultural perception which tied land to an 'office' and not to a 'person'.[52] Tax reductions and exemptions were enjoyed by high social classes, especially government functionaries, but they were also applicable in cases of privatised lands, notably endowments and *mülk*.[53]

As to tax farming, this economic instrument enhanced the private wealth of privileged families. The families, often bearing the title '*âyân*' (notables) or '*eşraf*' (gentlefolk), were often privileged due to a military serving background or *Şeriat* learned forefathers. They had a lavish lifestyle which was very dependent on their access to 'political power'. Hence, they were deeply occupied with tightening 'connections with high state officials' rather than engaging in any fruitful economic activity. Political connections were mutually beneficial. In return for the privileged status and economic stability granted to these families, the administration earned their loyalty defusing any political aspiration harmful to the Empire. In this formula, the administration retained the upper hand with its perpetual power to revoke any economic entitlement or social privilege if needed.[54]

These powers to grant and revoke privileges, to control and confiscate wealth 'made up much of Ottoman government business'. It enhanced governmental policies to secure a centralised form of governance and restrained wealth capabilities borne by private individuals or families. In the same realm, policies prohibiting private incorporation and other economic empowering forms safeguarded the patrimonial world-view that the sultan was the source of all economic good. According to Mardin, wealth in Ottoman society is tied to a person's 'social status' and the latter is dependent on 'political power'.[55] Weber explicates this condition as a 'status situation' where one's standard of life is dictated by one's social 'honour'.[56] This is different from the Marxist 'class situation' in which control of capital determines a person's social properties. In the latter case, individuals compete for 'means of production'.[57] In the former, they compete 'for influential connections that would bring state privileges'.[58]

Describing elders' empowerment in Ottoman Egypt of the time, Alan R Richards argues that the elders exhibited a 'notable rise in wealth and

---

[51] Starr (n 11) 48.

[52] Mardin (n 6) 28.

[53] S Shaw, 'The Nineteenth-Century Ottoman Tax Reforms and Revenue System' (1975) 6(4) *International Journal of Middle East Studies* 421, 421.

[54] Mardin (n 6) 26, 30–32. The policy of the automatic confiscation at death of private wealth was cancelled in 1826 (at 31).

[55] ibid 25, 29, 30, 32, 61.

[56] Weber (n 25) 932; ibid 28.

[57] F Parkin, *Marxism and Class Theory: A Bourgeois Critique* (London, Tavistock, 1979) 3–4.

[58] Mardin (n 6) 27.

power' which was clearly attributable to their 'political positions as inter-mediaries between the government and the peasants'.[59] His account asserts that the dependence of wealth on political power was not confined to urban cities like Istanbul, Ankara or Bursa, but also extended to other territories and rural areas of the Empire.[60]

A powerful communicator of the politics of status was the use of 'honorary titles'. These titles were important signifiers of social rank and one's proximity to political power. For example, members of the army and administration often bore the titles *Beşe, Ağa* and *Bek*. Judges, jurists and worship leaders were often referred to as *Efendi, Şeyh, Molla, Çelebi and Dede*. And though members of the ruled group did not usually carry titles, family members claiming to be 'descendants' of the Prophet were referred to as *Seyyid* or *Şerife*, similarly Muslim pilgrims were called *Elhac* or *Haci*. Bogaç Ergene and Ali Berker stress that honorary titles in Ottoman society did not only reflect a person's vocation but more so her socio-economic properties.[61]

Another important communicator of social status was dressing practices. The Ottoman administration went so far as to impose legislation specifying the sort of dress each individual had to wear according to one's social position, faith and profession. Colours and materials were specified for different groups, like military personnel and followers of different religions. These legislations were severely observed by the administration. According to Donald Quataert, dress codes were used by sultans to 'maintain and enhance legitimacy and power'. Doing so, sultans positioned 'themselves as guardians of the boundaries differentiating their subjects' and 'as the enforcers of morality, order, and justice'.[62]

Uniformity of dress, however, did not decrease Ottomans' care for their looks and social image. Though a man's house, for example, was often modest, his female family members were often accessorised with fancy items of personal ornaments, such as rings, gems and necklets. Boyar and Fleet note that some Ottoman women 'were clearly very costly to maintain'. Impoverishment per se did not impede the consumption of 'jewellery' which proved a fast track to social respect. Valuable ornaments were testifiers of honour and social esteem in Ottoman society. As important communicators of wealth and status, expensive ornaments were part of a dress code tremendously cherished by Ottomans.[63]

---

[59] A Richards, 'Primitive Accumulation in Egypt, 1798–1882' in H İslamoğlu-İnan (ed), *The Ottoman Empire and the World-Economy* (Cambridge, Cambridge University Press, 1987) 231.

[60] Quataert (n 19) 46.

[61] B Ergene and A Berker, 'Inheritance and Intergenerational Wealth Transmission in Eighteenth-Century Ottoman Kastamonu: An Empirical Investigation' (2009) 34 *Journal of Family History* 25, 29–30 (Ottoman titles as listed at 29).

[62] Quataert (n 19) 44; Boyar and Fleet (n 36) 101, 135–36.

[63] ibid 174–75 (Boyar and Fleet).

This reality in which wealth is intimately tied to social status and political power was not only sustained by religious beliefs but also consciously correlated with them to achieve legitimacy and political stability. According to Islam, God is the ultimate source of wealth, power and well-being. Those who desire His mercy and blessing need to abide His rules as commanded by Şeriat. Şeriat instructs Muslims to work for living and to do that decently. One must not beg if she is able to work. The Prophet says, for example, 'a person who unnecessarily continues to beg will stand before Almighty God [on the Day of Judgment] without a shred of flesh on his face'. A Muslim is instructed to turn to God, the source of all good and wealth, for her needs rather than to humans. 'If a person who is afflicted with poverty refers it to people, his poverty will never end. But if he refers it to God, God will soon give him sufficiency' so teaches the Prophet.[64]

Şeriat does not restrict any kind of occupation as long as it is ethical and righteous. It permits any kind of economic activity as long as it neither involves disapproved items, for example, corpses, alcohol, narcotics, immorality, nor ill-gotten gains, for example, usury (*ribā*), fraud, unfairness or games of chance. *Ribā*, for example, is considered a major sin which entails severe punishment on those practising it. Thus, the Quran warns those who take *ribā* to abstain from this wrong, otherwise 'God and His Messenger' will wage war on them. Humans who earn their living by *ribā* 'shall not stand on the Day of Resurrection except as that whom is beaten by Satan into insanity' warns the Quran. Furthermore, 'God deprives usurious gains of all blessing, whereas He blesses charitable deeds with manifold increase'.[65]

An economic activity which rests on chance or deception is prohibited by Şeriat. Earning one's living by injustice or usurpation is equally forbidden. Şeriat fervently warns of injustice. The Prophet says, 'Beware of injustice, for indeed injustice will be darkness on the Day of Judgment' and 'whoever cheats us is not one of us'. A person, who wrongfully appropriates the property of another person is deemed a sinner who will be severely punished. The Quran stresses God's commandment 'to deliver trusts back to their owners'. Disloyalty and betrayal of 'trust', teaches the Prophet, is one of three signs of the 'hypocrite'. Lying and breaking one's promise are the other two.[66]

Şeriat instructs Muslims to observe the divine rules pertaining to wealth and wealth acquisition, and warns against transgressions.[67] It holds that God has allotted each her determined share of wealth. 'We have

[64] F Bahammam, *Wealth in Islam*, Kindle edn (Birmingham, Modern Guide, 2012) locations 24–29.
[65] Quran 2:2 78–79; Quran 2:2 75–76. ibid locations 29–106 (Bahammam).
[66] Bahammam (n 64) locations 149–66, 172–94, 212, 276.
[67] ibid locations 308–99.

apportioned among them their livelihood in the life of this world and have raised some of them above others in degrees so that some may use others for service'[68] says the Quran. Each Muslim is accountable for the share of wealth she is entrusted with, and she will have to provide explanation for all her deeds on the Day of Judgment. Thus, the Quran warns that one's 'competitive longing for greater gains' that occupies a person till death will lead to Hell and be punished for all the pleasures enjoyed during life.[69]

These norms epitomise the economic doctrine of *Şeriat*.[70] According to this doctrine, wealth is perceived as a divine trust in the hands of humans who need to abide by the rules and answer to God for all their deeds. The *Şeriat* holds that a person who defies 'the terms' of one's trust has 'no faith'.[71] The Ottoman administration utilised these beliefs and correlated them with the worldly condition of its subjects. The ultimate aim was to legitimate the sultan's ruling powers and create a sense of togetherness for all Ottomans. To that end, the sultan reinforced his image as the 'ultimate sovereign of the Ottoman Empire administration', the legitimate representative of God on Earth and the fountain of all wealth and economic good. An Ottoman subject needs to abide by the rules of the sultan, otherwise she will be deprived of all good.[72]

In official documents, the sultan is referred to as 'the shadow of God on Earth', 'commander of the Faithful', 'imam of Muslims', 'protector of Islam', 'supporter of *Şeriat*', 'Sultan of Turks, Arabs and foreigners', 'King of earthly kings', 'granter of welfares', 'anchor of scholars', 'custodian of the Two Holy Mosques' and more. The sultan is capable of bestowing wealth and power on those he chooses. He is able to confer political and economic privileges as well as honours, titles and social status. He monitors money shifts and acquisitions and has all the power to eradicate privileges and confiscate wealth. This correlation facilitates one of the most valued assets of the regime—its legitimacy. The sultan's powers, we are reminded, are eventually 'nothing but a mediator for the enforcement of Islamic *Şeriat* rules'.[73]

These political and economic powers were not only exercised, but also displayed publicly and vocally. In fact, the sultan took all measures to advertise his power and wealth. Thus, for example, the sultan and his court of high officials, guards, servants and wives were all dressed luxuriously.

---

[68] Quran 43: 32.
[69] Quran 102: 1–8.
[70] M Abdul-Rauf, *A Muslim's Reflections on Democratic Capitalism* (Washington, DC, American Enterprise Institute, 1984) 19; S Sait and H Lim, *Paper 1: Islamic Land Theories and their Application* (Nairobi, UN-HANITAT, 2005) 10.
[71] Bahammam (n 64) location 277.
[72] Yediyildiz (n 34) 524–27.
[73] ibid.

The sultan held extravagant feasts attended by high-ranking subjects and aliens. Parades were held in his honour. His inspection tours of the local population with his formal staff and extravagant carts publicised his affluence and claim for the fatherly care of his people. His ubiquitous military officers, who were constantly roaming the land, publicised his control. All these were messengers of the sultan's portrait as the mighty protector of the Empire and source of all worldly good. According to Boyar and Fleet, extravagance and performance worked to sustain the 'legitimacy' of the sultan's dominion. Royal staging became part of the population's contentment and political stability. It sustained the sultan's superiority and ruling powers in the eyes of the public.[74]

Validity and stability were also enhanced by the sultan's religious image as caliph of Muslims. Sultans continued to use the title of caliph until the Turkish war of independence. The title appealed to the public and generated much fascination and reverence. It adorned the sultan's image radiating spirituality in every corner of the Empire. Myths ascribing blessing and malediction powers to the sultan were fervently disseminated.[75] It was another tool in the hands of the administration to enforce the sultan's ostensible authority and power, and to enhance correlation of religious beliefs with Ottoman life postulates.

In his study on the rational construction of 'Ottoman public identity' in the nineteenth century, Mardin discusses the use of Islamic rhetoric to generate a sense of shared identity. He cites a sultan edict issued following loss of fortresses in the war against the Russians. The edict describes the loss as offensive to Islam. It appeals to listeners' religious zeal noting each subject's duty to defend Islam and battle 'for the Glory of God'. The edict urges Ottomans to fight back and relaunch 'Mohammedan call to prayer' in the lost provinces. According to Mardin, while previous edicts urged 'unity' as well, the call to revive 'Mohammedan virtue' was novel. It elevated the role of religion as the 'new coordinating force' capable of forming 'solidarity, uniformity and responsibility' among Ottomans.[76] Such edicts marked the rise of the *ummah* rhetoric denoting 'the essential unity' of Muslims despite linguistic, ethnic and social differences.[77] It was a nineteenth-century strategy utilised by the administration to enhance its power and legitimacy.

This correlative strategy suited major demographic changes in the Empire at the time. On the one hand, the number of the general population was steadily decreasing. On the other, the number of Muslims was increasing. The decrease in the general population is mostly associated

---

[74] Boyar and Fleet (n 36) 28–32.
[75] ibid 31, 35–39.
[76] Mardin (n 6) 126–30.
[77] 'Ummah', *The Oxford Dictionary of Islam* (2003) 327.

with the 'loss of lands during wars', while the increase in the number of Muslims is often attributed to the mass immigration of Muslims from defeated areas to provinces of the Empire. For instance, in 1844, the total population of the Empire amounted to 35.35 million with the Muslim majority standing at 58.13 per cent and comprising 20.55 million. In 1906, the total population was estimated at 20.88 million with a Muslim majority of 74.26 per cent and 15.5 million subjects. These numbers continued to change in 1914, with the total number of the population dropping to 18.52 million, and the percentage of Muslims rising to 81.12 per cent.[78]

The systematic use of religion to enhance legitimacy and stability was not confined to administrative actions but extended to Ottoman Islamic art and architecture.[79] One of the founding postulates of Sunni Islamic art is the ban on portrayals of prophets, saints, humans and animals. According to Titus Burckhardt, this ban stands on two propositions. One is the rejection of deities holding that any portrayal, real or imagined, can turn into an object of sinful reverence and fallen exaltation. It reiterates the Islamic call that 'there is no divinity save God' (*'lā ilāha illa Llāh'*). The other proposition is the religious belief in God's perfection and the inimitability of His creation. For this reason, any human portrayal is a sin as it equates the error-prone productions of humans to God's perfect creation.[80]

Holiness in Islamic art is not accentuated by portrayal of the spiritual or temporal, but by inviting the beholder to contemplate the transcendent and eternal rather than the concrete and temporary. This is achieved by the extensive use of lines and intertwining forms. These abstractions prevent concentration on any fixed point offering instead a rhythmic sense of continuation and boundless flow of shapes. The aim is to avoid 'mental fixation' on any figure or object which might induce idolatry. Arabesque is a good example of such art. Arabesque is basically a form of decoration which rests on geometric abstracts, intertwining lines with repetitive symmetries. These designs dwell, sometimes, around a centre point bearing God's name (*Allah*). This form of art expresses the belief in 'Divine Unity' reflected by closed-ended designs symbolising 'harmony' of diversities and the circle of life. It is also reflected by open-ended lines which depict human longing for eternity. Anomalies are sometimes detected in line patterns which some have suggested are intentional errors by the artists to show modesty and human error as opposed to God's perfection.[81]

---

[78] Yediyildiz (n 34) 558, 612–17.
[79] See generally Z Zygulski, *Ottoman Art in the Service of Empire* (New York, New York University Press, 1991).
[80] T Burckhardt, *Art of Islam, Language and Meaning*, Kindle edn (Bloomington, IND, World Wisdom, 2009) locations 822–43.
[81] ibid locations 843–57, 1320, 1377, 1385, 1403, 1434–40.

According to Edward H Madden, these traits express a culture which is 'social and traditional' not 'idiosyncratic' or 'self-expressive'. Unlike Western art which accentuates specific historical and stylistic contexts, Islamic art represents religious postulates unbound by spatial or temporal dimensions. Thus, while Western iconography, for example, portrays biblical figures in mortal forms, Islamic iconography transcends mortality by using geometric forms and flowing lines. These exemplify core differences between Islamic and Western cultures. The late Ottoman Empire utilised Islamic art to enhance political legitimacy and 'Ottomanise' culture. This process, however, did not rest on a passive consumption of Islamic art, but on a rationalised endorsement of that art. Traditionally, Islamic art was neither objectified nor detached from its authentic context. Arabesque designs decorated actual doors and windows. Calligraphy ornamented grounds and ceilings. For this reason, the Western notion of museums where artistic objects were organised, categorised and displayed in laboratory conditions was alien to Islamic tradition.[82] But it was not so to late Ottoman tradition.

The late Ottoman Empire sought to utilise Islamic art and architecture in a systematic manner to produce and sustain a sense of 'heritage' and 'dynasty'. Religious art became a rationalised tool in a ceaseless process to Ottomanise culture and forge an 'Ottoman nation' transcending all lingo-ethnic differences among subjects of the Empire.[83] According to Wendy MK Shaw, late-Ottoman administrations endorsed the idea of museums holding many Islamic art exhibitions. These displays enhanced 'the construction of nationalist visions' says Shaw. They managed to reframe 'religion as belonging to the empire' she adds.[84] Islamic architecture was systematically treated as part of Ottoman architecture. A study titled 'The Fundamentals of Ottoman Architecture' was published in Istanbul in 1873 introducing a new genre of critical monographs asserting the so-called Ottoman architectural postulates.[85]

In contrast to the timeless aesthetics of Islamic designs, such monographs Ottomanised Islamic architecture by applying a spatiotemporal fixation. They 'historicised' and examined it by 'paradigms of stylistic change'.[86] In Ahmet Ersoy's view, the historiography of Ottoman architecture, as

---

[82] E Madden, 'Some Characteristics of Islamic Art' (1975) 33(4) *Journal of Aesthetics and Art Criticism* 423, 423–24; M Talili, *Conference Report: Clash of Civilizations or Clash of Perceptions?* (New York, Dialogues, 2002) 8, available at: www.centerfordialogues.org/publications_islam_and_the_West/Clash_of_Civilizations_or_Clash_of_Perceptions/clash_06.html.

[83] A Ersoy 'Architecture and the Search for Ottoman Origins in the Tanzimat Period' (2007) 24 *Muqarnas* 117, 117.

[84] W Shaw 'Islamic Arts in the Ottoman Imperial Museum, 1889–1923' (2000) 30 *Ars Orientalis* 55, 55; Deringil (n 2) 150–65.

[85] Ersoy (n 83) 134.

[86] ibid 122.

treated in the said monograph, accentuated 'political and cultural aspirations' of the regime. It glorified Islamic tradition and 'naturalised' its association with Ottoman culture, all with the aim of boosting the legitimacy of the ruling administration and safeguarding stability.[87] In similar vein at the time, many Ottoman mosques were built in a systematic manner. In Istanbul alone, dozens were erected, notably the Teşvikiye Mosque (1794–1854) of Şişli district, the Nusretiye Mosque (1823–26) located in the Beyoğlu district, the Dolmabahçe Mosque (1853–55) of the Beyoğlu district, the Ortaköy Mosque (1853–56) in Beşiktaş, the Pertevniyal Valide Sultan Mosque (1869–71), the Aziziye Mosque (1872–74) in Konya, and the Yildiz Hamidiye Mosque (1884–86) located in the Beşiktaş district.

According to Burckhardt, what is unique about the Ottoman mosque is that in contrast to European architecture which fervently separated 'art' from 'technique', Ottoman architecture maintained a natural link between the two. It consolidated 'beauty' and 'functionality' and maintained their unity. A construction was deemed aesthetic as long as it was useful. According to Burckhardt, this tie denoted humans' place intermediating between 'Heaven' and 'Earth'.[88] The Empire's attempt to monopolise Islam was not confined, however, to art and architecture but extended to the very core of Islamic religion, the holy Quran. Following a steady arrival of forbidden Iranian prints of the Quran into the Empire, the administration decided to forbid its printing save by the Empire's official press.[89]

This decision should not be interpreted as a sheer defensive measure against doctrinal threats generated by Shia prints. The ban on private Quran printing included prints produced in 'Sunni Kazan' and even prints produced by the most authoritative Sunni institution for the study of the Quran, 'al-Azhar'. The administration established a commission to inspect Quran prints and no printings were allowed without the explicit consent of that commission. According to Deringil, what was threatened here is not the Sunni doctrine of the Quran, or at least not only that, but more so 'the legitimacy of the Ottoman Caliphate'. Thus, 'it was no longer enough to be a Muslim, or indeed a Sunni' to be part of the *ummah*, says Deringil, a person needed to be Ottoman and abide her ruler.[90]

To sum up, it seems that the Ottoman perception of wealth was nurtured on both the distinctive socio-political condition of life in the late Empire and on a perception rooted in Islam and revitalised by the Ottoman administration. Wealth acquisition and materiality were controlled by a philosophy of accountability. They marked one's proximity to the ruler and testified social status. Ottoman subjects were entrusted

---

[87] ibid 132.
[88] Burckhardt (n 79) locations 2394–2560.
[89] Deringil (n 2) 53–56.
[90] ibid.

with their allotted share of wealth and the societal terms of their social stratum. Their actions and deeds were monitored and answerable to a higher source, the ruler. Violating the terms of this earthly trust entailed political, social and economic redresses and conceptual reframing.

OBSERVING OTTOMAN LAW AND CULTURE: THE EXCEPTIONAL
CASE OF *IMITATIO*

One of the developed forms of *mimesis* is *imitatio*. *Imitatio* is the Latin translation of 'the Greek term *mimesis*'. It denotes the masterly 'imitation of role models and the ability to make something new out of old traditions'. Unlike *mimesis*, *imitatio* does not rest on intuitive, spontaneous and organic imitation of the world, but on a rationalised process of 'reproduction' which targets 'trusted conventions' to create a novel copy. It transforms the organic traits of a work into artificial ones. *Imitatio* of art and literature was practised for centuries in Western civilisation producing many admired works from original ones. With the rise of modernity, however, this artistic practice was considered counterfeiting and was mostly discontinued.[91]

According to Matthew Potolsky, many cultures used *imitatio* to affirm 'unity' with past traditions. Roman culture, for example, proclaimed 'continuity' with Greek culture by skilfully reproducing Greek artwork. Similarly, Renaissance cogitators affirmed their ties to the past by imitating Roman literature. *Imitatio* used postulates of original works to reproduce new compositions. Yet unlike *mimesis* which is generated by genuine social and cultural practices, *imitatio* adds Potolsky 'is based on the conscious use of conventions'.[92] It is a purposeful process of imitation which can easily be used by any emulator to serve legitimation goals. This was the case with the Ottoman administration and the *Mecelle*.

The *Mecelle* was a work of *imitatio*. The Ottoman administration used *Şeriat* law to reproduce an original new piece of *Şeriat* law. This process did not rest on mere copying of available materials, but on a conscious and prudent process of reproduction. In this, what Deringil described as the '*Ottomanization* of *Şeriat*' was not mere reframing of Islamic law but more so laying a claim to 'unity' and 'continuity' with the glorified past of Islamic tradition. This step was part of a more grandiose plan to legitimise and normalise the Empire's ruling powers. The Ottoman administration consciously opted for a political and rational use of Islam to refashion its image and Ottomanise its culture. *Imitatio* was the best method to achieve

---

[91]   M Potolsky, *Mimesis* (New York, Routledge, 2006) 50–52.
[92]   ibid 51–54, 74–75.

those ends. It was a promising redress to the 'legitimacy crises' faced by the regime at the time.[93]

Resting on the unique socio-political condition of Ottoman society, the administration consciously generated a religious discourse of wealth which corresponded in many senses to the actual life conditions of its subjects. Religiosity was reproduced to serve politics. Religious accountability before God for one's wrongful deeds was remade into a legal liability which bore many traits of the original materials. This process of reproduction reciprocated with socio-political accountability for one's own actions before the sultan and his administration. The *Mecelle* reproduced the Islamic doctrine of *ġaṣb* with what the Ottoman condition could afford. The crux of Ottoman *ġaṣb* was neither the action involved nor any element of the enrichment incident. It was the question of each person's accountability for her deeds before a higher power.

In this, the *Mecelle* imitated a perception cut across the socio-ethnic diversities of the Empire's population. Though the *Mecelle* was written in Ottoman Turkish, it drew heavily on Arabo-Islamic terms, practices and ethics. Shortly after its promulgation, the *Mecelle* was officially translated into Arabic and was used in Arabic speaking regions as well. It was an important step in a comprehensive plan to reproduce Islam, Ottomanise it and claim ownership. The *Mecelle* was another tool by the Ottoman administration to regain power and stability formerly enjoyed by the regime. It was meant to generate the desired sense of *umma*, one nation of Muslims under God led by His earthly steward, the sultan and his administration.[94]

The *Mecelle* endorsed the powerful religious frame and terminology of *ġaṣb* to fashion the factual case of a wrongful enrichment. It correlated religiosity with reality, applying harsh judgements to such incidents. In those incidents, the enriched person does not simply take or use another person's property wrongfully. She actually commits a serious transgression against God's commandments and sinfully challenges the divinely and worldly shares of wealth allotted to her and the disadvantaged person. Consequently, she is held legally responsible for her wrongful deeds. This composed scene nurtures on the socio-political reality lived by Ottomans and works to reinforce it in a path to greater social stability and political legitimacy.

While the European legal right to wealth grew, conceptually at least, independent from political authority, an Ottoman's entitlement to wealth stood on the merits of a central power, the Divine and His shadow on Earth, the sultan. Each Ottoman is accountable for her deeds before both powers. An Ottoman must report on the way she acquires wealth, the way she spends it and what she engages in her legal *ẕimmit*. In this sense, a

---

[93] Deringil (n 2) 50, 166.
[94] Karpat (n 1).

share of wealth does not reach a person unmediated. It passes through imposed filters of God and the administration. These filters define who shares wealth, how it is shared and when wealth is to be handed back. In this reciprocal dialect, heavenly and earthly powers enforce and legitimise each other. Restitution, or clearing one's record (*zimmit*) to use the words of the *Mecelle*, meets expectations in terms of legal duty, religious commandments and socio-political expectations.

Restitution in the Ottoman law of wrongful enrichment is neither about restoring rights or objects as is the case in the European context, nor is it about rectification of one's wrongful behaviour as in the American context. It is an issue of trust, of social and religious expectations and of aligning to potent rules of religion and society. This was a novel creation by the Ottoman administration which rested on recycled tenets of religion and corresponded to the living conditions of Ottomans. Perhaps, in this, the Ottoman administration identified what Michel Foucault described a century later. He said that reality does not offer 'a legible face' which humans simply read. The world has 'no prediscursive providence' which acts on human lives, he adds. It must be humans who shape their reality. Or as Sara Mills explains the point more plainly: 'there is no intrinsic order to the world itself other than the ordering which we impose on it'.[95]

---

[95] S Mills, *Discourse*, 2nd edn (London, Routledge, 2004) 47.

Conclusions

ONE OF THE main objectives of this study is to elucidate the manner with which culture participates in the construction of law and meaning as regards wrongful enrichment. While former studies in the field have largely ignored the cultural perspective, the current study demonstrates how culture in fact informs the poetics of this law. To do that, the study had to abandon positivistic analysis and embrace, instead, a *verstehen* approach, seeking meaning elucidations. It targeted those distal powers of cultural perceptions which imbued legal crafting with distinctive patterning models. To that end, we were able to find significant affinity between exemplars traced on the level of legal forming and the dominant themes of wealth in each supra-culture. It is, thus, safe to claim that the ethical idea that 'nobody should be made richer through loss and wrong to another' though universal in its prescription, is essentially bound by the distinctive cultural perceptions which give it further shape and meaning.

As an artefact of both professional craftsmanship and cultural artistry, law displays discernible congruence to postulates of the legal profession as well as to those of cultural perceptions. Such congruence of law-as-knowledge is prone to be present in professional jargon, technical, stylish, mechanical and functional aspects of the law. Congruence of law-as-culture, on the other hand, is traceable mostly in the semantic moulds and significances which construct the imagery dimension of the law. These processes which lie in the expositional and descriptive layers of the law determine how the cognitive image is composed and how it communicates the legal message. In general, the more we zoom out of the image and evade traits of legal dynamics, the more we are revealed to culture's hidden epigraph. The aim of this study was not to trace cultural substance in legal content. This is a barren method with few discernible fruits. The aim was, instead, to investigate those postulates of legal crafting which seem to have cultural origins and happen to leave their mark on the final product.

Opting for a study of poetics was driven by several reasons. One is to avoid the largely dead-end attempts to trace direct gateways to culture, as if the law-as-culture question is merely one of content absorption. Second is to demonstrate how culture is present in legal poetics and not necessarily in legal dynamics, namely not in what law conveys but in how law conveys. Third is to show how cultural discourses and perceptions of wealth can provide a telling contextualisation of wrongful enrichment law. Fourth is to introduce comparative law-and-culture scholarship to the important role of poetics and mimesis. In fact, one of the working assumptions of this study is that culture only infrequently presents a direct and unmediated 'cause' of law. Claiming a necessarily cause–effect relationship between the two realms seems inaccurate and can be misleading. A study of the cultural context, on the other hand, elucidates the general settings for the examined law rather than the fuel for its dynamics. It traces the affinities between distinctive patterns of legal crafting and the unique cultural perceptions of wealth.

On more general and holistic levels, law is necessarily affected by culture but insistence on discerning immediate causes can be illusory. The main question as generated by this book was not whether culture affects restitution and unjustified enrichment law. As suggested by cognitive, linguistic and cultural studies, this tie is not only intuitive but inevitable. The question was rather how culture does that. The general predisposition is that law is unavoidably nurtured by discourses and themes of culture, but the question remains: how? To answer this question, the current study suggests a model of law as a mimetic artefact. According to this model, law like any other artefact possesses a mimetic trait which works to imitate postulates of its settings. Two sorts of notable postulates in legal crafting are those of the legal profession and those of the wider pool of meanings and concepts we call culture. With the power of mimesis, the law works to optimise meaning and to naturalise it. To evoke acceptance, law imitates life as we perceive it. It facilitates the communication of meaning as well as empowers the normative justification of the law. Law, thus, utilises mimesis to convey meaning, authority and legitimacy.

The current study examined the legal poetics of wrongful enrichment in three different setting: Europe, the United States of America and the late Ottoman Empire. Three pivotal differences were observed in crafting the case of intentional appropriation and exploitation of another's property. They could be respectively marked as Asset, Action and Accountability poetics, the 3A paradigm. European law constructs a scene which underscores the private domain of the disadvantaged person and his attachment to property. Wrongful enrichment, there, is mainly projected as a displacement of property and challenge to the private sphere, entailing restitution of the asset and reinstitution of the disadvantaged person back as lord of his domain. American law manifests a subtle care for the action involved. It embraces an ethical description of the wrongful conduct projecting the scene primarily as a person who makes a gain through wrongful conduct. This misconduct calls for restitution as behavioural rectification. And finally, the Ottoman *Mecelle* utilises powerful poetics of socio-religious accountability, representing the case as grave defilement of social and divine terms, and restitution as clearing one's personal record.

The cultural explication of discourses and perceptions of wealth suggested that these poetics, in fact, correspond to broad, albeit deeply-rooted, premises of culture. The European context marked the celebration and triumph of the proprietary and the growing alienation of wealth from questions of labour and conduct. The American context marked the continuing significance of the work ethic and the religious dualistic perception of life. It also signified the unique status of money in American society. The Ottoman context demonstrated an administration in 'crisis' which opted for the consensual language of Islam to boost its legitimacy and the sense of unity and solidarity among its subjects. Culture seemed to draw the line of normative legitimacy. In medieval Europe, wealth meant labour, religiosity and social merits. Wealth which did not abide those postulates was considered unacceptable, a sin and a risk to society. In the Renaissance and early modern Europe, wealth meant private domain and belongings. Encroaching on the wealth of a person was a direct challenge to his domain, and deprivation of his possessions. This perception was sharpened with the rise of modern political and economic ideas of property as a basic right and as capital.[1] The perceptions of wealth drew the lines protecting these new configurations. Crossing the lines was deemed a wrongful enrichment.

In America, wealth is perceived as personal effort, money and morals. America, thus, focuses on the active pursuit of money. American law abstains from halting the shift of wealth from one person to another unless a problem is observed. In a case of the intentional exploitation of another's property, the law intervenes to rectify the wrongful behaviour by way of restitution, or disgorgement to use a more sensible term. In the late Ottoman Empire, wealth was placed on the merits of a central power, namely God and His earthly representative, the sultan. A person's deeds with which he acquires wealth, spends it and engages in his *zimmit* makes him accountable before that central power. Ottoman wealth is, thus, a matter of trust, of socio-religious prescriptions and dishonour. The *Mecelle* correlated religiosity with reality, turning incidents of wrongful enrichment into the blameworthy acts of *ġaṣb* with all the religious and social baggage that comes with this religious terminology. This purposeful correlation promised a more stable Empire and a more legitimate regime.

The latter context puts us back before the inevitable question: why law imitates culture. Prompting this question raises the phenomenon of legal

---

[1] A Gambaro, 'Western Property Law' in M Bussani and F Werro (eds), *European Private Law: A Handbook* (Berne, Stämpfli, 2009) 47, 55; A Clarke and P Kohler, *Property Law: Commentary and Materials* (Cambridge, Cambridge University Press, 2006) 297; J Merryman, *The Civil Law Tradition: An Introduction to the Legal Systems of Europe and Latin America* (Stanford, CA, Stanford University Press, 2007) 18–20.

mimesis to the level of consciousness. If we can understand why this happens, we may be able to make purposeful, rationalised and, I dare say, artificial use of mimesis. This is hardly a novel suggestion. The concept of mimesis is originally borrowed from literary and artistic fields where it was occasionally put to such use. One of the various important functions of the term is its capability to generate 'a sense of reality'. This sense does not refer to the ontological reality, namely what lies out there, but to the epistemological one, namely how we know and perceive what is out there. In this sense, mimesis articulates the 'complicated set of ideas about how human beings think, feel and understand the world and each other' as uniquely developed within each supra-culture.[2]

The explications of the American and European contexts vis-a-vis the Ottoman one commit us to the preliminary answers we provided earlier as to why law imitates culture. The first is that using mimesis the law enhances our understanding of the subject treated. Using pertaining rubrics and themes of culture the legal artefact optimises meaning and public understanding. In this sense, mimesis actively participates in the process of meaning-making by providing cognitive significances already grounded and understood in our wider perceptions of life experience, thus helping us make clearer sense of the legal artefact.[3] The second is that mimesis institutes legitimacy. Like artistic work which draws its legitimacy from 'its relation to reality'[4]—again, as culturally construed—law enhances its legitimacy by resting on discourses and themes which enjoy wide cultural approbation.[5] Ronald Barthes describes this condition as the *continuing* reference of textuality to 'the numerous codes of knowledge or wisdom' produced by culture. Textuality injects the reader with a sense of the '*familiar*' and the *natural* utilising cultural conventions of the reader's world. *Mimesis* enhances legitimacy by appealing to what 'has already been read, seen, done' and 'experienced'. Rather than violating conventions, it adheres to them corresponding to people's life 'expectations'.[6]

One only needs to imagine the meaning chaos and legitimacy crisis produced if we implant the Islamic artefact of *ġaṣb* in American law. As elaborated in previous chapters, the perceptions of wealth in each context differ significantly. While both have religious roots, each culture utilises

---

[2] M Potolsky, *Mimesis* (New York, Routledge, 2006) 49, 105.

[3] W van Peer 'Where Do Literary Themes Come From?' in M Louwerse and W van Peer (eds), *Thematics: Interdisciplinary Studies* (Amsterdam, John Benjamines, 2002) 253, 253–60.

[4] H Blumenberg 'The Concept of Reality and the Possibility of the Novel' in R Amacher and V Lange (eds), *New Perspectives in German Literary Criticism* (Princeton. NJ, Princeton University Press, 1977) 30 cited in M Potolsky, *Mimesis* (New York, Routledge, 2006) 93.

[5] *cf* S Mills, *Discourse* (London, Routledge, 2004) 46.

[6] R Barthes, *S/Z: An Essay*, trans R Miller (New York, Hill and Wang, 1974) 18, 20, 206; Potolsky (n 2) 109–110.

a totally different aspect of religiosity. Furthermore, American culture stresses progressive thinking, the power to be 'reborn', to fight one's way to the top and to be a self-reliant self-made man. These values contradict head-on the Ottoman understanding of social and religious accountability, with the Ottoman conservative life philosophy and with the Ottoman traditional submissiveness to higher forces. In this thought experiment two scenarios are feasible. The first is that the 'alien' rules would soon find their way out of the legal corpus. The second is that culture would enforce 'American' interpretations of these norms which would make it possible to bypass the mimesis failure produced by the implant.

In addition, the Ottoman experience with *imitatio*, or the so-called 'Ottomanisation' of Şeriat, reveals the possible use and abuse of legal poetics to achieve ideological or political ends. It demonstrates an extreme attempt to boost a sovereign's legitimacy by deliberate work of *mimesis*. Though Şeriat law was 'the law of the land' also prior to the Ottomanisation process, what was novel was the production of a learned and systematic mimesis by Şeriat law of the socio-political reality lived by Ottomans. Ottoman *imitatio* was, thus, not aimed only at artefact-reality relation, but also on artefact-audience one.[7] The 'Ottomanization of' Şeriat, to use Selim Deringil's term, constituted a conscious labour of constructing a recognisable imaginary world, which aspired to convince Ottomans, first that it was a genuine continuation of their own world, and second that this imaginary world may and, more so, should be used for interpreting and conceiving the real one they inhabit.[8]

These observations are inextricably linked to the cause versus justification debate presented in the introduction of this book. If legal poetics are indeed important to questions of legitimacy, the persistence of cultural elucidations of law seems an important measure for the preservation of legal authority and possibly the legal system altogether. Mimesis is a critical factor for the legitimacy of any legislative and judicial act in the eyes of the public. This may be a less subversive terminology to that of 'power' struggles often used in critical studies.[9] As explicated in previous chapters, mimesis may and could appeal to the wider circle of meanings and values which ties together the people of a certain nation, region or political entity, and defines their collective identity. Therefore, it could be argued that one way to safeguard the legal ethos of objectivity and neutrality lies in its inner capacity to imitate themes and values sustained by the wide cultural circles.

---

[7] ibid 49.

[8] *cf* M Brinker, 'Theme and Interpretation' in W Sollors (ed), *The Return of Thematic Criticism* (Cambridge, MA, Harvard University Press, 1993) 21, 30; Deringil (n 15) 50.

[9] See, eg, J Conley and W O'Bar, *Just Words: Law, Language and Power* (Chicago, IL, Chicago University Press, 2005) 6–9.

On the level of restitution and unjustified enrichment law doctrine, it is possible to add the following two observations. First, that though this law appeals to a moral—some say positivistic—idea, it perpetually converses with specific cultural discourses of wealth that give it shape and meaning. And second, that the general moral or positivistic idea against improper enrichment could also be articulated (not necessary explained) in terms of legitimacy and appeal to culture. While wrongful enrichment could be termed as a shift of wealth which contests our sense of morality and justice or which the law prohibits,[10] it could also be termed as that which culture cognitively perceives and verbally conceives as so. In this respect, it is possible to deem it a deprivation of legally owned wealth in Europe, a reaping of profit through misconduct in America, and a defilement of social and religious expectations in the late Ottoman Empire.

Some studies have analysed the ramifications of the use of restitution law in human rights abuses. These studies assess, inter alia, the power of a restitution-for-wrong claim to generate and mutate cultural meanings. Notable examples are those discussing pecuniary reparations for human rights abuses.[11] One of the chief questions examined is whether claims brought under these laws by victims of the Holocaust, slavery, Second World War forced labour, and massacres serves to 'commoditise' human suffering.[12] A main argument suggests that putting price tags on serious crimes against humanity using the daily rhetoric of private law disputes threatens to tamper with our basic understanding of heinous atrocities. These implications could indeed be inevitable when we attempt to 'measure' complex moral issues using simple monetary scales.[13]

Our study, however, may add two further remarks on this topic. First is that the question whether restitution law terminology commoditises human suffering should not be discussed in universal terms as, if restitution law means the same everywhere, it should rather be addressed with culture in mind. For example, it could be prudently argued that a European sense would prefer to discuss the 'appropriating of humans'

---

[10] H Dagan, *The Law and Ethics of Restitution* (Cambridge, Cambridge University Press, 2004)12–25.

[11] See generally M Bazyler, 'The Holocaust Restitution Movement in Comparative Perspective' (2002) 20 *Berkeley Journal of International Law* 11; M Bazyler, *Holocaust Justice: The Battle for Restitution in America's Courts* (New York, New York University Press, 2003).

[12] A Sebok 'Two Concepts of Injustice in Restitution for Slavery' (2004) 84 *Boston University Law Review* 1405; Dagan, *The Law and Ethics of Restitution* (n 10) 246–54; H Dagan, 'Restitution and Slavery: On Incomplete Commodification, Intergenerational Justice, and Legal Transitions' (2004) 84 *Boston University Law Review* 1139; D Klimchuk, 'Unjust Enrichment and Reparations for Slavery' (2004) 84 *Boston University Law Review* 1257.

[13] G Taylor, 'Where Morality Meets Money' in M Bazyler and R Alford, *Holocaust Restitution: Perspectives on the Litigation and its Legacy* (New York, New York University Press, 2006) 163, 163–164.

rather than the 'monetising of human suffering' which seems an American way of articulating the problem. Different articulations appeal to different discourses, hence, different rhetorics and considerations. Second, that commodification is not the only issue on the table. Restitution law relies on a variety of cultural themes and discourses. It is by no means confined to themes of money and commerce. American culture, for example, has a very powerful right–wrong discourse which is grounded in religious values and cuts across perceptions of wealth. A legislative or judicial strategy which consciously and purposefully utilises the ideas of wrongfulness and religious values could be very appealing to American ears and can balance the negative ramifications of money talk in these cases. Restitution law could be discussed with a conscious intention to sustain an equilibrium between the different themes involved, or to put it more generally, employing *imitatio* to serve desired ends in enrichment law can be a very useful strategy. In this use, *imitatio* invites culture to imitate law.

On the whole, the book encourages better cross-cultural understanding between three major 'civilisations' of our contemporary world: the American, the European and the Islamic. Two sources I came across were anecdotal yet intriguing on this point. One was Donald Quataert's *The Ottoman Empire, 1700–1922*, which mentioned that long ago 'Viennese mothers put their children to bed warning them to behave lest the "Turks" come and gobble them up'.[14] Another was Selim Deringil's *The Well-Protected Domains* which cited a letter written on 28 November 1895 by the Ottoman ambassador to Washington saying: 'Although it is undeniable that the United States of America has recorded great progress in science, technology and industry', 'there is no respect for religion or rulers, and they do not hesitate to attack even their own president in the most scandalous language, to the extent of calling President Cleveland a drunk'. 'Families are ruined every day by such malicious attacks. Therefore, it would be correct to say that this is a savage country'.[15] While each story probably had its presumed stimuli, they both involved some deep-rooted cross-cultural misrepresentations which we ought to recognise and avoid.

The current book has not dealt with unintentional wrongs, nonproprietary wrongs or cases involving public authorities. It also did not treat cases of enrichment not classified under the rubric of wrongs, such as mistaken payments or other cases of impaired consent. It may be, thus, prudent to confine our observations and conclusions to the cases we considered. Furthermore, the study refrains from pondering the actual

---

[14] D Quataert, *The Ottoman Empire, 1700–1922* (Cambridge, Cambridge University Press, 2007) 1–2.
[15] S Deringil, *The Well-Protected Domains: Ideology and Legitimation of Power in the Ottoman Empire 1876–1909* (London, Tauris, 2011) 141.

dynamics of the law and limits its frontier to the study of legal poetics. It appeals to culture in general refraining from discussing varieties, specifications and intra-differences in each. On the one hand this could be a drawback, on the other it stresses the importance of macro-level studies which give us a broad-brush idea of what is out there. In this respect, the study abstains from examining political, class, ethnic and cultural struggles and controversies within each context, favouring instead what seems basic and dominant postulates in the wealth perceptions of each supra-culture.

While each limitation of the abovementioned provides a prospective route for future research, for example, a study on the comparative national levels or broadening the type of cases, I wish to point out a few more routes which could prove particularly fruitful. First, since the discourses and perceptions of wealth may prove relevant to other fields of law, such as contract, tort and property laws, it may be possible to find similar traits in the legal poetics of these fields as well. This could, and should, be verified for two reasons: (1) the ceaseless harmonisation projects of EU and US law have encompassed these fields as well; (2) *mimesis* and the poetics of the law are inextricable to the sustaining of legitimacy. Second, further research could empirically examine the cogitated dependency of legitimacy on legal poetics. Third, it could investigate rhetorical uses of textuality and its appeal to cultural conventions and social values. And finally, it is possible to utilise the model of law as a memetic artefact in the field of legal historiography and to use it as an additional tool to validate and crosscheck observations on the development of law.

This book has been an expeditionary journey to a *terra* which is mostly *incognita*, and for that sake it is important to admit forthrightly that it is not necessarily the only or even the best way to map what is out there. Hence, perhaps it is useful to conclude this humble journey with the words of Clifford Geertz:

> Cultural analysis is intrinsically incomplete. And, worse than that, the more deeply it goes the less complete it is. It is a strange science whose most telling assertions are its most tremulously based, in which to get somewhere with the matter at hand is to intensify the suspicion, both your own and that of others, that you are not quite getting it right.[16]

I hope this study, adventurous, daring and incomplete as it is, encourages others to explore new ways of looking at the human artefact we call law.

---

[16] C Geertz, 'Thick Description: Toward an Interpretive Theory of Culture' in C Geertz (ed), *The Interpretation of Cultures* (New York, Basic Books, 1973) 3, 29.

Bibliography

Books

Abdul-Rauf, M, *A Muslim's Reflections on Democratic Capitalism* (Washington DC, American Enterprise Institute, 1984).

Agassi, J, *ha-Ni'urut ha-ḥadasha* (*The New Enlightenment*) (Ben-Shemen, Modan, 2012).

al-Dimashqi, 'a, *Sharḥ Īmān al-Tahawi* (*Explanation of the Taḥawī Faith*) (Beirut, al-Risālah, 1997).

al-Qarnī, 'a, *al-Fiqh al-Muyassar* (*Accessible Jurisprudence*) (Riyaḍ, Obeican, 2009).

al-Qubbaj, S, *Majallat al-Aḥkam al-'dlyyah: Maṣāḍiraha wa-'tharaha fī Qwanīn al-Sharq* (*Ottoman Civil Code: Its Sources and Effect on the Laws of the Islamic East*) (Ammān, Alfatḥ, 2008).

al-Sanhūri, A, *al-Waṣīṭ fī Sharḥ al-Qānūn al-Madanī* (*The Mediator in the Explanation of Civil Law*) vol I (Cairo, Dar el-Nashr lel-Jame'at Al-Masryyah, 1952).

al-Sharqawi, W, *Naẓaryat al-ethra' bilā sabab taṭbīqātihā fī al-fiqh al-eslamī* (*The Theory of Unjustified Enrichment in Applications of Islamic Jurisprudence*) (Alexandria, Dar el-jami'a al-jadīda lil-nashr, 2009).

al-Zarqa, M, *al-Madkhal al-Fiqhī al-'ām* (*General Introduction to Fiqh*) (Damascus, Dar al-Kalam, 1998).

Aldrich, N, *Old Money: The Mythology of Wealth in America* (New York, Allworth, 1996).

Almog, S, *Mishpat yi Sifrut bi'idan Digitali* (*Law and Literature in the Digital Age*) (Shrigim-Leon, Nevo, 2007).

Alpa, G and Zeno-Zencovich, V, *Italian Private Law* (Oxford, Routledge-Cavendish, 2007).

Althen, G and Bennett, J, *American Ways: A Cultural Guide to the United States* (Boston, MA, Intercultural, 2011).

Alvarez, C and Picazo, D, *Manuel de la Cámara Alvarez and Díez-Picazo, Dos estudios sobre el enriquecimiento sin causa* (Madrid, Civitas Ediciones, 1991).

Amsterdam, A and Bruner, J, *Minding the Law* (Cambridge, MA, Harvard University Press, 2002).

Andersen, H, *Eventyr fortalte for Børn* III (*Fairy Tales Told for Children*) (Copenhagen, Reitzel, 1837).

Anderson, P, *Lineages of the Absolutist State* (London, Verso, 1974).

Applebaum, H, *The American Work Ethic and the Changing Work Force* (Westport, CT, Greenwood Press, 1999).

Appleby, J, *The Relentless Revolution: A History of Capitalism*, Kindle edn (New York, Norton, 2010).

Aquinas, T, *Summa theologica* (Public Domain, 1485) (online).

Aristotle, *Aristotle's Theory of Poetry and Fine Art*, trans S Butcher (New York, Dover, 1951).

Arneil, B, *John Locke and America: The Defence of English Colonialism* (Oxford, Clarendon Press, 1996).

Bacon, F, *Novum Organum* (*New Instrument*) trans P Urbach and J Gibson (eds) (Illinois, Open Court, 2000).

Bahammam, F, *Wealth in Islam*, Kindle edn (Birmingham, Modern Guide, 2012).

Bahn, P and Tidy, B, *Archaeology: A Very Short Introduction* (Oxford, Oxford University Press, 2000).

Bailey, F, *British Policy and the Turkish Reform Movement: A Study in Anglo-Turkish Relations, 1826–1853* (Cambridge, MA, Harvard University Press, 1942).

Barthes, R, *S/Z: An Essay*, trans R Miller (New York, Hill and Wang, 1974).

Baz, S, *Sharh al-Majallah* (*Commentary on the Ottoman Civil Code*) (Beirut, Dar al-'elm lel-Jamī', 1998).

Bazyler, M, *Holocaust Justice: The Battle for Restitution in America's Courts* (New York, New York University Press, 2003).

Beatson, J and Schrage, E (eds), *Cases, Materials and Texts on Unjustified Enrichment* (Oxford, Hart Publishing, 2003).

Becker, C, *The Declaration of Independence: A Study in the History of Political Ideas* (New York, Peter Smith, 1933).

Bellah, R, Madsen, R and Sullivan, W et al, *Habits of the Heart: Individualism and Commitment in American Life* (Berkeley, CA, University of California Press, 1996).

Bendix, R, *Max Weber: An Intellectual Portrait* (London, University of California Press, 1977).

Benedict, R, *Patterns of Culture* (Boston, MA, Houghton Mifflin, 1934).

Benedict, R and Mead, M, *An Anthropologist at Work* (New Jersey, NJ, Rutgers-State University of New Jersey, 2011).

Bennett, B, *Logically Fallacious* (Subury, eBookIt, 2012).

Berger, J, *Ways of Seeing* (London, Penguin Modern Classics, 2009).

Berkes, N, *The Development of Secularism in Turkey* (London, Hurst & Company, 1998).

Birks, P, *An Introduction to the Law of Restitution* (Oxford, Oxford University Press, 1985).

—— *Unjust Enrichment* (Oxford, Oxford University Press, 2005).

Blackstone, W, *Commentaries on the Laws of England*, vol 2 (Chicago, University of Chicago Press, 1979).

Boeckx, C, *Language in Cognition: Uncovering Mental Structures and the Rules Behind Them* (West Sussex, Wiley-Blackwell, 2010).

Brownie, D, *Ashburner's Principles of Equity* (London, Butterworth & Co, 1933).

Buckland, W and McNair, A, *Roman Law and Common Law: A Comparison in Outline* (Cambridge, Cambridge University Press, 1965).

Burckhardt, J, *The Civilization of the Renaissance in Italy*, trans S Middlemore (London, Penguin, 1990).

—— *Art of Islam, Language and Meaning*, Kindle edn (Bloomington, IND, World Wisdom, 2009).

Burrows, A, *The Law of Restitution* (Oxford, Oxford University Press, 2011).

Butler, C, *Modernism: A Very Short Introduction* (Oxford, Oxford University Press, 2010).

Byyūmī, A, *Lughat al-Qānūn fī Daw' Lughat al-Naṣ: Dirāsa fī a-Ttamāsuk al-Khaṭṭ ī (The Language of Law in Light of Text Language: A Study in Textual Cohesion)* (al-Maḥ alla al-Kubra, Dar al-Kutub al-Qānūnyyah, 2010).

Campbell, J and Robinson, H, *A Skeleton to Finnegans Wake: Unlocking James Joyce's Masterwork* (Novato, CA, New World Library, 2005).

Campbell, N and Kean, A, *American Cultural Studies: An Introduction to American Culture* (Oxford, Routledge, 2012).

Clapham, C, *Third World Politics: An Introduction* (Madison, WI, University of Wisconsin Press, 1985).

Clarke, A and Kohler, P, *Property Law: Commentary and Materials* (Cambridge, Cambridge University Press, 2006).

Cole, M, *Cultural Psychology: A Once and Future Discipline* (Cambridge, MA, Harvard University Press, 2003).

Conley, J and O'Barr, W, *Just Words: Law, Language and Power* (Chicago, IL, University of Chicago Press, 2005).

Coombe, R, *The Cultural Life of Intellectual Properties: Authorship, Appropriation, and the Law* (Durham, NC, Duke University Press, 1998).

Creasy, E and von Hammer-Purgstall, J, *History of the Ottoman Turks: From the Beginning of Their Empire to the Present Time*, vol II (London, Richard Bentley, 1856).

Cucker, F, *Manifold Mirrors: The Crossing Paths of the Arts and Mathematics* (Cambridge, Cambridge University Press, 2013).

Culler, J, *Literary Theory: A Very Short Introduction* (Oxford, Oxford University Press, 2000).

Dagan, H, *Unjust Enrichment: A Study of Private Law and Public Values* (Cambridge, Cambridge University Press, 1997).

—— *The Law and Ethics of Restitution* (Cambridge, Cambridge University Press, 2004).

—— *Reconstructing American Legal Realism and Rethinking Private Law Theory* (Oxford, Oxford University Press, 2013).

Dannemann, G, *The German Law of Unjustified Enrichment and Restitution: A Comparative Introduction* (Oxford, Oxford University Press, 2009).

Dante, A, *Divine Comedy* (Hollywood, Simon & Brown, 2013).

Datesman, M, Crandell, J and Kearny, E, *American Ways: An Introduction to American Culture* (New York, Pearson Education, 2005).

Davies, M, *Property: Meanings, Histories, Theories* (New York, Routledge-Cavendish, 2007).

Deringil, S, *The Well-Protected Domains: Ideology and Legitimation of Power in the Ottoman Empire 1876–1909* (London, Tauris, 2011).

Descartes, R, *Discourse on the Method of Rightly Conducting One's Reason and of Seeking Truth in the Sciences* (Charleston, NC, BiblioBazar, 2007).

Doyle, K, *The Social Meanings of Money and Property: In Search of a Talisman* (Thousand Oaks, CA, Sage, 1999).

Dworkin, R, *Law's Empire* (Cambridge, MA, Harvard University Press, 1986).

Eaton, J, *Handbook of Equity Jurisprudence* (St Paul, MN, West, 1923).

Edgerton, S, *The Renaissance Rediscovery of Linear Perspective* (New York, Basic Books, 1975).

Eisenman, R, *Islamic Law in Palestine and Israel: A History of the Survival of Tanzimat in the British Mandate and Jewish State* (Leiden, Brill, 1978).

el-khafīf, A, *al-Żamān fī al-Fiqh al-Islāmī (Żamān in Islamic Jurisprudence)* (Cairo, Dar el-fikr el-Arabi, 2000).

Engel, D and McCann, M, 'Introduction: Tort Law as Cultural Practice' in D Engel and M McCann (eds), *Fault Lines: Tort Law as Cultural Practice* (Stanford, CA, Stanford University Press, 2009).

Evans, M, *America: The View from Europe* (San Francisco, CA, San Francisco Book, 1976).

Farnsworth, W, *Restitution: Civil Liability for Unjust Enrichment* (Chicago, IL, University of Chicago Press, 2014).

Feldman, N, *The Fall and Rise of the Islamic State*, Kindle edn (New Jersey, NJ, Princeton University Press, 2008).

Findley, C, *Bureaucratic Reform in the Ottoman Empire: The Sublime Porte, 1789–1922* (New Jersey, NJ, Princeton University Press, 1980) 149.

—— *The Turks in World History* (Oxford, Oxford University Press, 2005).

Fischer, C, *Made in America: A Social History of American Culture and Character* (Chicago, IL, University of Chicago Press, 2010).

Fish, S, *Is There a Text in This Class? The Authority of Interpretive Communities* (Cambridge, MA, Harvard University Press, 1980).

Foley, M, *American Credo: The Place of Ideas in US Politics* (New York, Oxford University Press, 2007).

Foster, N and Sule, S, *German Legal System and Laws* (Oxford, Oxford University Press, 2010).

Foucault, M, *The Archaeology of Knowledge* (London, Routledge, 2002).

Gadamer, H, *Method and Truth* (London, Continuum International, 2004).

Garnsey, P, *Thinking about Property: From Antiquity to the Age of Revolution* (Cambridge, Cambridge University Press, 2007).

Giglio, F, *The Foundations of Restitution for Wrongs* (Oxford, Hart Publishing, 2007).

Glendon, M, Carozza, P and Picker, C, *Comparative Legal Traditions in a Nutshell* (St Paul, MN, West, 2008).

Glenn, H, *Legal Traditions of the World* (New York, Oxford University Press, 2007).

Glenny, M, *The Balkans—Nationalism, War, and the Great Powers, 1804–1999* (New York, Penguin, 2001).

Goody, J, *Capitalism and Modernity: The Great Debate* (Cambridge, Polity, 2004).

Gordley, J and von Mehren, A, *An Introduction to the Comparative Study of Private Law: Readings, Cases, Materials* (Cambridge, Cambridge University Press, 2006).

Gray, R, *A History of American Literature*, Kindle edn (West Sussex, Wiley-Blackwell, 2012).

Grund, F, *The Americans in their Moral, Social, and Political Relations*, vol II (London, Longman and Company, 1837).

Gurevich, A, *Categories of Medieval Culture*, trans G Campbell (London, Routledge & Kegan Paul, 1985).

—— *The Origins of European Individualism*, trans K Judelson (Oxford, Blackwell, 1995).

Haider, A, *Durar al-Ḥukkam fī-Sharḥ Majallat al-Aḥ kām (Perils of the Rulers Explaining the Ottoman Civil Code)* vol I, trans F El-husseini (Beirut, al-Nāsher Dar al-Kutub al-'ilmyyah, 1925).

—— *Durar al-Ḥukkam fī-Sharḥ Majallat al-Aḥkām* (*Perils of the Rulers Explaining the Ottoman Civil Code*) vol II, trans F El-husseini (Beirut, al-Nāsher Dar al-Kutub al-'ilmyyah, 1925).

Hobsbawm, E, *Nations and Nationalism Since 1780: Programme, Myth, Reality* (Cambridge, Cambridge University Press, 2012).

Hochschild, J, *Facing Up to the American Dream* (New Jersey, NJ, Princeton University Press, 1996) xvii.

Hofstede, G, Hofstede, GJ and Minkov, M, *Cultures and Organizations: Software for the Mind* (New York, McGraw-Hill, 2010).

—— *Cultures and Organizations: Software for the Mind*, Kindle edn (New York, McGraw-Hill, 2010).

Howell, M and Prevenier, W, *From Reliable Sources: An Introduction to Historical Methods* (Ithaca, NY, Cornell University Press, 2001).

Huber, J and Form, W, *Income and Ideology: An Analysis of the American Political Formula* (New York, Free Press, 1973).

Huntington, S, *Who Are We?: The Challenges to America's National Identity* (New York, Simon & Schuster, 2004).

Imber, C, *Ebu's-Su'ud: The Islamic Legal Tradition* (Stanford, CA, Stanford University Press, 2009).

Jardine, L, *Worldly Goods: A New History of the Renaissance* (London, Macmillan, 1996).

Jespersen, O, *Growth and Structure of the English Language* (Leipzig, BG Teubner, 1912).

Joerges, C, *Bereicherungsrech als Wirtschaftsrecht: Eine Untersuchung zur Entwicklung von Leistungs- und Eingriffskondiktion* (Köln, Otto Schmidt, 1977).

Joseph, S, Schultz, J and Castan, M, *The International Covenant on Civil and Political Rights* (Oxford, Oxford University Press, 2004).

Joyce, J, *Finnegans Wake* (New York, Penguin Books, 1999).

Kahn, P, *The Cultural Study of Law* (Chicago, IL, University of Chicago Press, 1999).

Karpat, K, *The Politicization of Islam: Reconstructing Identity, State, Faith, and Community in the Late Ottoman State* (Oxford, Oxford University Press, 2001).

Keener, W, *A Treatise on the Law of Quasi-Contract* (New York, Baker, Voorhis and Company, 1893).

Khusru, M, *Mir'āt Asāsyyat* (*Mirror of Fundamentals*) (Istanbul, Busnawi, 1872).

Kia, M, *Daily Life in the Ottoman Empire* (Santa Barbara, CA, Greenwood Press, 2011).

Kluegel, J and Smith, E, *Beliefs About Inequality: Americans' Views of What Is and What Ought to Be* (New Jersey, NJ, Transaction Books, 2009).

Knowlton, E, *Joyce, Joyceans, and the Rhetoric of Citation* (Gainesville, FL, University Press of Florida, 1998).

Kolvicki, J, *On Images: Their Structure and Content* (Oxford, Oxford University Press, 2009).

Kramsch, C, *Language and Culture* (Oxford, Oxford University Press, 2001) 13.

Lacorne, D, *Religion in America: A Political History*, trans George Holoch, Kindle edn (New York, Columbia University Press, 2011).

Lakoff, G and Johnson, M, *Metaphors We Live By* (Chicago, IL, University of Chicago Press, 2003).

Lamont, M, *Money, Morals, and Manners: The Culture of the French and American Upper-Middle Class* (Chicago, University of Chicago, 1994) 4.

Lapham, L, *Money and Class in America: Notes and Observations on Our Civil Religion* (New York, Weidenfeld & Nicolson, 1988).

Le Goff, J and Barrow, J, *Medieval Civilization 400–1500* (Oxford, Blackwell, 1991).

Leeming, D and Page, J, *Myths, Legends, and Folktales of America: An Anthology* (Oxford, Oxford University Press, 1999).

Locke, J, *An Essay Concerning Human Understanding* (London, Willian Tegg, 1849).

—— *Two Treatises of Government* (Cambridge, Cambridge University Press, 1988).

Lodder, A, *Enrichment in the Law of Unjust Enrichment and Restitution* (Oxford, Hart Publishing, 2012).

Lorand, R, *Aesthetic Order: A Philosophy of Order, Beauty and Art* (London, Routledge, 2000).

Mâle, E, *Religious Art in France of the Thirteenth Century* (Mineola, NY, Dover, 2012).

Mardin, Ş, *Religion, Society and Modernity in Turkey* (New York, Syracuse University Press, 2006).

Marshall, G, *In Search of the Spirit of Capitalism: An Essay on Max Weber's Protestant Ethic Thesis* (London, Hutchinson, 1982).

Marx, K, *Early Writings* (Harmondsworth, Penguin, 1975).

Marx, K and Engels, F, *The Economic and Philosophic Manuscripts of 1844 and the Communist Manifesto*, trans M Milligan (New York, Prometheus Books, 1988).

Mason, H, *European Masters: Voltaire* (London, Hutchinson, 1975).

Mautner, M, *Mishpat yi Tarbut (Law and Culture)* (Ramat-Gan, Bar-Ilan University Press, 2008).

—— *Law and the Culture of Israel* (New York, Oxford University Press, 2011).

McClanahan, R, *Word Painting: A Guide to Writing More Descriptively* (Cincinnati, OH, Writer's Digest Books, 2000).

McCormick, J, *Europeanism* (Oxford, Oxford University Press, 2010).

McElroy, J, *American Beliefs: What Keeps a Big Country and a Diverse People United* (Chicago, IL, Ivan R Dee, 1999).

Merryman, J, *The Civil Law Tradition: An Introduction to the Legal Systems of Europe and Latin America* (Stanford, CA, Stanford University Press, 2007).

Miles, M and Huberman, M, *Qualitative Data Analysis: An Expanded Sourcebook* (Thousand Oaks, CA, Sage, 1994).

Miller, P, *Errand into the Wilderness* (Cambridge, MA, Harvard University Press, 2000).

Mills, S, *Discourse* (London, Routledge, 1997).

—— *Discourse*, 2nd edn (London, Routledge, 2004).

Minkov, M, *Cross-Cultural Analysis: The Science and Art of Comparing the World's Modern Societies and Their Cultures* (Thousand Oaks, CA, Sage, 2013).

Morris, C, *The Discovery of the Individual: 1050–1200* (Toronto, University of Toronto Press, 2004).

Munzer, S, *A Theory of Property* (Cambridge, Cambridge University Press, 1990).

Murphy, A, Jordan-Bychkov, T and Jordan, B, *The European Culture Area: A Systematic Geography* (Lanham, Rowman & Littlefield, 2009).

Murphy, G, *The Big Book of Concepts* (Cambridge, MA, Massachusetts Institute of Technology, 2004).

Nussbaum, S, *American Cultural Baggage: How to Recognise and Deal with it* (New York, Orbis Books, 2005).

O'Toole, P, *Money and Morals in America: A History* (New York, Clarkson Potter, 1998).

Optem, *The Europeans, Culture and Cultural Values, Qualitative Study* (June 2006).

Ostergren, R, and Bossé, M, *The Europeans: A Geography of People, Culture, and Environment* (New York, Guilford, 2011).

Palmer, G, *The Law of Restitution*, vol 1 (New York, Little, Brown and Company, 1978).

Pamuk, Ş, *A Monetary History of the Ottoman Empire* (Cambridge, Cambridge University Press, 2001).

Parkin, F, *Marxism and Class Theory: A Bourgeois Critique* (London, Tavistock, 1979).

Pattison, G, *Art, Modernity and Faith: Restoring the Image* (Norwich, SCM, 1998).

Pels, D, *Property and Power in Social Theory: A Study in Intellectual Rivalry* (London, Routledge, 1998).

Pertusier, C, *Picturesque Promenades in and near Constantinople and on the Waters of the Bosphorus* (London, Phillips, 1820).

Pinker, S, *The Language Instinct: How the Mind Creates Language* (New York, Harper Perennial Modern Classics, 2007).

Pirenne, H, *Belgian Democracy: Its Early History*, trans J Saunders (Kitchener, Batoche Books, 2004).

Plato, *Republic*, trans A Bloom (New York, Basic Books, 1991).

Polking, K, *Writing A to Z* (Cincinnati, OH, Writer's Digest Books, 1990).

Posner, R, *Law and Literature: A Misunderstood Relation* (Cambridge, MA, Harvard University Press, 1988).

Potolsky, M, *Mimesis* (New York, Routledge, 2006).

Proulx Lang, A, 'Poggio Bracciolini's De Avaitia: A Study in Fifteenth Century Florentine Attitudes Toward Avarice and Usury' (MA thesis, Montreal, Sir George Williams University, 1973).

Quataert, D, *The Ottoman Empire, 1700–1922* (Cambridge, Cambridge University Press, 2007).

Rapaille, C, *The Culture Code: An Ingenious Way to Understand Why People Around the World Live and Buy as They Do* (New York, Broadway, 2007).

Rifkin, J, *The European Dream*, Kindle edn (New York, Penguin, 2004).

Rodgers, D, *The Work Ethic in Industrial America, 1850–1920* (Chicago, University of Chicago Press, 1979).

Rorty, R, *Philosophy and the Mirror of Nature* (Princeton, NJ, Princeton University Press, 1981).

Rubin, A, *Ottoman Nizamiye Courts: Law and Modernity* (New York, Palgrave Macmillan, 2009).

Sahlins, M, *Culture and Practical Reason* (Chicago, IL, University of Chicago Press, 1978).

Sait, S and Lim, H, *Paper 1: Islamic Land Theories and their Application* (Nairobi, UN-HANITAT, 2005).

Salzmann, Z, Stanlaw, J and Adachi, N, *Language, Culture and Society: An Introduction to Linguistic Anthropology* (Boulder, CO, Westview, 2011).

Sapir, E, *Selected Writings in Language, Culture and Personality*, (ed) D Mandelbaum (Berkeley, CA, University of California Press, 1985).

Say, J, *A Treatise on Political Economy, or, the Production, Distribution, and Consumption of Wealth* (New York, Cosimo, 2007).

Schlatter, R, *Private Property: The History of an Idea* (New York, Russell & Russell, 1973).

Scott, J (ed), *Cases of Quasi-Contract* (New York, Baker, Voorhis and Company, 1905).

Shaw, S and Kural Shaw, E, *History of the Ottoman Empire and Modern Turkey: Reform, Revolution, and Republic—The Rise of Modern Turkey 1808–1975*, vol II (New York, Cambridge University Press, 1997).

Sidky, H, *Perspectives on Culture: A Critical Introduction to Theory in Cultural Anthropology* (New Jersey, NJ, Pearson, 2004).

Simmel, G, *The Philosophy of Money*, trans T Bottomore and D Frisby (London, Routledge, 2004).

Smith, E, *Commercial Real Estate: Listing Properties* (Chicago, IL, Dearborn, 2002).

Starr, J, *Law as Metaphor: From Islamic Courts to the Palace of Justice* (Albany, NY, State University of New York, 1992).

Steiner, E, *French Law: A Comparative Approach* (Oxford, Oxford University Press, 2010).

Stimson, F, *Glossary of Technical Terms, Phrases, and Maxims of the Common Law* (Boston, MA, Little, Brown and Company, 1881).

Tawney, R, *Religion and the Rise of Capitalism* (New Jersey, Transaction Publishers, 2008).

'The Hildebrandslied', trans F Wood (Chicago, University of Chicago Press, 1914).

Tierney, B, *The Idea of Natural Rights: Studies on Natural Rights, Natural Law, and Church Law 1150–1625* (Cambridge, Wm B Werdmans, 2001).

Tuck, R, *Natural Rights Theory: Their Origin and Development* (Cambridge, Cambridge University Press, 1979).

Ubicini, A, *Letters on Turkey: An Account of The Religious, Political, Social, and Commercial Condition of the Ottoman Empire, Part I: Turkey and the Turks*, trans Easthope (London, John Murray, 1856).

Underhill, J, *Humboldt, Worldview and Language* (Edinburgh, Edinburgh University Press, 2009).

—— *Ethnolinguistics and Cultural Concepts: Truth, Love, Hate and War* (Cambridge, Cambridge University Press, 2012).

van Caenegem, R, *An Historical Introduction to Private Law*, trans D Johnston (Cambridge, Cambridge University Press, 2003).

Virgo, G, *The Principles of the Law of Restitution* (Oxford, Oxford University Press, 2006).

Voltaire, *Candide, ou L'optimisme* (Paris, Siréne, 1759).

—— *Candide and Other Stories* (Oxford, Oxford University Press, 2008).

Webb, C, *Reason and Restitution: A Theory of Unjust Enrichment* (Oxford, Oxford University Press, 2016).

Weber, M, *Economy and Society: An Outline of Interpretive Sociology*, G Roth and C Wittich (eds) (Berkeley, CA, University of California Press, 1978).

—— *The Protestant Ethic and the Spirit of Capitalism: And Other Writings* (New York, Penguin, 2002).

Whorf, B, *Language, Thought and Reality: Selected Writings of Benjamin Lee Whorf* (New York, Technology, 1956).

Wilburg, W, *Die Lehre von der ungerecgtfertigten Bereicherung nach österreichischem und deutschem Recht* (Graz, Leuschner & Lubensky, 1934).

Wood, E, *The Origin of Capitalism: A Longer View* (New York, Verso, 2002).

Woodward, F, *The Law of Quasi Contracts* (Boston, MA, Little, Brown and Company, 1913).

Wuthnow, R, *God and Mammon in America* (New York, Free, 1994).

Zelizer, V, *The Social Meaning of Money* (New Jersey, NJ, Princeton University Press, 1997).

Zimmermann, R, *The Law of Obligations: Roman Foundations of the Civilian Tradition* (Cape Town, Juta, 1992).

Zygulski, Z, *Ottoman Art in the Service of Empire* (New York, New York University Press, 1991).

Book Chapters

Abacherli, M, 'Nuẓum al-Dawlah al-'uthmānyah' ('Systems of the Ottoman State') in E İhsanoğlu (ed), *al-Dawlah al-'uthmānyah: Tarīkh Waḥadārah* (*The Ottoman State: History and Civilization*) vol I, trans Ṣ Sa'dāwy (Cairo, Maktabat al-shurūq al-Dawlyah, 2010).

Aydin, M, 'al-Nuẓ um al-Qānūnyya fī al-Dawlah al-'uthmānyah' ('Legal Systems in the Ottoman State') in E İhsanoğlu (ed), *al-Dawlah al-'uthmānyah: Tarīkh Waḥadārah* (*The Ottoman State: History and Civilization*) vol I, trans Ṣ Sa'dāwy (Cairo, Maktabat al-shurūq al-Dawlyah, 2010).

Aynès, L, 'Property Law' in G Bermann and E Picard (eds), *Introduction to French Law* (AH Alphen aan den Rijn, Kluwer Law International, 2009).

Baker, J, 'The Use of Assumpsit for Restitutionary Money Claims 1600–1800' in E Schrage (ed), *Unjust Enrichment: The Comparative Legal History of the Law of Restitution* (Berlin, Duncker & Humblot, 1995).

Barker, K, 'Understanding the Unjust Enrichment Principle in Private Law: A Study of the Concept and its Reasons' in J Neyers, M McInnes and S Pitel, *Understanding Unjust Enrichment* (Oxford, Hart Publishing, 2004).

Beydilli, K, 'al-Dawlah al-'uthmānyah min Mu'āhadat Qynarjah al-Ṣughrah ḥatta al-inhyār' ('The Ottoman State from the Treaty of Küçük Kaynarca Until the Collapse') in E İhsanoğlu (ed), *al-Dawlah al-'uthmānyah: Tarīkh Waḥadārah* (*The Ottoman State: History and Civilization*) vol I, trans Ṣ Sa'dāwy (Cairo, Maktabat al-shurūq al-Dawlyah, 2010).

Birks, P, 'Restitution for Wrongs' in E Schrage (ed), *Unjust Enrichment: The Comparative Legal History of the Law of Restitution* (Berlin, Duncker & Humblot, 1995).

Blumenberg, H, 'The Concept of Reality and the Possibility of the Novel' in R Amacher and V Lange (eds), *New Perspectives in German Literary Criticism* (Princeton, NJ, Princeton University Press, 1977).

Brinker, M, 'Theme and Interpretation' in W Sollors (ed), *The Return of Thematic Criticism* (Cambridge, MA, Harvard University Press, 1993).

Brooks, P, 'Introduction' in T Todorov, *Introduction to Poetics*, trans R Howard (Minneapolis, MN, University of Minnesota Press, 1984).

Cartwright, J and Hesselink, M, 'Case 9' in J Cartwright and M Hesselink (eds), *Precontractual Liability in European Private Law* (Cambridge, Cambridge University Press, 2008).

Coombe, R, 'Contingent Articulations: A Critical Cultural Studies of Law' in A Sarat and T Kearn (eds), *Law in the Domains of Culture* (Ann Arbor, MI, University of Michigan Press, 2003).

Feenstra, R, 'Grotius' Doctrine of Unjust Enrichment as a Source of Obligation: Its Origins and its Influence in Roman–Dutch Law' in E Schrage (ed), *Unjust Enrichment: The Comparative Legal History of the Law of Restitution* (Berlin, Duncker & Humblot, 1995).

Gambaro, A, 'Western Property Law' in M Bussani and F Werro (eds), *European Private Law: A Handbook* (Berne, Stämpfli, 2009).

Geertz, C, 'Ideology as a Cultural System' in C Geertz (ed), *The Interpretation of Cultures* (New York, Basic Books, 1973).

—— 'Thick Description: Toward an Interpretive Theory of Culture' in C Geertz (ed), *The Interpretation of Cultures* (New York, Basic Books, 1973).

—— 'Local Knowledge: Fact and Law in Comparative Perspective' in C Geertz (ed), *Local Knowledge—Further Essays in Interpretive Anthropology* (New York, Basic Books, 2000).

—— 'The Way We Think Now: Ethnography of Modern Thought' in C Geertz (ed), *Local Knowledge—Further Essays in Interpretive Anthropology* (New York, Basic Books, 2000).

Hall, S, 'The Work of Representation' in S Hall (ed), *Representation: Cultural Representations and Signifying Practices* (London, Sage, 1997).

Hallebeek, J, 'Developments of Mediaeval Roman Law' in E Schrage (ed), *Unjust Enrichment: The Comparative Legal History of the Law of Restitution* (Berlin, Duncker & Humblot, 1995).

Halperin, J, *The French Civil Code*, trans Tony Weir (New York, UCL, 2006).

Hedetoft, U, and Hjort, M, 'Introduction' in U Hedetoft and M Hjort (eds), *The Post-national Self* (Minneapolis, MN, University of Minnesota Press, 2002).

Hirsch, S and Lazarus-Black, M, 'Introduction—Performance and Paradox: Exploring Law's Role in Hegemony and Resistance' in S Hirsch and M Lazarus-Black (eds), *Contested States: Law, Hegemony and Resistance* (New York, Routledge, 1994).

Inalcik, H, 'The Nature of Traditional Society: Turkey' in R Ward and D Rustow (eds), *Political Modernization in Japan and Turkey* (Princeton, NJ, Princeton University Press, 1964).

Joffé, G, 'Regionalism—A New Paradigm?' in M Telò (ed), *European Union and New Regionalism* (Hampshire, Ashgate, 2007).

Kaelber, L, 'Max Weber and Usury: Implications for Historical Research' in L Armstrong, I Elbl and M Elbl (eds), *Money, Markets and Trade in Late Medieval Europe: Essays in Honour of John HA Munro* (Leiden, Koninklijke Brill NV, 2007).

Khadduri, M and Liebensky, H (eds), *Law in the Middle East* (Washington DC, The Middle East Institute, 1955).

Krebs, T, 'Unrequested Benefits in German Law' in J Neyers, M McInnes and S Pitel (eds), *Understanding Unjust Enrichment* (Oxford, Hart Publishing, 2004).

Lapuente, S, 'Negotoirum Gestio' in S van Erp and A Vaquer (eds), *Introduction to Spanish Patrimonial Law* (Granada, Comares, 2006).

—— 'Undue Payment' in S van Erp and A Vaquer (eds), *Introduction to Spanish Patrimonial Law* (Granada, Comares, 2006).

Lehmert, M and Rainer, M, 'Austrian Law of Unjust Enrichment' in E Schrage (ed), *Unjust Enrichment and the Law of Contract* (Hague, Kluwer Law International, 2001).

Leiter, B, 'American Legal Realism' in M Golding and W Edmundson (eds), *The Blackwell Guide to the Philosophy of Law and Legal Theory* (Oxford, Blackwell, 2005).

Ligüerre, C, 'Disgorgement of Profits Under Spanish Law: Gain Based Remedies throughout the World' in E Hondius and A Janssen (eds), *Disgorgement of Profits* (Cham, Springer, 2015).

Moulton, I, 'Whores as Shopkeepers: Money and Sexuality in Aretino's *Ragionamenti*' in J Vitullo and D Wolfthal (eds), *Money, Morality, and Culture in Late Medieval and Early Modern Europe* (Surrey, Ashgate, 2010).

MacKinnon, M, 'The Longevity of the Thesis: A Critique of the Critics' in H Lehmann and G Roth (eds), *Weber's Protestant Ethic: Origins, Evidence, Contexts* (Cambridge, Cambridge University Press, 1995).

Mattila, H, 'Legal Vocabulary' in P Tiersma and L Solan (eds), *The Oxford Handbook of Language and Law* (Oxford, Oxford University Press, 2012).

Miller, J, and Taylor-Mitchell, L, 'To Honor God and Enrich Florence in Things Spiritual and Temporal: Piety, Commerce, and Art in the Humiliati Order' in J Vitullo and D Wolfthal (eds), *Money, Morality, and Culture in Late Medieval and Early Modern Europe* (Surrey, Ashgate, 2010).

Murray, J, 'The Devil's Evangelists? Moneychangers in Flemish Urban Society' in J Vitullo and D Wolfthal (eds), *Money, Morality, and Culture in Late Medieval and Early Modern Europe* (Surrey, Ashgate, 2010).

Nisbett, R, and Norenzayan, A, 'Culture and Cognition' in D Medin and H Pashler (eds), *Stevens' Handbook of Experimental Psychology: Cognition*, vol 2 (New York, Wiley, 2001).

Ocak, A, 'al-Ḥayat al-Dīnyya wa al-Fikryya' ('The Religious and Intellectual Life') in E İhsanoğlu (ed), *al-Dawlah al-'uthmānyah: Tarīkh Waḥadārah* (*The Ottoman State: History and Civilization*) vol II, trans Ṣ Sa'dāwy (Cairo, Maktabat al-shurūq al-Dawlyah, 2010).

Okay, O, 'Dirasah Awalyah 'n al-ḥayah al-Fikryah Khilāl 'hd al-Taghrīb' ('Initial Study of the Intellectual Life in the Westernisation Era') in E İhsanoğlu (ed), *al-Dawlah al-'uthmānyah: Tarīkh Waḥadārah* (*The Ottoman State: History and Civilization*) vol II, trans Ṣ Sa'dāwy (Cairo, Maktabat al-shurūq al-Dawlyah, 2010,).

—— 'al-Adab al-Turky fī 'ṣr al-Taghrīb' ('The Turkish literature in the Westernisation Era') in E İhsanoğlu (ed), *al-Dawlah al-'uthmānyah: Tarīkh Waḥadārah* (*The Ottoman State: History and Civilization*) vol II, trans Ṣ Sa'dāwy (Cairo, Maktabat al-shurūq al-Dawlyah, 2010).

Pease, D, 'National Identities, Postmodern Artifacts, and Postnational Narratives' in D Pease (ed), *National Identities and Post-Americanist Narratives* (Durham, NC, Duke University Press, 1994).

Richards, A, 'Primitive Accumulation in Egypt, 1798–1882' in H İslamoğlu-İnan (ed), *The Ottoman Empire and the World-Economy* (Cambridge, Cambridge University Press, 1987).

Savage, J, 'From American Democracy to French Empire: Race and the Law in Tocqueville's Liberalism' in N Persram (ed), *Postcolonialism and Political Theory* (Lanham, MD, Lexington Books, 2007).

Schacht, J, 'Law and the State: Islamic Religious Law' in J Schacht and C Bosworth (eds), *The Legacy of Islam* (Oxford, Clarendon Press, 1974).

Smith, L, 'Property, Subsidiarity, and Unjust Enrichment' in D Johnston and R Zimmermann, (eds), *Unjustified Enrichment: Key Issues in Comparative Perspective* (Cambridge, Cambridge University Press, 2004).

Taylor, G, 'Where Morality Meets Money' in M Bazyler and R Alford, *Holocaust Restitution: Perspectives on the Litigation and its Legacy* (New York, New York University Press, 2006).

Todeschini, G, 'The Incivility of Judas: "Manifest" Usury as a Metaphor for the "Infamy of Fact" (*infamia facti*)' in J Vitullo and D Wolfthal (eds), *Money, Morality, and Culture in Late Medieval and Early Modern Europe* (Surrey: Ashgate, 2010).

van Peer, W, 'Where Do Literary Themes Come From?' in M Louwerse and W van Peer (eds), *Thematics: Interdisciplinary Studies* (Amsterdam, John Benjamines, 2002).

Vaquer, A, 'Unjustified Enrichment' in S van Erp and A Vaquer (eds), *Introduction to Spanish Patrimonial Law* (Granada, Comares, 2006).

Viney, G, 'Tort Liability' in G Bermann and E Picard (eds), *Introduction to French Law* (AH Alphen aan den Rijn, Kluwer Law International, 2009).

Vitullo, J and Wolfthal, D, 'Introduction' in J Vitullo and D Wolfthal (eds), *Money, Morality, and Culture in Late Medieval and Early Modern Europe* (Surrey, Ashgate, 2010).

Vitullo, J, and Wolfthal, D, 'Trading Values: Negotiating Masculinity in Late Medieval and Early Modern Europe' in J Vitullo and D Wolfthal (eds), *Money, Morality, and Culture in Late Medieval and Early Modern Europe* (Surrey, Ashgate, 2010).

von Caemmerer, E, 'Bereicherung und unerlaubte Handlung' in H Dölle, M Rheinstein and K Zweigert (eds), *Festschrift für Ernst Rabel*, vol 1 (Tübingen, Mohr, 1954).

Wendehorst, C, 'No Headaches over Unjust Enrichment: Response to Daniel Friedman' in K Siehr and R Zimmermann (eds), *The Draft Civil Code for Israel in Comparative Perspective* (Tübingen, Mohr Siebeck GmbH & Co., 2008)

Whittaker, S, 'The Law of Obligations' in J Bell, S Byron and S Whittaker (eds), *Principles of French Law* (Oxford, Oxford University Press, 2008) 294.

Yediyildiz, B, 'al-Mujtama' al-'Uthmānī' (*Ottoman Society*) in E İhsanoğlu (ed), *al-Dawlah al-'uthmānyah: Tarīkh Waḥadārah* (*The Ottoman State: History and Civilization*) vol 1, trans Ş Sa'dāwy (Cairo, Maktabat al-shurūq al-Dawlyah, 2010).

Journal Articles and Book Reviews

Asfour, N, 'Book Review: The Measure of Injury: Race, Gender and Tort Law' (2011) 7 *Law, Culture and the Humanities* 142.

—— 'Law and Literature: Jewish and Christian Models' (2012) 6(2) *Pólemos* 263.

Bazyler, M, 'The Holocaust Restitution Movement in Comparative Perspective' (2002) 20 *Berkeley Journal of International Law* 11.

Birks, P, 'A Letter to America: The New Restatement of Restitution' (2003) 3(2) *Global Jurist Frontiers* 20.

Bissenove, A, 'Ottomanism, Pan-Islamism, and the Caliphate Discourse at the Turn of the 20th century' (2004) 9(1) *Barqiyya* 2.

Bourdieu, P, 'The Force of Law: Toward a Sociology of the Juridical Field', trans R Terdiman (1987) 38 *Hastings Law Journal* 805.

Boyar, E and Fleet, K, *A Social History of Ottoman Istanbul* (Cambridge, Cambridge University Press, 2010).

Boyer, P, *American History: A Very Short Introduction*, Kindle edn (Oxford, Oxford University Press, 2012).

Burrows, A, 'Quadrating Restitution and Unjust Enrichment: A Matter of Principle' (2000) 8 *Restitution Law Review* 257.

—— *The Law of Restitution* (Oxford, Oxford University Press, 2011).

—— *A Restatement of the English Law of Unjust Enrichment* (Oxford, Oxford University Press, 2012).

Busnelli, F, Camandé, G and Cousy, H et al (eds), *Principles of European Tort Law: Text and Commentary* (Vienna, Springer, 2005).

Cohen, A, 'An Evaluation of "Themes" and Kindred Concepts' (1946) 52(1) *American Journal of Sociology* 41.

—— 'On the Place of "Themes" and Kindred Concepts in Social Theory' (1948) 50(3) *New Anthropologist: New Series* 436.

Coombe, R, 'Critical Cultural Study of Law' (1998) 10(2) *Yale Journal of Law & the Humanities* 463.

Dagan, H, 'Restitution and Slavery: On Incomplete Commodification, Intergenerational Justice, and Legal Transitions' (2004) 84 *Boston University Law Review* 1139.

Davis, W, '"Anticritical Last Word on The Spirit of Capitalism", by Max Weber' (1978) 83(5) *American Journal of Sociology* 1105.

Dawson, J, *Unjust Enrichment: A Comparative Analysis* (New York, William S Hein & Co, 1999).

de Tocqueville, A, *Democracy in America*, vol 1, trans H Reeve, Kindle edn (Public Domain, 1835).

—— *Democracy in America*, vol 2, trans H Reeve, Kindle edn (Public Domain, 1840).

Dutta-Bergman, M and Doyle, K, 'Money and Meaning in India and Great Britain: Tales of Similarities and Differences' (2001) 45 *American Behavioral Scientist* 205.

Edelman, J, 'Unjust Enrichment, Restitution, and Wrongs' (2000–01) 79 *Texas Law Review* 1869.

Elkin-Koren, N and Salzberger, E, 'Towards an Economic Theory of Unjust Enrichment Law' (2000) 20 *International Review of Law and Economics* 551.

Erdmann, G and Engel, U, 'Neopatrimonialism Reconsidered: Critical Review and Elaboration of an Elusive Concept' (2007) 45(1) *Commonwealth & Comparative Politics* 95.

Ergene, B and Berker, A, 'Inheritance and Intergenerational Wealth Transmission in Eighteenth-Century Ottoman Kastamonu: An Empirical Investigation' (2009) 34 *Journal of Family History* 25.

Ersoy, A, 'Architecture and the Search for Ottoman Origins in the Tanzimat Period' (2007) 24 *Muqarnas* 117.

Ferrari, S, 'Adapting Divine Law to Change: The Experience of the Roman Catholic Church (with some reference to Jewish and Islamic Law)' (2006) 28(1) *Cardozo Law Review* 53.

Gergen, M, 'What Renders Enrichment Unjust?' (2000–01) 79 *Texas Law Review* 1927.

Giglio, F, 'A Systematic Approach to "Unjust" and "Unjustified' Enrichment"' (2003) 23(3) *Oxford Journal of Legal Studies* 455.

Harel, A and Lorberbaum, Y, 'Hirhurim 'l Sakanot Mishpat yi Tarbut' ('Reflecting on Dangers of Law and Culture') (2011) 40 *Mishpatim* 939.

Hill, J and Mannheim, B, 'Language and Worldview' (1992) 21 *Annual Review of Anthropology* 381.

Hohfeld, W, 'Fundamental Legal Conceptions as Applied in Judicial Reasoning' (1913) 23 *Yale Law Journal* 16.

Inalcik, H, 'Capital Formation in the Ottoman Empire' (1969) 29(1) *Journal of Economic History* 97.

Jasso, G, 'Culture and the Sense of Justice: A Comprehensive Framework for Analysis' (2005) 36(1) *Journal of Cross-Cultural Psychology* 14.

Karababa, E, 'Approaching Non-Western Consumer Cultures from a Historical Perspective: The Case of Early Modern Ottoman Consumer Culture' (2012) 12(1) *Marketing Theory* 13.

Klimchuk, D, 'Unjust Enrichment and Reparations for Slavery' (2004) 84 *Boston University Law Review* 1257.

Kluckhohn, C and Hoebel, E, 'Covert Culture and Administrative Problems' (1943) 45(2) *American Anthropologist* 213.

Kornhauser, M, 'The Morality of Money: American Attitudes Toward Wealth and the Income Tax' (1994) 70(1) *Indiana Law Journal* 119.

Kull, A, 'Rationalizing Restitution' (1995) 83(5) *California Law Review* 1191.

Laycock, D, 'The Scope and Significance of Restitution' (1989) 67 *Texas Law Review* 1277.

MacQueen, H, 'Book Review: Unjust Enrichment: A Study of Private Law and Public Values' (1998) 47 *International & Comparative Law Quarterly* 740.

Madden, E, 'Some Characteristics of Islamic Art' (1975) 33(4) *Journal of Aesthetics and Art Criticism* 423.

Mautner, M, 'Three Approaches to Law and Culture' (2011) 96(4) *Cornell Law Review* 839.

McInnes, M, 'The Canadian Principle of Unjust Enrichment: Comparative Insights into the Law of Restitution' (1999) 37 *Alberta Law Review* 1.

Moore, S, 'Law and Anthropology' (1969) 6 *Biennial Review of Anthropology* 252.

Northrop, F, 'Jurisprudence in the Law School Curriculum' (1948–49) 1 *Journal of Legal Education* 482.

Opler, M, 'Themes as Dynamic Forces in Culture' (1945) 51(3) *American Journal of Sociology* 198.

—— 'The Context of Themes' (1949) 51(2) *American Anthropologist* 323.

Pound, R, 'Sociology of Law and Sociological Jurisprudence' (1943) 5(1) *University of Toronto Law Journal* 1.

Rendleman, D, 'Restating Restitution: The Restatement Process and its Critics' (2008) 65 *Washington and Lee Law Review* 933.

Rogers, J, 'Restitution for Wrongs and the Restatement (Third) of the Law of Restitution' (2007) 42 *Wake Forest Law Review* 55.

Rotherham, C, 'Unjust Enrichment and the Autonomy of Law: Private Law as Public Morality' (1998) 61 *Modern Law Review* 580.

Ryan, G and Bernard, H, 'Techniques to Identify Themes' (2003) 15(1) *Field Methods* 85.

Schlechtriem, P, 'Unjust Enrichment by Interference with Property Rights' in *International Encyclopedia of Comparative Law*, vol X (2007).

Sebok, A, 'Two Concepts of Injustice in Restitution for Slavery' (2004) 84 *Boston University Law Review* 1405.

Shaw, S, 'The Nineteenth-Century Ottoman Tax Reforms and Revenue System' (1975) 6(4) *International Journal of Middle East Studies* 421.

Shaw, W, 'Islamic Arts in the Ottoman Imperial Museum, 1889–1923' (2000) 30 *Ars Orientalis* 55.

Sherzer, J, 'A Discourse-Centered Approach to Language and Culture' (1987) 89(2) *American Anthropologist* 295.

Smith, K and Stone, L, 'Rags, Riches and Bootstraps: Beliefs about the Causes of Wealth and Poverty' (1989) 30(1) *Sociological Quarterly* 93.

Sweeney, T, 'English Judges and Roman Jurists: The Civilian Learning Behind England's First Case Law' (2012) 84(4) *Temple Law Review* 827.

Veenstra, J, 'The New Historicism of Stephen Greenblatt: On Poetics of Culture and the Interpretation of Shakespeare' (1995) 34(3) *History and Theory* 174.

Weinrib, E, 'Legal Formalism: On the Immanent Rationality of Law' (1987–88) 97 *Yale Law Journal* 958.

—— 'Restitutionary Damages as Corrective Justice' (1999) 1 *Theoretical Inquiries in Law* 1

Wendehorst, C, 'The State as a Foundation of Private Law Reasoning' (2008) 56 *American Journal of Comparative Law* 567.

—— 'The Draft Principles of European Unjustified Enrichment Law Prepared by the Study Group on a European Civil Code: A Comment' (2006) 7 *CC ERA Forum* 244.

Wilburg, W, 'Zusammenspiel der Kräfte im Aufbau des Schuldrechts' (1964) 163(4) *Archiv für die civilistische Praxis* 346.

Encyclopaedias

Encyclopedia of the Ottoman Empire (2009).

Encyclopedia of Transnational Crime and Justice (2012).

Oxford Dictionary of Sociology 3rd edn (2009).

The Catholic Encyclopedia (1909) (online).

Dictionaries

Merriam-Webster's Collegiate Dictionary, 11th edn, Kindle edn (2006).

The Oxford Dictionary of Islam (2003).

Miscellaneous

ALI, Founding Charter (23 February 1923) (online).

ALI, *The Report of the Committee on the Establishment of a Permanent Organization for the Improvement of the Law* (Washington DC, ALI, 1973).

American Congress, 'Declaration of Independence (July 4, 1776)' in P Henry, B Franklin and T Jefferson et al (eds), *15 Documents and Speeches That Built America*, Kindle edn (Seattle, WA, Amazon Digital Services, 2011).

The Bible KJV (Genesis, Psalms, John, Matthew).

European Convention on Human Rights (Rome, 4 November 1950).

Déclaration des droits de l'homme et du citoyen, 1789 (online).

Franklin, B, *Poor Richard's Almanack* (Philadelphia, PA, Franklin, 1734, 1737, 1756).

The Talili, M, Conference Report: 'Clash of Civilizations or Clash of Perceptions?' (New York, Dialogues, 2002) (online).

Obama, B, victory speech following re-election (7 November 2012) (online).

Pope John XXII , *Cum Inter Nonnullos* (12 November 1323) (online).
Quran.
Trump, D, Inauguration Speech (21.1.2017) (online).
World Values Survey Data analysis tool waves 1981–84, 1990–94, 1995–98, 1999–2004, 2005–09, 2010–14 (online).

Transliteration Sources

ALA-LC Arabic (2012) Romanising Table (online).
ALA-LC Hebrew and Yiddish (2011) Romanising Table (online).
Eleazar Birnbaum 'The Transliteration of Ottoman Turkish for Library and General Purposes' (1967) 87(2) *Journal of the American Oriental Society* 122.

Index